Thimbleriggers

thimblerig *rigged, rigging, n.*

1. a sleight-of-hand swindling game in which the operator palms a pellet or pea while appearing to cover it with one of three thimblelike cups, and then, moving the cups about, offers to bet that no one can tell under which cup the pellet or pea lies

The Random House Dictionary of the English Language

Thimble riggers

THE LAW *v.* GOVERNOR MARVIN MANDEL

BRADFORD JACOBS
Foreword by William Manchester

The Johns Hopkins University Press
BALTIMORE AND LONDON

The Johns Hopkins University Press, Baltimore, Maryland 21218
The Johns Hopkins Press Ltd., London

*The paper in this book is acid-free and meets the
guidelines for permanence and durability of the
Committee on Production Guidelines for Book Longevity of
the Council on Library Resources.*

Library of Congress Cataloging in Publication Data

Jacobs, Bradford.
    Thimbleriggers: The law v. Governor Marvin Mandel.

    Bibliography: pp. 253–56
    Includes index.
    1. Mandel, Marvin, 1920–   . 2. Corruption (in
politics)—Maryland.   3. Maryland—Politics and government—1951–   . I. Title.
F186.35.M36J33   1984   975.2′043′0924   84–7879
ISBN 0-8018-3170-9

To Molly, Brucie, and Sally

"Goodness. Yeah, just plain, simple goodness," *Governor Stark* was saying. "Well you can't inherit that from anybody. You got to make it up, Doc. If you want it. You got to make it out of badness. Badness. And you know why, Doc? . . . Because there isn't anything else to make it out of. Did you know that, Doc? . . ."

Adam wet his lips and said, "there is one question I would like to ask you. It is this. If, as you say, there is only the bad to start with, and the good must be made from the bad, then how do you ever know what the good is? How do you even recognize the good? . . ."

"Easy, Doc, easy."

"Well, answer it."

"You just make it up as you go along."

"Make up what?"

"The good. What the hell else . . . what the hell else you think folks been doing for a million years, Doc? When your great-great-grandfather climbed down out of the tree, he didn't have any more notion of good or bad, or right or wrong, than the hoot owl that stayed up in the tree. Well, he climbed down and he began to make good up as he went along. He made up what he needed to do business, Doc. And what he made up and got everybody to mirate on as good and right was always just a couple of jumps behind what he needed to do business on. That's why things change, Doc. Because what folks claim is right is always just a couple of jumps short of what they need to do business on. . . . Now, an individual, one fellow, he will stop doing business because he's got a notion of what is right, and he is a hero. But folks in general, which is society, Doc, is never going to stop doing business. Society is just going to cook up a new notion of what is right. Society is sure not ever going to commit suicide. At least, not that way and of a purpose. And that is a fact. Now, ain't it? . . ."

"It is?" *Adam* said.

"You're damned right it is, Doc . . ."

—Robert Penn Warren,
All the King's Men

vii

Contents

Foreword

It is not true, as the inscription on the Justice Department building in Washington proclaims, that "The Place of Justice is a Hallowed Place." Usually it is a shabby place, inhabited by shifty-eyed bondsmen and seedy bailiffs, whose halls and chambers somehow give the impression that over the years a great deal has been swept under the rug. Yet all in all, most courts get the job done. There are probably fewer crooked judges in the Maryland Free State than there are, say, card sharps in the elegant Maryland Club or illiterate reporters on Baltimore's *Sunpapers*.

Of course, most Americans never stand in the dock. However, Americans are not entitled to sanctimony. With the exception of those who possess a personal code of honor—they are few, and growing fewer—the majority of our citizenry become spineless when confronted by temptation. The guilty are everywhere. Winsome, freckle-faced boys fix soapbox derbies by the cunning use of tiny motors. West Point cadets cheat on examinations. Athletes throw games or shave points. Celebrities urge us to buy products they know are worthless. Olympians inject illicit drugs into their veins to boost their performance. And, as Bradford Jacobs points out, the chief executive officers of mighty firms suborn foreign governments. Lockheed is one example. The International Telephone and Telegraph Company is another. Who can forget the highly incriminating memorandum of Dita Beard, ITT's salty Washington lobbyist, implicating Harold S. Geneen and ending, "Please destroy this, huh?"

What separates the unjust from the just is opportunity. When it knocks, most swing wide the welcoming door, grinning glittering grins of cupidity. Although it is untrue that every man has his price, it can be argued that the greater the opportunity, the higher the likelihood that it will be seized. We place our greatest trust in our public servants, and the highest per capita concentration of felons in the country, if you exempt prisons, is found on Capitol Hill. In the ITT caper, during which $400,000 changed hands, the culprits were the president of the United States, the president's chief of staff and his attorney general, and the lieutenant governor of California. They explained that the swag wasn't for them; it was all for the party. The evasion was typical. Unscrupulous politicians enjoy an infinite capacity for rationalization. Robert Penn Warren dissected those of Louisiana's Huey Long in *All the King's Men*, Edwin O'Connor stripped Boston's Jim Curley in *The Last Hurrah*, and now Mr. Jacobs gives us this fascinating political autopsy of Maryland's Marvin Mandel. Long defended his extortions on the ground that he had used the money for the people's best interests, which he alone knew; Curley said he was getting even with the Brahmins who had cheated the Irish, though he never revealed how this justified hiring a contractor so fraudulent that one of his office buildings collapsed (fortunately, at night). Mandel saw no need to make any accounting whatever. Of all Mr. Jacobs's revelations, perhaps the most significant is that Mandel, emerging from federal prison, spoke not a word of remorse. Indeed, in a moment of supreme chutzpah, he told reporters that as a result of his prison experience, he might "lend" himself to a study of convict rehabilitation. That Mandelism belongs in *Bartlett's*.

Who was this knave of knaves?

To the day he took his oath in Annapolis, and led his constituents in a stirring rendition of "O, Tannenbaum," his life had been exemplary. A Polish Jew whose father owned a small liquor store in the vast black slum of West Baltimore, Marvin had sold newspapers at Pimlico Racetrack, performed well on baseball diamonds and in boxing rings, and married his high-school sweetheart, Barbara Oberfeld. Barbara, a k a "Bootsie," became as able a politician as her husband; many thought her abler. Together they reared two children, repeatedly campaigned for office, and when Governor Spiro Agnew became vice-president, moved into

Government House, the splendid Annapolis home of Maryland's chief executives.

Had life any more to offer? Well, yes, Marvin thought it had. Like Nelson Rockefeller, who had sacrificed a good shot at the White House by trading in an old wife for a new, Agnew's successor found himself irresistibly drawn to one Jeanne Dorsey, a blonde divorcee nearly twenty years his junior and the daughter of an impoverished but genteel Eastern Shore family. With increasing frequency, he slunk away to trysts with La Dorsey, as Mencken would have called her, in remote St. Mary's County. Word got around; inevitably the highway he traveled was rechristened the Road to Mandel's Lay. He was deliriously happy. But the serpent of Eden had set Mandel up; Eve had handed him the apple and he had sunk his teeth in it, and now he had to leave the garden.

He didn't want to leave. Where else but in the gubernatorial mansion should a governor live? A better question, said Bootsie, was where should she live? According to some ancient scrolls, Eve was Adam's second wife; her predecessor, Lilith, had been hard on Adam and harder to get rid of. As Maryland's First Lady, Mandel's Lillith announced, she had no intention of leaving the gubernatorial mansion. So her husband moved into a Hilton Hotel. But a reelection campaign was imminent; he had to straighten out his domestic life before going to the voters, and so he yielded to all of Bootsie's demands. The divorce cost him some $400,000. He was returned to office, and then, in a series of intricate, shady moves, he completed the grant of precious racing days to a run-down race track and covered up the grant. The track's owners, Mandel cronies all, were enriched. So was the Governor. The losers were the people of Maryland, who had been betrayed for a bribe. Agnew, their last governor, had been a crook. Now the same federal prosecutors who had unmasked Agnew nailed Mandel, and he found himself doing time in Florida, working in the prison laundry.

Mr. Jacobs digs much deeper than that—among his book's other treasures is an incomparable history of Maryland politics— but he keeps the unfortunate Governor where he belongs, writhing in the spotlight. He has his own, closely reasoned interpretations of Mandel's fall, and since he has been a professional observer of Maryland politics for nearly forty years the story will get a more thoughtful reading than mine. I never met any of the chief characters in his tale; during my seven years as a *Sunpapers* reporter, I covered only one legislative session. But I see *Thimbleriggers* as a political morality tale, more a study in ethics than political science.

As long as insecure men reach offices of great public trust, we shall always have the Mandels with us. England, for a brief period, enjoyed governments free from the threat of greed. Between the rise of Chatham and the fall of Lloyd George, the British electorate chose a succession of leaders from an affluent, well-educated oligarchy. The Liberal government that took office in 1906 is unequalled in the history of free nations: it was brilliant, visionary, wise. Among its many achievements were the foundations of the welfare state: pensions, health insurance, unemployment compensation, slum clearance. But there was a trick. Members of Parliament had to enjoy financial independence because they were not paid. Once that changed, the Labour party emerged and grew. Today, ironically, a substantial number of seats are held by workingmen whose lifestyle depends on their salaries as MPs. If unseated, and forced to return to the lathe or the shop bench, they would slide down the greasy pole of recognition; therefore they always vote at their party's call and never think of thinking for themselves at all. Was 1906 better? Yes, but it was a freak of chance; that lightning will never strike again. Republics, as Plato knew, never last. We must settle for democracy and risk the Mandels.

Is reform hopeless? To a similar question Mencken replied: "I am a pathologist, not a chiropractor." But there is a better answer. For every bribed official, there is a briber, and we should start by unmasking him. As long as one standard is applied to politicians and another to those in private life, the old rigmarole will go on. Mr. Jacobs is clearly troubled by this. Selective justice isn't justice at all. In this sense society is in fact conned, switched, and double-shuffled.

Even the publication of all legal proceedings is a service. It is also, sad to say, rare. But its possibilities are immense. Early in the 1950s a large group of law-enforcement officials convened in Baltimore, and during their first evening they visited "The Block," the city's notorious hive of sin. Stag parties were arranged; convention delegates paired off with prostitutes and found solitude upstairs. At the height of these festivities, Baltimore's vice squad struck. It was pure chance; they were looking for something else. Faced with flagrant evidence of lechery, however, the raiders arrested not only the girls, but also their customers. Once the men's names were on the police docket, they were public record. The *Evening Sun* published them, and the Associated Press put them on the wire. Many an assistant states attorney, many a magistrate, returned home to face a furious wife. It not only was justice; it was also retribution. But that was thirty years ago. Mandel's friends, netted under different circumstances, provide an encore.

William Manchester

Wesleyan University
February 1984

Introduction

I, Marvin Mandel, do swear that I will support the Constitution of the United States; and that I will be faithful and bear true allegiance to the State of Maryland, and support the Constitution and Laws thereof; and that I will, to the best of my skill and judgment, diligently and faithfully, without partiality or prejudice, execute the office of Governor according to the Constitution and Laws of this State, that I will not directly or indirectly, receive the profits or any part of the profits of any other office during the term of my acting as Governor. (Constitution of Maryland)

What Marvin Mandel and his friends conspired to do sounds pretty simple. It was this: To double overnight an investment in a dusty, rundown Maryland racetrack, and to lie to the public about what they were up to.

Furthermore, the friends conspired to buy, with bribes to the Governor, the political leverage needed at the legislature to pump up their racetrack.

And the Governor conspired to help them by throwing his weight behind the relevant bills.

At least that's what a federal jury found unanimously, and it wasn't so simple as it sounds. One federal prosecutor estimated later that 25 percent of Marylanders remained unpersuaded, or at least cloudy about what had happened.

What exactly did Marvin Mandel do, people asked, that was wrong?

Why did he do it? Who was hurt?

Hadn't earlier Maryland governors done things just as wrong—and gotten away with it?

How much did a mistimed romance, operated in the dark and on the cuff, have to do with Mandel's fall? How about anti-Semitism?

Those were the broad questions. Lawyers were more specifically disturbed. Some pointed doubtfully to hearsay evidence brought to bear at the trial of the Mandel circle. Federal intrusion into a state's affairs bothered others. So did the odd-sounding charges—mail fraud by a public official, racketeering. Disconcertingly, a "shark" precipitated a mistrial. Also, the Court of Appeals seemed to try standing awkwardly on its judicial head.

And this steady refrain, in airy nonsequitur: Apart from all that, Marvin Mandel was a pretty good governor, wasn't he?

It was the pileup of such questions which prompted the writing of this book. If so much hung so unclear to so many, then one of the foundations of popular government was seen to wobble. This was the capacity of government to police its own backyard and, no less important, to carry public opinion along. It is nowhere written that democracy, to survive, must stumble along unclean, secretly unclean at that. Maybe a book would throw a few helpful beams upon an uncommonly complex, troublesome case.

This book does not answer all the questions. It brings on no sizzling new revelations. Nor is it the latest entry into the modish how-to field, not *How to Understand—and to Cherish—Your Corrupt Public Officials*. It aims only at clarification, at synthesis, at making sense out of confusion. It aims also at objectivity.

There is included a glance backward in time at earlier Maryland governors, as well as at the dynamics of political corruption as they unfolded after the Civil War into contemporary attitudes. What emerges is that, in response to the growth of political corruption in Maryland, reformism grew, too, and steadied into political fact. Unfortunately for Marvin Mandel, history betrayed him. Danger signs, though plainly marked by 1970, caught him looking, delicately bemused, in quite another direction.

Closest scrutiny here goes to the Mandel affair itself as a logical culmination of both trends seen earlier in motion, widespread corruption and the struggle against it. If only indirectly, the Mandel circle did recognize that what it had set afoot was wrong.

Its members contrived a cover-up that, in its Byzantine intricacies, made the Watergate cover-up look like hide-and-go-seek.

Ironically, it was this very cover-up that queered the game. Jurors reported after the trial that they thought Marvin Mandel had lied on the witness stand and that, despite some sympathy for him, lies so transparent could scarcely have rolled forth from an innocent man. And if Mandel was guilty so were the rest.

A relatively recent development recounted here is the maturing of legal enforcement machinery used to peel back the aforementioned cover-up. This offers a possible answer to one of the more persistent questions: Why Maryland? Is this a uniquely dirty little state (described by Marvin Mandel, in his preconviction posture, as "a postmark for corruption")?

The answer seems to be no. Maryland simply achieved a quicker, more professional, momentum than other states in turning its rascals out. Led by Barnet D. Skolnik, already the seasoned scourge of one vice-president and two Maryland county executives, the team fielded by the U.S. attorney's office proved itself heavily armed, resourceful, convincing. At the end, however, its victory over the Mandel circle turned narrow and marred.

Where the enforcement machinery sagged was at the Fourth Circuit Court of Appeals in Richmond, Virginia. Prosecutors, defendants, and onlookers alike were left cross-eyed by this court's bewildering zigs and zags. No small factor in the near-upset at Richmond was the canny maneuvering demonstrated by Arnold M. Weiner, Mandel's lawyer and the lead counsel for the defense. Badly out-gunned by the federals and their cannonade of documents, Weiner nevertheless played with devilish ingenuity upon Skolnik's uncertain linkage between the bribers and the bribed, between the quid and the quo. Judge Robert L. Taylor would later call Weiner "one of the finest lawyers in the country—and honest, too."

Throughout, inevitably, the book focuses on Marvin Mandel. It is to measure his behavior against the behavior of predecessors that the selected historical portions are lowered as a backdrop. It was his personal involvement in a conspiracy which lifted tensions, which gave investigators their sense of high mission. It was his crossover between wives which forced a sort of drama and, for some, piquancy. His powers as governor furnished the conspiracy its pivot, his evasive manner contributed to the conspirators' exposure.

Marvin Mandel is the book's central figure, all right, and just there arises its central flaw.

Too little is set forth on the Mandel background and home life, on his own views of what befell him and why. Too few clues are offered to illuminate what, by way of inner motivations, makes this unhappy man tick. What does appear had to be gathered in, perforce, from others not necessarily close to him. Marvin Mandel himself, understandably weary of these painful matters, declined repeated invitations to review them once again. He apparently advised his family to do the same. With two exceptions, his codefendants stood silent on advice of their lawyers.

Even so, as a matter of dramatis personae, a portrait of the six defendants together is paintable. Ranged personally at varying distances from the Governor, their mutual magnet, the five codefendants are a disparate lot. Closest stood Irvin Kovens, a Mandel crony and booster from early manhood, and W. Dale Hess, so matey in their time as young legislators he was called "Marvin's mother." Kovens—tall and stooped, expensively dressed, faintly menacing—had family money and made much more in a Florida land deal. Hess came on the sly rustic, jester to the gubernatorial court, shooter of sharp angles, sudden millionaire. Both had a little trouble with syntax, also with the line separating right from wrong.

Smoother spoken by far, but a step further back personally from Mandel, were the insurance brothers, Harry W. Rodgers III and his brother, William, called by reporters "Billy Who?" The Harry Rodgers role, as crack corporate executive, was to hold together and guide the Tidewater Insurance Associates, a frankly political trough at which two governors, J. Millard Tawes and Marvin Mandel, fed and flourished—for a while. The William A. Rodgers role was relatively insignificant: he was called driver of the getaway car.

Almost as incidental to the main proceedings was Ernest N. Cory, Jr., a lawyer-fixer of rural stripe, opportunist, and eager hanger-on. Cory never made the first rank. Instead he let himself be hustled about as messenger and as instant camouflage by men younger, tougher, smarter. But Cory had ridden pink-coated to foxhounds and so, whether the others cared or not, supplied a half-comic, half-gentrified note otherwise lacking.

So stood the Mandel circle, strewn in two-way dependence about their patron, the Governor.

All but Cory, whom he scarcely knew, Marvin Mandel thought of as his closest, most trusted friends. Mandel, Kovens, Hess, and the Rodgers brothers dined, drank, shot wild ducks, vacationed, partied. Their wives shared much of the friendship. Presents were exchanged, birthdays celebrated, jokes played. What bound them originally and held them for years was the jobbing at two levels, above and beneath the table, of a steady stream of money for election purposes. They were very good at that.

Of the lot only Mandel was poor, only he was genuinely interested in the study of government and, consequently, he more than the others was personally retiring. But only Mandel carried the authority and presence of the governor's office, and this more than made up for the rest. It was he as their companion who furnished them all whatever style or station they acquired.

This relationship was not unprecedented. Spiro Agnew too had close political friends of the money-raising variety, but in the crunch the difference was drastic. It was four of Agnew's friends who, to save themselves, pointed accusing fingers at him: all went free. Each of Mandel's friends, by contrast, held loyal to his leader: all served time of one sort or another.

As a result, the two cases while seemingly parallel were built on grounds far apart. Direct evidence did in Agnew, who half-acknowledged his own guilt. But circumstantial evidence, bottomed on the damning documents, brought down Mandel. He and his friends stonewalled to the end.

One result was that where little public confusion followed the Agnew case the Mandel trial left behind it puzzles spinning at many levels. Herewith an attempt to resolve a few.

Acknowledgment is a staple in the code of book writers, a genteel band. But how acknowledge so much to so many? Start where? How stop? I can hardly go back to the late Ed Young, my first city editor, who sent me forth as a political reporter. I mustn't impose on Bradford Shea, my new grandson, who because of the name may some day have to bear burdens now undreamed-of. The point is, as with total peace, total acknowledgment is totally impossible. I can reach out a grateful hand here only to a few, then hope those somehow left unacknowledged will come forward once again, with forgiveness. The many individuals who shared their knowledge of the events related in this book are listed in the Notes on the Sources at the end of the volume. I thank them too.

Ted Lippman, the *Baltimore Sun*'s elegant columnist, led me to think a book was possible. Jack Goellner, director of the Johns Hopkins University Press, became my editor, my publisher, my friend, and, that uncommon species, a gentle camel driver. Jacqueline Wehmueller as copy editor proved tougher, thank God.

Jean Hare, departmental secretary for the *Evening Sun*'s editorial writers, scooped up without complaint an endless flood of letters and clippings, telephone messages and appointments. John Hudgins, departmental messenger, Xeroxed until his back hurt. Cindi, of Totally Typing, was totally efficient.

It is counted a grace note for the writer to say a word about his own family. In this case, there's more than grace. On one hand see three years of snappish mornings and morose evenings, sullen silences and irrational outbursts. On the other hand, witness forbearance at breakfast, encouragement at night, understanding all the time. The three of them—Molly and both our daughters, Brucie and Sally—read chapter by chapter and managed perceptive comments on each. To them I owe much.

Chronology

1968

November. Maryland Governor Spiro Agnew is elected vice-president. Marvin Mandel is chosen by the Maryland legislature to succeed him in 1969.

1970

November. Marvin Mandel is elected governor by popular vote.

December. Mandel is involved in a fatal automobile accident while returning, postmidnight, from parts unknown. Jeanne Dorsey's name is first heard in State House gossip. Later, when Barbara Mandel receives a diamond bracelet, some say it's a pacifier.

1971

April. Irvin Kovens makes private inquiries about buying Marlboro Racetrack. He is told he can't because of previous contractual commitments. Nor can his wife or children.

May. Mandel vetoes the Marlboro expansion. This veto reduces the value of Marlboro. At Kovens's suggestion, Tubby Schwartz buys 15,000 shares.

December. The rest of Marlboro stock is bought for $2 million. The secret buyers are Dale Hess, Harry and William Rodgers—all close friends of Mandel—and Ernest Cory. Publicly, Eugene Casey is called the new owner and president. Later, Schwartz will say he owns the track.

Hess acquires a 9 percent interest in Security Investment, Inc., an interest he will later value at $725,000. A few days later, Hess gives Mandel four-ninths of his own share. This is worth at least $300,000.

Mandel is given, virtually free, a $35,000 share in Ray's Point Farm, a real estate enterprise owned by Hess, the Rodgers brothers, and others. Later, the Governor's name is erased from the records.

1972

January. Legislators, including most of the Governor's followers, vote to override Mandel's veto of the Marlboro bill, in effect reinstating the expansion and once again doubling Marlboro's value.

March. Mandel backs a bill to fatten Marlboro still more. Fifty-eight new racing days would be added, for a total of ninety-four. Because all would be used at one of the larger tracks—larger crowds, larger betting pool, larger profits—the Marlboro investment would be maximized. True owners are still secret.

April. Rumors arise. A senate rebellion, led by a midnight filibuster, kills the Marlboro expansion, temporarily.

December. Marlboro's secret owners arrange a merger with Bowie Racetrack. The gain is huge. They get their original investment back, plus 30 percent of the merged tracks, plus the land under abandoned Marlboro, then valued at $1.5 million. All this within one year, using capital almost entirely borrowed.

1973

April. Facing a new law requiring public officials to disclose their holdings, Mandel secretly cancels his interest in Security Investment.

May. Mandel's circle raises $917,000 to reelect him, more than a year in advance of the election. Serious challengers back off.

July. Mandel leaves his wife, Barbara, declaring himself in love with another woman, Jeanne Dorsey. Later, Kovens lends Mandel $150,000 to underwrite the divorce. Hess helps out, screened behind the Pallottine Fathers.

1974

April. Hess and Harry Rodgers are formally notified that they are under investigation by the federal grand jury.

Hess writes a letter that he back-dates six years earlier, before Mandel was governor. It explains away Mandel's income from Security Investment as old legal fees earned from Hess.

August. Barbara Mandel's divorce becomes final. A half-hour later, Marvin Mandel marries Jeanne Dorsey.

November. Mandel is reelected governor by a two-to-one majority.

1975

February. Mandel denies at a news conference any knowledge that Hess and Rodgers own Marlboro.

April. Mandel repeats his denial of knowledge of Marlboro ownership.

September. Mandel is notified that he, too, is under grand jury investigation.

November. Mandel, with five others, is indicted for mail fraud and racketeering.

1976

December. The first trial ends in a mistrial because jurors learn of two separate attempts to influence their decision. Two men are later convicted.

1977

August. All six defendants—Mandel, the two Rodgers brothers, Hess, Kovens, and Cory—are convicted at the end of a second trial.

1979

January. A three-judge panel of the Court of Appeals vacates the convictions, citing error by the judge in district court. They vote two for vacating, one for upholding.

July. A six-judge holding by the same court splits three to three. The effect is to reinstate the original convictions.

November. Eight judges split four to four on whether to hear the defendants' appeal again. Convictions remain in effect.

1980

May. Mandel begins serving nineteen months in federal prison at Eglin Air Force Base, Florida.

1981

December. Mandel is released from prison and returns home. The others are already free.

1.

Vindication,
for Awhile

B y 4:30 P.M., when her telephone buzzed, Pat O'Meara had made a satisfying dent in a three-year stack of courtroom jetsam. There were statute references, motions to quash, defense briefs—all left over from the Marvin Mandel case, most tumultuous by far the firm of Melnicove, Kaufman & Weiner had ever handled. It was January 11, 1979, and after three years the case hung in uneasy limbo. There had been a conviction, but it was now on appeal in Richmond, Virginia, where the Fourth Circuit Court sits. Luck could go either way, but Pat O'Meara had no reason to expect a decision that Thursday.

It looked like rain when she glanced out her sixth-floor office window at Baltimore's oil-gray inner harbor. A nice humdrum day: she clicked her teeth in contentment. She had purposely put on her flat heels and a dress she wouldn't, well, wouldn't wear in the Easter parade. A nice humdrum cleanup day, with the partners mostly out of town or anyway out from underfoot. Pat O'Meara reached for the buzzing telephone.

Arnold Weiner? The Governor's lawyer?

Sorry, he was in Philadelphia for the day. Al Figinski, his partner? Well, he had gone to a bar association meeting outside of Towson. Couldn't she take the message . . . who was this calling, anyway?

The soft Virginia syllables she heard could not temper the metallic words they formed. "Fourth Circuit . . . Richmond . . . assistant clerk . . ."

1

Pat O'Meara felt her spine tingle and, as became a seasoned legal secretary, instantly put the tingle down. Was this the Mandel case? Yes, it was. The assistant clerk sounded a little superior when he said he had to talk to a partner about that, a secretary wouldn't do. Pat O'Meara got Phyllis Brown, the firm's lawyer for technical matters, on the line. Sensing something big, she took out her stenographer's pad, then listened in.

On came the Virginia voice, rattling off whereases and accompanying judicial throat-clearings. Dutifully Pat O'Meara scribbled shorthand notes: Arnold Weiner was due back that night and would want the word. But which way was the damned court panel ruling? Conviction affirmed? Vacated . . . Well, what?

At last, near the very end, the assistant clerk got out the telling decision, the critical words. "Vacated . . . remanded," Pat O'Meara heard Richmond say, and for a moment a ringing in her ears blocked out all else. Later she was to learn that two of the three judges held with the Mandel defense, that one dissented. What mattered just then was that, at two to one, the panel seemed to be switching on the sunshine again. Not quite seventeen months earlier, when Marvin Mandel had been convicted by a federal jury of mail fraud and racketeering, all the lights had gone off. Now, suddenly, there were the lights blazing—or so it seemed that hitherto gloomy Thursday, and for the moment it was enough and maybe too much. The world had turned.

Pat O'Meara is a disciplined woman not given to soap opera whimsey, but the case had gotten to her all through the trial. She pulled for Marvin Mandel to win. She grieved at his conviction and felt outright exultant at this reprieve. Now, she knew she must get the glad word to him at once before the news media could pounce. Already a television reporter had caught some whiff of court action and was calling in for details. Pat O'Meara firmly put the call on hold, then dialed the Governor at the modest office he had rented fifteen miles south of Baltimore at the Post Office building in Arnold, Maryland. He was just leaving, and her call caught him alone.

"We've got it," she told him. Only the words were matter of fact. Breathless, her voice hung at the edge of tears. Marvin Mandel's ear caught the happy excitement at the Baltimore end of the line.

"Mrs. O, Mrs. O," he said over and over, almost stroking her with the affectionate nickname as if the two were battle-worn teammates, which is about what they had become. Each savored the moment. But each quickly realized it had to be cut short, that further events pressed for unfolding. Pat O'Meara hung up, thereafter to undergo a five-hour barrage of newsmen's calls. By 10:30 that night, she had had all four of the Baltimore television stations on the line, the Washington stations, the wire services, the *Baltimore Sunpapers* and the *Baltimore News-American*, the *New York Times*, the *Washington Post* and *Star*. One voice she was hugely relieved to hear: it was that of Arnold Weiner, homeward bound from Philadelphia and calling in from a roadside telephone booth shortly after 5. Given the good Richmond news, Weiner sprang back in his car to race south on the Kennedy Highway for Baltimore, quietly humming to himself.

When Pat O'Meara's husband picked her up at 11 for supper, she lit the last cork-tipped Tareyton of four packs smoked through that afternoon. She realized that, except for a Coke or two from the office refrigerator, nothing had passed her lips in almost twelve hours. But she had been the first to bring to Marvin Mandel, and the world that with various sentiments watched him, Richmond's delightful thunderbolt. Next, the impulse she had conveyed would move forward, if at a level less orderly and more exuberant. Marvin, for example, had Jeanne to tell.

Maddeningly, Jeanne didn't answer the telephone. The Governor—yes! He would govern again, if only for the five days until Wednesday—could hear the phone buzzing at the small estate the couple had taken a few months earlier at Glen Oban, a leafy suburb twenty minutes' ride north of Annapolis. Where was Jeanne, this fiercely protective new wife of his? Where was this vibrant blonde who had plucked him from a stable workaday marriage of thirty-two years and thrust him, some said with a cruel leer, straight up to the jailhouse door?

How those two had writhed under that scornful reading, how they had lashed out at real enemies and at many more imaginary ones. With what frantic intensity they had insisted that Marvin was innocent and that, as Jeanne kept saying, everyone who knew him admired him and loved him. With what bleeding they had heard the government set forth its damning evidence: the "cheapest, meanest, dirtiest, trick I ever saw," Jeanne said of the revelations of Marvin's private finances. Finally, devastatingly, the eighteen iron blows from a hesitant jury: guilty, guilty, guilty . . . For Marvin and Jeanne it had been three years of purgatory, and suddenly, this ecstatic turn. But Jeanne didn't know, and Marvin couldn't get to her. Why, oh why wouldn't she answer?

Jeanne was taking a shower. The rush of water muffled all sounds, including the telephone. But wait . . . wasn't that a noise at the back door? Jeanne, wet as a fish, shampoo in both ears, clutched at a towel. It was Marvin bursting in, not five minutes after grabbing the state police car waiting outside the Arnold Post Office.

"It's been reversed!"

Jeanne stood there dripping. Mystified, she dabbed the towel at her hair.

"What are you talking about?"

"It's been reversed!"

"Do you mean? . . ."

"Yes!"

Jeanne cried. Marvin cried. They laughed too.

What happened next? a reporter asked the following morning. "I don't have to tell you what happened next," Jeanne said.

What would happen beyond that was, just then, less predictable. The time bracket is important. Here it was Thursday evening, and Marvin Mandel's term as governor would run out the following Wednesday. That was the day Harry Hughes, elected in November, was to be inaugurated his successor. There loomed a full five days during which all the considerable powers of a Maryland governor were Mandel's to exercise once again—if he chose to. He had but to snap his fingers, then ascend the throne as if the horrible trial had never happened.

Would he turn vengeful? Quickly sign up a lot of old friends in state jobs? Fire his political enemies? Jigger the state budget? Maybe hand last-minute pardons to a couple of convicted criminals? Mainly, what would he do about Blair Lee, the too-loyal, now-tortured acting governor?

Blair Lee had been first the beneficiary and then the victim of the Mandel saga, of what he himself wistfully called life's "little ironies." Up he had gone to lieutenant governor on the Mandel slate in 1970 and again in 1974, then—on his own, for governor—disastrously down in 1978. Running in that Democratic primary, he met a reformist surge against what Mandel and his circle seemed to stand for. Lee stumbled badly. Trying a straddle, he loudly proclaimed the Mandel "stain" to be gone. But onlookers discerned, tucked away among the Lee assistants, the Mandel campaign consultant, the Mandel patronage boss, the Mandel chief of staff. What was this? Milking votes from both sides? Mandel diehards on one hand, unforgivers on the other? Lee had correctly sensed a public ambivalence about the Mandel case, but this contrivance was too clever, too cynical. Democrats voted with zest to bring up instead the fresh face of Harry Hughes and, in the fall election, that choice had been confirmed. So what now?

Was all this political purging abruptly reversed by a two-to-one court decision, by only a partial panel court made up of non-Maryland judges at that? Here was an ironical if hopeless puzzle to Lee who, given an earlier court decision, might well have been trying on his own inaugural robes. But an irrelevancy to Mandel. Perhaps understandably, he chose not to worry about Lee's personal ironies but to relish to the full what he was certain was his triumphant, and justified, recall from the darkness of three years past.

It was familiar adversaries, the news media, which furnished the jubilant Mandel his first opportunity to work off a resentment long stored up, now festering. Print personal embarrassments, would they? Humiliate him with published details of custom sports jackets, of diamonds, of Florida vacations, of divorce arrangements paid for by his friends? Violate his privacy, bait him at news conferences, lecture him in righteous editorials? . . . Well, now, that worm had turned. In hand was the most explosive news break of his career and in the careers of many of the reporters covering him . . . look, Jeanne, through that window. There's a couple of the bastards outside the house right now. Screw them. He would cut them off where it hurt worst. At this electric moment, he would cut them off from himself.

Out went word from the Glen Oban living room to state troopers gathered on the wintry driveway: keep the press off my back. Three police cars moved to block both approaches; reporters were told to step back, the Governor had nothing to say to them. Next a follow-up order: get a police car ready to take Jeanne and me to Annapolis . . . no, I just thought of something . . . get more cars . . .

At 7:15, reporters saw four police cars turn south on Ritchie Highway, toward Annapolis. In the back seat of the last car, Marvin and Jeanne smiled and waved gaily. Newspeople sprang to their own cars, hurried in pursuit—then hell and son of a bitch! Where was Mandel? The Mandel-bearing police car had somehow melted out of sight. Back to the Mandel compound hustled three cars full of growling reporters. But on to Annapolis, some at 80 mph, sped nine others, anxiously hunting a quarry all knew to be foxy. For the quarry had indeed fled but, foxlike, had taken cover. Marvin and Jeanne, still euphoric, laughed in delight as deluded pursuers milled about in the gathering darkness.

Their police cruiser had pulled just off Ritchie Highway at a side road. Past them as they watched, Jeanne through happy tears, hurried a carful of reporters, a carful of print photographers, then the television exotics with their cams mini and maxi. All this journalistic firepower primed and loaded, but the target inexplicably out of sight. Journalism had known few moments more maddening.

The Mandels had known few moments more delicious. It was not alone that the appeal had worked at Richmond, that the appeals court had turned back the hated guilty verdict. Marvin's name stood clear at last of the three-year shadow: He was an honest man again in the eyes of the law, wasn't he? Jeanne's blind fierce faith had been justified after all, right? Right, and to celebrate they had just given one in the eye to their tormentors in the press, by now charging in bafflement about slushy county roads leading nowhere. Warm and chuckling, feeling richly vindicated, Marvin and Jeanne settled back against the cushions as the police cruiser swung out on the highway again, this time for Annapolis at last. There, at the scene where nine years earlier Marvin had achieved the political throne, they would taste triumph all the more savory for rancid doubts raised and now suddenly quashed. It was 7:30, and snowflakes winked out in the dark water below as the police car crossed the Severn River Bridge.

To ordinary Marylanders elsewhere, the news bounced briskly across the state. Reporters left tricked and cursing in Annapolis furnished a sardonic frieze but their personal irritations were, as always in journalism, immaterial. What mattered was that Pat O'Meara was busy, back at the Baltimore law firm, feeding out the essential news break: Marvin Mandel had beaten the rap, or certainly seemed to have. Smoothly the home office news people sensed commanding importance, tapped out special bulletins. Instantly wire services moved copy: great presses paused, refitted, spun slowly, then faster. Quicker still, electronic impulses flickered, living-room screens carried the message Pat O'Meara had picked up from Richmond. Some who heard it shared the Mandels' near-ecstasy. Some did not. A sample of reactions is revealing, notably of tensions bottled up within the Mandel circle itself.

Irvin Kovens was not ecstatic, at least not in a conventional clap-hands way. A gruff man of imposing presence, Kovens had been tagged "the Czar" at the trial where with Mandel and four others he was convicted of a massive, highly imaginative fraud upon Maryland citizens. Just after the Richmond reversal, an *Evening Sun* reporter reached him by telephone at the Cricket Club in North Miami, Florida. What was Kovens's reaction now?

"Go get Mandel," Kovens said. "This is his day. Let him get all you sons of bitches who chopped him up. You 'expletives' [the *Evening Sun* daintily reported] called him a crook, you called him a thief. . . . I'm as bitter with the *Sunpapers* as with the U.S. attorney's office."

W. Dale Hess, wryly called "Country Boy" in several incriminating documents, was more serene. A former Future Farmer of America graduated to millionaire political fixer, Hess said the turnabout "brings back your faith." Just which faith, he did not say.

A not altogether innocent bystander was William Rodgers. On getting the word from Richmond, Rodgers loosed a noisy neighborhood party to celebrate. There was champagne and, as a grace note, the host sent an obscene message to a Baltimore newspaper editor.

From the remaining two defendants—Harry Rodgers, William's younger but sharper brother, and the more or less pathetic Ernest Cory, Jr.—the post-Richmond response trailed off in prudent silence.

So it went with the Marlboro six, this little band that thought it had chanced upon a system to beat the horse races, a system quicker and surer than the tedious walk to the $2 bettors' window. In a different way, they bet $2 million, hoping for $4 million or more back. Their misfortune was to win, for a while.

These six stood at the center of the judicial splash suddenly thrown up by the doubts of two judges in Richmond. In widening circles about them, ripples touched others at varying distances. A close Mandel aide, Frank Harris, in nonpolitical life a railroad engine driver, said, "I'm happy . . . just had some gin." Ben Cardin, a Mandel political ally elevated to Speaker of the House of Delegates: "I hope this puts an end to it." Thomas H. Franz III, a troubled juror who had hung back thirteen days from the word *guilty*, said, "I'm not surprised. I was hoping for reversal." Of these, none discerned the tentative nature of the two-to-one ruling. All assumed the Mandel circle stood finally exonerated.

No more doubt had Paul Maggio, a 44-year-old guard at the Baltimore jail, who nevertheless took a different view. To a *Sun* reporter running an opinion survey, Maggio said, "They should have hung that bum [Mandel]. . . . All you've got to do if you want to be a thief is turn politician." If this sentiment came harshly from an apostle of law and order, the mood seemed not uncommon. Other observations rounded up in a newspaper survey conducted at three shopping centers in Baltimore County divided two to one against the Richmond decision, meaning against the Mandel group. Still, the troublesome point remained: one in three consulted at random stood with Mandel and not against him.

The government was badly jolted. Privately, members of the United States attorney's office were horror stricken; publicly, they kept silent. Judge Robert Taylor, the elderly jurist in whose rulings the higher court found what it called error, was also unconvinced but sorrowfully wordless. Overall the prosecuting machinery was left in an unaccustomed, unwelcome posture. It seemed to have won a ragged victory with the onlooking public, only to lose out—also raggedly—in the eyes of the law. What now?

One trial had been strangely aborted, the second finally fought through to a close, anguished finish. Now, in effect, prosecutors were hurled back to stand where they had stood three years earlier. Was still a third trial on the same weary, chewed-out evidence inescapable in the Richmond finding? Or was there another, shorter, way out? Glumly prosecutors put their heads together.

Against the night sky the dome of Maryland's elegant old State House is lit up to butter-colored yellow. It seems to warm Annapolis's colonial streets especially for Marvin and Jeanne as the police car clears the river. Airily, they put aside the pain endured through the three years since Marvin's indictment. Any suggestion of a cloud on the future is disdained: The breaks are turning their way, aren't they? Who could stop them now? Not the prosecutors left mute in Baltimore, not the hated press with its mutterings about a "premature" celebration. Certainly not Blair Lee, victim of his unwisely divided loyalties. Not even Harry Hughes, cold and unforgiving toward Mandel but still hesitant, personally, about striking his own gubernatorial stance. Nobody could stop them in the five days, beginning tomorrow, which stretch ahead to the Hughes inauguration. Let's embrace the present, let's live the next few days as we never lived before.

Which is what they did. Whereupon the once-shattered world of Marvin Mandel, defying Humpty Dumpty, began on this magical evening to reassemble its scattered fragments.

Eye-corner glimpses convey the scene unfolding, a smoke-filled resurrection. Dinner that night is private at the home of a close friend from the golden days before indictment. The company is impromptu and effervescent. Enter another crony from State House days, the Mandel patronage chief, Maurice Wyatt: Irish vivacity abounds. Soon a larger welcome beckons. Well lubricated and launched, the little party moves across Annapolis to the rooftop lounge of the favored legislative pub, the Hilton.

At the hotel's door, a half-dozen legislators clutch Marvin's hands, clap his back, sneer happily at the prosecutors left undone. Marvin sounds his theme for the evening, indeed for weeks to come. He is vindicated, he says, his name is cleared, he is the Governor again. Yeah, Marvin, yeah, cry the hangers-on. They form a chorus half-admiring, half-sycophantic. You're vindicated, yeah. They elbow into the crowded elevator beside him and Jeanne.

The Hilton's management has its own political opportunism. In the top-floor bar, its broad windows disclosing pin-point reflections off the dark harbor water, doors are kept open past closing hours by "special request." New admirers cluster about, a table for eight is quickly filled. Marvin Mandel, quietly radiant in vindication, is the automatic center. He sips Old Grand-Dad and water, lights his trademark meerschaum. He says yes, he is vindicated, the court system does work after all. A couple of Philadelphia reporters happen by; noncommittally they say well, now, well, well. Jeanne looks on, glowing.

The little party swells and contracts, changes and revolves, then slides off into the night. It is a rolling restoration. Marvin and Jeanne move arm-in-arm at its heart: 58 years old, he is short, wiry, trendily dressed; she is 41, taller by a half-head, befurred as for the opera. Does Jeanne choose Marvin's clothes? Never mind who pays for them. Together they amble into a main street bar: old Annapolis hands hurry up, beam at Marvin, hug Jeanne. Marvin says the news is great, it's great. It's vindication. On they move. They do not drink, they just kibitz, smile endlessly, bask in approval. No unkind word is said or, if one is, it goes unheard. For a while reporters tag along, scooping up every tiny scrap for tomorrow's papers. It's increasingly thin stuff, because all Marvin says is vindication, vindication, vindication. Reporters drift off.

By 2 A.M. Marvin and Jeanne are tired and getting hungry. Chick 'n' Ruth's delly stands open and, as always, is hospitable to the Mandels: their eminence makes Chick Levitt feel important. In return, Chick has roped off a special booth they are to sit in. Long ago he put in a little sign saying "Governor's Office" and installed a red telephone to make Marvin feel at home and comfortable. They sit there again, still treasuring the news only nine hours old and now freshly buoyed by the Annapolis reception. They tell Chick how fine it feels to be vindicated. Chick says it's only right. They linger late over empty coffee cups, contentedly squeezing the last drops from an evening rich and sweet. Vindication, it's wonderful.

Five more sweet days lie ahead. But, unmentioned, the edge of premonitions not so sweet arise about what Day Six and Day Seven and the days beyond may hold for Marvin. Reluctantly, they turn back to Glen Oban. The dawn of Friday, or Day One, brightens the Severn.

The following Wednesday, five days ahead, had to be the end of something and the beginning of something else. Everyone knew that. But the end of how much? The beginning of what else? And how about the meantime?

The Hughes inaugural was immovably scheduled for January 17, graven in the state constitution, formally confirmed by vote of the people. That was clear. But who was the outgoing governor to be, the newly resuscitated Mandel or Blair Lee, acting governor now dangling on a Mandel whim? That was the first puzzle, a small one and formalized but titillating all the same.

Second, and deeper laid, was the puzzle of the next turn, if any, predictable in the mail fraud case. Had Mandel really won through? Was the prosecution actually ready to quit, to abandon three years of work to what struck some as no more than judicial pettifoggery? Federal surrender seemed unlikely, as one longshot began to beckon. Prosecutors debated with increasing enthusiasm a petition to the full seven-member Court of Appeals, asking for a rehearing. Court precedent frowned on rehearings unless the issue was of overriding importance. Still, couldn't the prosecutors produce legal questions too pointed to be brushed aside by the judges as routine, as disposable by a two-to-one panel decision? Scenting a recoup, the U.S. attorney's office poked about among precedents for support. Not all moods were so ponderous.

It was twelve minutes past noon, Friday, and Michael S. Silver's glittering eyes swept across the backs of bureaucrats bent low over desks in the outer office of acting Governor Lee. Silver raised his fist, blew high a cloud of rich cigar smoke, then shouted: "The muldoons are back!"

Bureaucrats started nervously. Once Silver had been Marvin Mandel's deputy patronage chief, a sort of jobholder's executioner. But now he was a has-been, an unhorsed curiosity around the State House. So he must be kidding, mustn't he? Well, these muldoons, these Mandel hatchetmen, kept multiplying. They wore dark glasses, Runyonesque hats pulled low.

"Out! Out! Out! Out! Out!" snapped one.

Another, with a sinister leer: "We've got to change a few nameplates."

"Did you get the old nameplates out like we told you?"

"They polished up?"

Maurice Wyatt couldn't keep his boyish face altogether straight. He leaned over one toothsome secretary, murmuring: "Honey, you can keep your job. We're not going to fire you."

In a splutter of laughter the game was up, but the muldoons— or "Mandelniks," as prosecutors privately called them—had got welcome relief. In a scene otherwise strained and lugubrious, they injected a fey, even manic note. They rescued the five-day

Mandel restoration from a parody of Napoleon's one hundred days between Elba escape and Waterloo collapse. Mandel himself, however, may have missed the point. Napoleon-like, he advanced upon Annapolis as if there were no Waterloo in his future, hence no more Richmond court to stumble over, certainly no shadow of federal prison, no St. Helena, waiting at Eglin Air Force Base. For Marvin Mandel in public, at least, was a governor newly rampant.

Yes, he was pleased with the decision, he told a news conference. Yes, there was vindication, the stain was removed. More even than the now-familiar words, the scene he set conveyed a sense of righteous triumph deeply felt, of scheming enemies properly put down. For a stage, he chose the handsome old conference room just outside the governor's office. For gubernatorial costume, he dressed up in dark blue pinstripes and polka-dot tie. For a back-up chorus, he kept Jeanne close at hand, blue eyes alight, vigorously nodding blonde curls. What most firmly convinced the fifty reporters gathered in—here, the audience he played to—was the Mandel manner long put on for news conferences.

Half-irritated, half-condescending, he toyed with the questions. No, he had not yet decided about taking back the governor's office. Yes, he would talk to acting Governor Lee about that. When? Oh, he didn't see any hurry. As of old, Marvin Mandel smiled his small half-smile, relishing his first day of restoration, particularly the opportunity it brought to confound the news people yet again. Twenty microphones besought clear-cut answers, but besought in vain. Jeanne beamed in sunny delight. Soon the reporters trailed out muttering. Mandel was back and evasive. What else was new?

The climax Friday was a largely liquid lunch staged behind closed doors in what had been the Governor's patronage office. There was a sheetcake proclaiming "Welcome back Governor Mandel," a knife, and some napkins. The muldoons were there, and Mandel. A lone free-lance photographer was permitted inside to record things, then was hurried out. The general press was not admitted, a stab unlikely to add to Mandel's journalistic stature. And maybe it wasn't the seemliest of celebrations. The *Baltimore Sun*, ever for propriety, sniffed that "for this one improbable day, Marvin Mandel was back in the saddle."

Others were warmer. Through the legislature, just then gathering for its annual session, Mandel loyalists hurried forward. Delegate Daniel Minnick kissed his leader, then tried in vain to draw Mandel into a personal appearance before the House of Delegates. Minnick said, "There would have been an ovation." Senator Roy Staten took the same worshipful view and, apparently without irony, a more revealing one. "When Marvin Mandel was governor," Staten stated approvingly, "he extended power to all the people. Contractors and developers and everyone got in, not just the political clubs." An illuminating observation, considering that it was mostly contractors and developers, not the political clubs at all, who caused Mandel's fall.

But time was short, only five days. Suddenly, it was Wednesday, the day Mandel's leftover term finally melted away, the day Hughes's fresh term began. Both men had played out the time stiffly, correctly. Hughes had campaigned against the Mandel record and let it be known he didn't want Mandel present at his inauguration. For his part, Mandel bowed to the incoming governor's wish. "It's his day," he said. If Mandel showed no spite, he also showed no repentance. Apparently, he felt neither.

Prior to Wednesday, he had tidied up such loose ends as Blair Lee. Move over, he told Lee on Sunday, I'm coming back formally. Monday he did, for the 45½ hours remaining. In fact, Lee personally had cleared out Saturday, including his own furniture from the governor's residence. An untidiness did linger, it turned out. As governor, Harry Hughes suggested that when the Mandels had moved out of the residence so had many thousand dollars worth of goods—notably, a dozen Waterford crystal champagne glasses and $489 worth of dog food—that were not rightly theirs. The Mandels denied it. A suit and counter suit would follow, but Wednesday no one foresaw that contretemps.

Wednesday was inauguration day. It marked the formal arrival of a new governor dedicated to a clean sweep-out of Mandel detritus, including the dressed-up version Blair Lee had fruitlessly offered at the polls. Inexorability filled the air. The Mandels' five-day bubble, an oddity in any case, finally burst. Marvin tried hard, that last half-day, to keep some sort of flag flying. Also to keep the resentment—he thought himself innocent, wrongly convicted, still in peril from the courts—locked cold and hard in his chest. Earlier, before Lee took off, the two had been able to joke a little about which one was to sit at the governor's desk, which was to sign a minor proclamation. The jokes seemed wan. Lee's sense of humor soon frayed.

"I'll be glad when this crap's over," he said.

"This shit," Mandel said.

Now it was over—or almost. That final morning in the office, with Harry Hughes's inauguration only an hour away, Mandel glanced about the lofty, old-fashioned walls. What stood out were the neatly squared stains left by pictures and plaques taken down, packed, moved off. Jeanne was there, as always, making cheerful sounds. Also an adopted son, then 13, called Paul Dorsey—the family name of Jeanne's first husband. Ellen Mandel, Marvin's 30-year-old daughter, moved restlessly in and out: the conviction had hit Ellen hard. A state trooper waited patiently for orders. From outside the tootling of a band, a tune-up for the Hughes inaugural ceremonies, could be heard. By fifteen minutes before noon there wasn't much left to say. Unobtrusively the others slipped out a side door, hoping to catch the back elevator and dodge the inaugural crowd below. For a moment Marvin Mandel stood in the empty, bare office alone.

He didn't stay long. Soon he shuffled an overcoat over his suit—vested, broad-lapeled, brass-buttoned—and clapped on an Alpine hat gaily banded in feathers. In his left hand he brandished the meerschaum like a weapon. One glance around, then off to join the others at the back elevator. It was locked, a security measure. Around to the front the little party went, down the broad marble staircase to the legislative floor. Legislators and inaugural hangers-on swamped them, smiling, hand-shaking, back-patting. Just what they had hoped to escape. When at last they broke free into State Circle—under the slush an elegant colonial vestige—Jeanne paused for a moment to look back. Then on to the Hilton and coffee and a bottle of champagne that turned out to be flat.

Harry Hughes, tall and imposing in the full morning dress he had rented the day before, was taking over. Maryland's venerable inaugural ceremony unrolled for him as flawlessly as if regulated by quartz clockwork. A solemn oath and a worn family Bible, high-ranked judges and political favor seekers, a band and a choral group and those Marylanders, muffled against the cold, who detect in any inaugural ceremony something moving and even stately. The deep roll of "Maryland, My Maryland," still the most poignant of state songs, left few without an inner tingle.

That tingle, in the view of Harry Hughes, was fine but not altogether substantial. As the governor freshly installed, as the champion chosen by an all-time record majority to turn the rascals out, he wanted there to be no doubt that rascals were henceforward unwelcome in Annapolis. At three critical points in the Hughes inaugural address, the word *different*—different, that is, from the immediate past—pointedly rang out. So did the phrases "scandal, shock, and shame" and "shadow of collective guilt." Then, soothing but firm, Governor Hughes promised for the future "moral conduct . . . beyond reproach." Harry Hughes promised other things too, but his main point was sharp and hard.

Marvin and Jeanne were not there to hear. Because the incoming governor had not wanted them, their five-day resurrection trailed off at a table in the Hilton coffee shop, the now ex-Governor suddenly mindful of history. Only his family and two newspaper reporters were there to hear him, but he began what promised to be a long process, maybe a career, of helping history out. Quickly the ex-gubernatorial ticking-off of good things in his record—school construction and judicial appointments, consolidated offices and tax restraint—began to pall on Jeff Price, the Sun's man. Price had heard all that before. Tactfully, he thought, he ordered up a bottle of good French champagne, hoping to inject a little sparkle into Marvin's historical drone. But no: there wasn't any sparkle. The champagne had been frozen, its bubbles flattened out. Marvin thought that was funny: just the shabby treatment, he said, he expected of the *Sunpapers*. A better bottle put things right.

Shortly even that last bubble flattened out too. Her mouth working, Jeanne began to show the strain. She glanced through the coffee shop window, up the hill toward the south portico of the State House where Governor Hughes was pointing his finger at "scandal, shock, and shame." Jeanne turned back to the table and kissed Marvin. Then she said: "Can we have a private moment?"

A ugustus W. Bradford was a poor but apparently honest country boy who came to Baltimore, married a rich judge's daughter and, with a heavy-handed shove, was elected governor of Maryland in 1861. It's the heaviness of that shove—at the time, some called it corrupt—which brings Governor Bradford in just here. That, plus the fact that if I as his great-grandson didn't raise this matter someone else would—someone out to score points about a cover-up. So here he is, straight from the family closet.

The starting point is the scare Abraham Lincoln had felt earlier in 1861. Following Fort Sumter, the Deep South had gone pell mell into rebellion. Hard by Washington's southern and western flanks, Virginia bristled defiance of the Stars and Stripes. President Lincoln glanced southward and shuddered. Then his eyes turned the other way.

What of Maryland? What of his nearest neighbors, what of his escape route north in the event the Confederates stabbed across the Potomac, maybe to seize him personally, perhaps to hang him? The often sardonic Lincoln found that prospect all too real and quite unlaughable.

The Maryland scene that spring offered the President cold comfort. Just across the District line, the state flapped uneasily in contrary airs. Slavery had long been the bulwark of Maryland tobacco fields, of the agricultural economy common to both Eastern and Western shores of the Chesapeake Bay. For them, secession seemed the logical answer. True, the rolling northern and western counties stood solidly loyal, but Baltimore City was a political maelstrom. Raw, untested immigrants packed its waterfront wards; blacks, freedmen or escaped, slunk frightened through the city shadows. A mercantile class seemed started and stable, but who knew which way the city police force might swing? Baltimore's mayor himself?

Where in Maryland, Lincoln wondered, lay law and order? Where ran a defensible road north?

As a wartime president already half-encircled by rebels, Lincoln couldn't afford not to know. He had to secure his communications to the all-important strength fanning out northward behind him. According to the National Intelligencer, an organ of the Lincoln administration, "The secession of Maryland, from its geographical position, necessarily destroys the national government altogether." But Maryland wasn't sitting tame and still, inviting the federal lasso.

A splutter of events in April, 1861, showed the rebel fevers alight in the Old Line State.

In response to Lincoln's call for help, a regiment of Massachusetts militia started south for Washington by rail. When forced to change stations on foot in Baltimore, militiamen were fallen upon and stoned by a rioting mob: casualties were the first of the young Civil War. The response of Baltimore authorities was revealing. Instead of taking steps to protect future federal soldiery in transit, they undertook to keep them out altogether. City officials burned a half-dozen railroad bridges north of Baltimore: but isolation was precisely what frightened Lincoln most. Nor were state officials more reassuring. Maryland legislators, muttering openly about secession, had to be hustled out of Annapolis to Frederick, thought to be more loyal terrain.

Lincoln got the message. He sent Maryland back one sharper still. The message was military: prominent men were put behind bars in Fort McHenry; the right of habeas corpus was suspended; grumbling newspaper editors were jailed. General Benjamin F. Butler—called "Beast" in the Deep South—proclaimed in May that he had "taken possession" of Baltimore. He would rule the obstreperous city from behind his guns emplaced on Federal Hill. In June, thanks to the lowering presence of the military, a special

17

congressional election produced a handsome victory for the new Union party, the president's choice. Now Lincoln had the reins safely in his hand.

The governorship of Maryland was the state's political rallying point, its moral voice and its inspiration. And, that fall, the governorship had to be decided. It had to be decided, Lincoln concluded, right and not wrong—meaning his Union way instead of "Secessia." The June congressional election had taught him how.

Augustus Bradford, by now a Baltimore lawyer dabbling in Whig politics, had turned out to be something of an orator: the necessity of preserving the Union and the Constitution was the refrain he shared with Lincoln. He seemed just the man, the newborn Union party thought, to carry its banner for governor. The State Rights party was of a different mind. It nominated Benjamin C. Howard of Pikesville. Many thought he could make a strong showing by exploiting pro-Southern sentiments.

What ensued that November varied in intensity, depending on which disputatious newspaper you read. That federal troops policed the balloting is beyond doubt: this was called justified as keeping order and protecting voters' rights. That some voters were apparently protected more than others is the point.

Let a neutral historian, Charles Branch Clark, a history professor at Washington College, give his account: The omnipresence of federal troops on election day, Clark writes, was in "brazen violation" of Maryland's right to conduct its own elections. "The manner of Bradford's election," Clark went on, "is perhaps the least satisfactory feature of his entire career, private and public."

Bradford probably wasn't told, Clark says, what troopers were actually doing, but "from a moral point of view, a large proportion of the [Bradford] vote was secured by intimidation, the illegal voting of soldiers, and the unlawful use of soldiery."

His guess is that Bradford probably would have won anyway. Still, the actual voting results offer an unmistakable signal to all seasoned political reporters that at least some ballot boxes were fiercely joggled. Bradford carried every Maryland subdivision except St. Mary's, Charles, and Calvert counties, in southern Maryland, and Talbot county on the Eastern Shore. The final total stood Bradford, 57,502; Howard, 26,070.

That meant a majority of 30,000 out of slightly more than 82,000 votes cast, a phenomenal two-to-one victory. Ironically, the Baltimore South commented: "Federal troops from every section of the country aided their Union friends here, and deposited their ballots in as many wards and precincts as suited their convenience." Another South-leaning paper observed of the Bradford majority: "Thirty or three hundred thousand—we have forgotten which." The election was illegally won, the paper hinted, whatever the size of the majority. So who cared?

Who cared most was President Lincoln. Now he would not be encircled in the White House, captured and hanged. Now the road north stood clear and safe, now the North's vast superiority in manufacturing could be marshaled against the Confederacy from Washington, not from some refugee capital jerry-built in Philadelphia or New York. For Augustus Bradford was governor of Maryland, and Maryland stood loyal to the Union. Here was a military operation and a military result. Politics came along second.

As it happened, the governor was shortly to part company politically with the president who had furnished him so useful a military boost. It was on the subject of slavery—more specifically, on whether the state or the nation should prescribe the rules for freedom—that Bradford demurred in his inaugural address of 1862. Once again, he spoke out strongly for Union and Constitution. However, he considered abolition of slavery Maryland's own responsibility to carry out and emancipation proclaimed from Washington an interference with state rights.

Border-state sensitivity perhaps. The Baltimore Sun agreed, ambivalently. That was of lesser importance. What mattered most was that the Union stood undisfigured, its southern head still firmly attached to its northern body. Maryland furnished the all-important linkage between shoulder-bone and brain.

Today, a century and a quarter later, let critics be damned.

2.

Gorman and
the Bad Seed

P olitical power is a fluid substance, a watery current canalized between good men banked up on one side, bad men on the other. The aromas of self-interest, whether grabby or enlightened, arise from its surface. So constituted, this streaky old river has meandered through history since the day the first man elbowed the second man aside—and the second man elbowed back. A smoother-sounding name than political power is government. Because the river changes course but never stops flowing, it links tomorrow to yesterday on a tide liquid and restless but, so far, without ebb. One historical rill is pertinent here because it links two Maryland governors widespread in time, Albert C. Ritchie and Marvin Mandel. An earlier tributary is rich with pollution that both Ritchie and Mandel, in contrasting ways, had to contend with many years downstream. Its uncelebrated source was Arthur P. Gorman, United States senator from Maryland.

These linkages hold clues, though seldom direct answers, to questions the Mandel story raises in many minds. No one can tell with precision why Marvin Mandel did what he did. No one knows, certainly, why a man of his demonstrated judgment nevertheless stumbles or is dragged from a high political pedestal to the humiliation of indictment, of trial, of conviction, of counting laundry in a federal prison in Florida. Much may be traced to Mandel directly—his upbringing and his associates, his personality and his philosophy. All that is central, if open only to subjective measure. There is more.

20

How much of Marvin Mandel's fate was determined by pressures outside the man himself? Where lurk the pitfalls in the political system he inherited? What impulses and temptations are bred into the exercise of power in a governing apparatus rooted two centuries deep, indeed among the thirteen original states? How much of this system is old, how much new? To what extent did a shift from old to new values, from permissive to stern, catch Mandel unaware? Or, if aware, then helpless to scramble to safety across the line freshly drawn between right and wrong?

No analysis suddenly bathes the Mandel scene in a clear, all-revealing light. But the very ambiguities provoke inspection, so a little history can be illuminating here. A dutiful record—of state taxes, transportation trends, school needs—is left for other hands, other objectives. Besides, that Mandel was pretty good at governing Maryland is largely conceded. What's considered here instead is confined to those events either directly pertinent to his misfortune or not so directly, to coloring in ethics of time segments unfolding.

It is historically convenient to install Albert Ritchie at the beginning of an era and Marvin Mandel at or near an era's end. To be sure, much of the political heritage common to both governors—iron-handed Gorman and the spirited reaction he provoked—preceded Ritchie. Of what is to follow Mandel beyond the subdued mood Harry Hughes adopted as his successor, much remains undisclosed. The era's cutoff points are ragged, not neat. And yet the fifty-year stretch marked out between the beginning of one governorship, in 1919, and the beginning of the other, in 1969, does show a texture sufficiently characteristic to be of a single, recognizable piece. Its nature is plain: it is the flowering, thrips and all, of modern government in Maryland.

Ritchie only began the modernizing. Where he installed fresh professional techniques at the end of World War I, Mandel and others picked them up down the line and improved them. Where Ritchie accepted with watchful reserve most of the crusty politicians of an earlier generation, and flourished, Mandel was less adroit. He failed to sense the sharp shift of ethics beneath his feet in his own generation, and so fell. No full understanding of the perilous fissures disastrously opened in Mandel's world is possible without, first, a glimpse at the relatively serene world of Albert Ritchie.

Physically, no two men could look less alike than this pair of governors who, as bookends do, prop up between them the annals of a half-century of a state's struggle to govern itself. Ritchie in the 1920s was called "the Gibson man," a man so tall, so ruddy faced and silver haired that a national magazine placed him, along with Charles Lindbergh and a half-dozen movie stars, among the ten handsomest Americans. Mandel is not so blessed. He is short, five feet six, and sallow, with hair between gray and vanishing. Eyes deep and shadowed impose upon him prematurely the melancholy air of an overage croupier at Las Vegas.

Contrasts don't stop with appearance. Where Ritchie radiated old-line, Maryland-Virginia gentility, Mandel is a recruit from the wrong side of the wrong tracks. The descendant of Jewish immigrants so Polish, so "downtown," as to be ruled off the "uptown" turf thought hallowed by their earlier German counterparts. Ritchie was a gregarious denizen of the Maryland Club, a talker, fraternizer, drinker; Mandel is so shy his first wife, Barbara, had to nudge him into his freshman political handshakings. Ritchie sat comfortably at the center of a worldly Baltimore establishment that Mandel—suspecting himself an automatic outcast, partly for ethnic reasons—profoundly distrusts. Both were lawyers, but of what a different stripe: Ritchie jousting with vast utilities, Mandel scrounging his first guys-and-gals clients in Baltimore's tawdry Block. As to personal money, Ritchie inherited a modest nest egg, sat modestly on it. Not Mandel. Born to a hard-scrabble house, he learned skillfully to hone other people's money into his own sharpest election sword. Later, miscalculating, he found himself skewered on the same borrowed blade.

The short of it is this: Albert Ritchie was a political grandee, to the manner born, the last but one of this waning species to sit in the governor's chair. He is commonly written down as Maryland's greatest. Mandel was a political foundling, born to what people call street smarts. But he let his organizer's competence bordering on brilliance betray his personal judgment, which, once elevated clear of the streets, looked not so smart after all. He too might have been rated greatest. Instead he fades into history as Maryland's first governor to busy himself, in his post-Annapolis years, stacking other convicts' clean underwear.

Ritchie and Mandel do show one resemblance, somewhat strained. Both took legacies from a political ancestor they held in common, Arthur Gorman. These two legacies, however, were significantly different. As a United States senator, Gorman had proved himself Maryland's most ruthless practitioner of the spoilsman's art. He had fitted together a statewide machine ("ring" was the reformer's epithet) worthy of two contemporaries, the Tweed Ring in New York and the Gashouse Ring in Philadelphia. As a successor to power, Ritchie spurned Gorman's political distortions and personal exploitations: he held himself up in gleaming, if unspoken, contrast. What Ritchie did condescend to take in hand for his own use were many of the party "bosslets," born and bred in the Gorman Ring, then left unbespoke at Gorman's death. Mandel, enough younger to be Gorman's great-grandson, came along too late to enjoy so tangible a political bequest as a team of tested vote getters. The old ring had rusted out long since. All that came down to him from Gorman was the part Ritchie left untouched: the tradition of making politics pay, plus Gorman's deaf ear to pained outcries from the moralists. Even that legacy was too much, measured by the standards of the 1970s. A federal grand jury held the Mandel inheritance invalid, indeed criminally corrupt.

It was an inheritance all the same, and Mandel was not the only Maryland legatee. Gorman's taking way took root, discreetly underground, and nourished a political tradition in Maryland seldom dragged effectively to light. Beginning in the 1960s, however, federal prosecutors strode aggressively upon the field. Once-vaunted state officials began to wilt and fall, not-so-innocent victims of new legal machinery at last formidable enough to challenge on equal terms the political machinery behind which Gorman's heirs once felt themselves safely barricaded. Gorman had died in 1906 at 68, to reappear as antihero in a symbolism longer than his own life.

Moralizing aside, Gorman deserves historical acknowledgment. He was a leader of unique capacity, and small matter, in history's cold eye, that he led down instead of up. He personified a tradition destined to color Maryland political life for generations to come, though the color, to be sure, was black, not white. A man of these seminal, if splendidly villainous, qualities can scarcely be ignored. This is especially true when the central figure under study, and a political descendent of Gorman, stands convicted of the same kind of corruption to which Gorman long ago gave its highest, most perverse polish. Mandel might well have misstepped anyway, Gorman or no Gorman, but as it happens he had a political forefather who bowed to none in creative amorality. Gorman may be where the Mandel matter begins, so a word here about a century-long linkage.

Mood was of first importance to Gorman's rise. What this flawed genius discerned gathering about him early in the 1870s was unprecedented opportunity and, with it, a handy sort of moratorium on ethics. Following the Civil War Maryland was brushed by a national eruption out of the sleepy agricultural innocence prevalent before Fort Sumter changed America forever. Northern industry and northern trading had won the war, hadn't they? Marylanders like others must learn their lesson, mustn't they? Out rang a righteous yes, whereupon there appeared in the state a trickle of bankers and industrialists, railroaders and contractors. Up to then, farming and a little farm trade had been the Maryland style. Now a substance unfamiliar but inviting, big money, sparkled in the air. Not so sparkling were the swindlers and the bribers, the manipulators and the thimbleriggers, who trotted happily along too. Against them state law lay largely flaccid, especially so when the exploiters began to eye the levers of state government itself. A robber barony waited in the wings.

Because his father had toyed with politics in Howard County, young Gorman's instinct turned naturally to votes and legislative bills and political jobs. To these governmental familiars the newly bustling times suggested the addition of a fresh ingredient, freshly sovereign. It was political bribery. As a promising legislator, Gorman reached out to the new businessmen who were eager to spend money to make more. Politics is the way, he counseled them, then showed them exactly how that was so. The rest is political history, the history of a state machine that fed on a business clientele, that grew formidable enough to balk a president of the United States, that finally provoked an outrage of Maryland reformers to destroy it—or almost. Outright "Gormanism," as the reformers called it through curled lips, was permitted to flourish in Maryland only during the twenty years between 1875 and 1895. Some states were never so deeply infected. In others—hardboiled New York, New Jersey, Pennsylvania; gang-ridden Illinois; the vanquished, starveling South; the damn-your-eyes, shoot-'em-up Westerners—a few comparable machines comparably venal afflicted state or city governments well past the half-way mark of the twentieth century. Still, in their relatively short day,

Gorman and his Baltimore City satrap, I. Freeman Rasin, managed to treat Marylanders to a cheerful extravaganza of politics gone bad easily rivaling the hairiest. Sketches of the old artist's masterpieces sharpen the point.

Creation of the Chesapeake & Ohio Canal Co. was originally a prudent step, state subsidized, taken to bind together watery Maryland's growing trade routes to the West. Gorman perverted it. As a payoff for political favors, he was given control of the C&O as its president: thereafter he extracted as salary enough money for a comfortable personal living, as patronage enough political jobs to build a subservient vote-getting machine, as a statewide organization enough election-time leverage to install at Annapolis a controlling bloc of legislators who, in 1881, elevated Gorman to the United States Senate. That the C&O, so abused, ultimately fell to financial floundering was irrelevant to Gorman.

The Baltimore Gas and Electric Co. was already a near-monopoly enjoying rates still unregulated by state government. It was, nevertheless, subject to state taxes. Gorman-led legislators invented the "bell-ringer," a proposed utility tax so alarmingly steep it brought G&E lobbyists scurrying to Annapolis armed with cash by the bagful. The Gorman machine solemnly accepted G&E contributions, relented on the utility tax, and thus muscled itself up for future elections. Baltimore rate payers absorbed the extra cost.

Grover Cleveland vowed, following his election as president in 1884, to get cheaper imports through to American consumers by lowering the high tariff wall erected against them as protection for domestic business interests. Not cheaper sugar, not with Senator Gorman, friend of the big sugar people, guarding the Senate gate. So damaging was the sugar amendment Gorman tacked on Cleveland's low-tariff bill, so transparent the financial boon to Gorman's sugar friends, that the president could not restrain his anger. Publicly he pointed to Gorman, who had materially boosted the Cleveland nomination a few years earlier. "Party perfidy, . . ." the president said, "Dishonor." Whatever the Gorman motivation, it was not legitimate concern for his own constituency: Maryland grew no sugar, refined little. Other explanations were heard.

Baltimore blacks demonstrated a loyalty to Abraham Lincoln's Emancipation Proclamation and, to the Democratic machine's annoyance, a pronounced tendency to vote Republican. Gorman undertook to stop that, indeed to stop black voting altogether. One way was to pay black voters to avoid the polls on election day. Another was to disfranchise them by legislative act, and Gorman tried both. Conversely, other and more pliable ethnics— notably, Baltimore's immigrants from Germany and Ireland, Italy and Poland—were enlisted as election day repeaters. They were marched from polling place to polling place, voting all the day. Beyond that, tombstones were researched, registered, voted. Tiny rooming houses in the new slum areas ballooned with registered voters, sometimes one hundred to the room. Such votes, delivered on time, carried a market value to aspirant judges, senators, court clerks—all subject to election. To them the Gorman machine offered the best line of goods in town.

Little effort was made, in this blunt-spoken epoch, to pretty up what most people knew to be true. One graduate of the Gorman school would later explain: "Politics is my business and I make it pay. I would be a fool not to." Or, as the *Baltimore Sun* put the same idea, the Gorman machine was "corrupt to the core," if "intelligently run"—not quite balanced phrases suitable for a left-handed epitaph. Imitations of the Mandel era?

Today Arthur Gorman cannot be lightly written off as a political dinosaur, a creature only of his time and soundly trampled by the onrush of Marylanders righteous and higher minded. Times did change for the better and political mores with them, but much change was more an evolution in form than a revolution in substance. Gorman himself, had he lived on to the 1970s, might have recognized his original fingerprints on threads at least loosely connecting a century of successors to power in Maryland. The Gormanish threads culminate—or may culminate; we have still to see how durable this latest reform phase is—in the federal crackdown that suddenly began to close prison doors behind men who once thought themselves politically immune. To this extent Marvin Mandel's observation is legitimate: what he did and was imprisoned for is scarcely unprecedented in Maryland politics. But there is a difference, if not between what was done earlier and what later.

The difference lies instead in the new public refusal to tolerate transgressions of the high-handed Gorman variety. Also, maybe more important, in the rise of a newly authoritative machinery for catching Gorman-like figures all but undreamed-of in Gorman's time. A federal intrusion into state affairs, once thought safely roped off by the United States Constitution, began in the 1960s. This intrusion was all but unhobbled politically, hence effective legally. It rolled up erring politicians wholesale to the sound of broad public applause. Marvin Mandel and his friends were not the first to fall or the last. What they failed to understand—the friends showed little remorse on conviction, Mandel himself none at all—was that they were not part of static, justifying history. Instead, the history they were part of was a history moving on.

The Gorman episode carries in it at least three trends in Maryland public life which strongly illuminate where history came from and where, in the Mandel case, it was to lead. One trend was the gathering of political power into a single dominant hand or circle, hence a leverage organized about pressure points strewn throughout the state. Next was exploitation of the political patronage accruing—jobs and money, legal and illegal—to secure the machine's base and to arm it for election battles. Finally, to Gorman's dismay, a third but contrary trend materialized. This one was the gradual awakening of Maryland reformers provoked by the simple slovenliness of the government Gorman produced, also by the naked extortions imposed upon professionals and businessmen. These three Gorman-time legacies were to linger, in varying styles but in comfortable coexistence, at least until they produced the final Mandel crash in 1979.

Some argue that Maryland's anti-Gorman reform movement that flowered toward the end of the century was, at bottom, self-seeking and revanchist. Many years later, when federal prosecutors had him encircled, Mandel would advance the same complaint. It's another case of the political outs, he said, trying to get back in. In the Gorman case, the complaint carried just enough truth to sustain a superficial argument. Gorman had indeed put out of joint the rural noses of members of a reigning squirearchy who, in the ancient British sense, thought themselves born to rule more or less benignly. On these the arrival of Gorman inflicted a rude shock. But there were others too, men of good will who were genuinely infuriated by the Gorman excesses. A commanding call for something better emerged from the throats of lawyers, doctors, educators, and those businessmen persuaded by the new notion that enlightenment too, not just slickness, could turn a profit. Soon even some Republicans, long bottled up by the Gorman Democrats, joined in. Baltimore newspapers, hitherto upholders of "happiness in a guarded way," caught the scent of a gathering political kill.

First blood was drawn in the 1882 elections. Reformers pushed onto the Baltimore judicial bench a slate of relatively nonpolitical lawyers against furious machine opposition. By 1895, reform was in full voice. Reform struck Gorman at a vital point, his hold on the legislature, where Maryland's members of the United States Senate were then chosen: Gorman's own seat was undermined, a Republican was dispatched to Washington in his place. The machine wasn't destroyed, but it was decapitated and dismembered, then left to flop about for two largely headless decades.

Today the Gorman machine seems almost statesmanlike in retrospect. Other states displayed pockets of political depravity Marylanders never dreamed of. At the federal, even presidential, level Credit Mobilier and Teapot Dome stood for political profit grabs that push the C&O Canal and the Mandel circle's little fling with Marlboro Racetrack into the category of elbowing at a volleyball game. But shadings of villainy are not the point. The significance here of the rise and fall of Arthur P. Gorman is its backlighting of the Mandel case, its sinking of roots sturdy and corrupt. It represents the early establishment of a Maryland tradition destined to plague for a century those Marylanders determined to believe that popular government aims at bettering the life of the governed, not at boodling in a political backroom. In a more wholesome sense, and closer to chronology, the fall of Gorman meant the rise of the reformists and the dawn of modern Maryland government, Albert Ritchie presiding.

W hatever else they say," Marvin Mandel said, his stern fate closing around him, "they can't say I wasn't a good governor."

Let's see:

Where Governor Mandel excelled was as politician and legislator, as compromiser and deal maker. He was always the artful Speaker of the House of Delegates, even when elevated to the governor's chair. He made things work. "Marvelous Marvin," State House reporters called him. They were not entirely cynical.

He played legislators as one would keys on a piano. There came the strong, progressive proposals made by the state Constitutional Convention: at a special referendum, however, voters had flinched. Later, bit by bit, Governor Mandel eased many of the new proposals into law. There followed consolidation of 248 ding-a-ling agencies into 12 major departments. A rationalized system of state law courts took shape, then a long-needed public defender system, a mass transit agency. In his first two legislative sessions, 93 of 95 Mandel-backed proposals were enacted, little else. He kept the state budget commendably tight.

What some would call his outsider's hypersensitivity began to show, at first rather attractively. He disliked the presumption of commercial pets long hungrily feeding at Annapolis's table, the established service firms. Coldly Marvin Mandel steered state business—bonds, insurance, heavy construction—elsewhere.

Later, in extremis, he suspected aloud that the whole established world was plotting against him, from Baltimore's elitist Maryland Club right down to the president of the United States.

Durable reform eluded him. Appointment of state officials and judges was one giveaway. Too often he turned his back on the best brains in the state. Too often he looked for guidance instead to Dale Hess and Irvin Kovens, to his in-house staff of fast-talking persuaders—a dismaying number of whom later followed their leader, for separate reasons, into trouble with the law.

Where he met outright failure was his taking on, apparently genuine at first, of the moral and ethical leadership of Marylanders. Maybe it wasn't Shakespearean, but it was something close to authentic tragedy when at his trial on mail fraud charges the Governor was forced to read aloud from the very state code of ethics he had ordered into effect (for others, not himself). It was a high-minded code that, point by point, lay degraded in the grim evidence piled up against him. In the witness chair, under all eyes, he first ate his own words, then tried in vain to spit them out. That was the day disaster caught up with Marvelous Marvin.

So in perspective how good was he as governor?

He was excellent in legislating, competent at administering, an embarrassment at acknowledging the difference, publicly perceived, between right and wrong. One explanation was his preoccupation with short-range government humdrum, his consequent astigmatism when long, philosophical vision was called for. Another explanation was his chronic distaste for confrontation. Never one to seize a strong lead for a good cause or against a bad one, he was a temporizer, a wait-and-see artist of the politically possible. Maybe, he was fond of saying, something could be worked out.

Some important things couldn't.

3.

Ritchie and
the Good Seed

Albert Ritchie looms a massive, compelling presence in Maryland political history. He was elected governor four times where all before had been turned out briskly at the end of one term. A Baltimorean, he shunted aside a seemingly endless stream of county moguls who had come to think of the governor's mansion, or Government House, as theirs by regional right. Flinty political bosses found themselves no longer issuing orders but taking them; Ritchie, flintier still, was the only boss who mattered. He shook the nineteenth-century hayseeds out of Maryland's hair, seized upon a tenuous reform movement and made of state government a model for others to copy.

Political leaders elsewhere soon recognized that something special was taking place in Maryland. Ritchie had given voice to a deep national trend, then responded to calls for guidance from a dozen cities across the nation. In 1932, during the Democratic National Convention at Chicago, a Ritchie drive for the presidential nomination foundered only upon collision with the steely machinery that was to lift Franklin D. Roosevelt to the stars. Ritchie's death four years later drew editorials not alone from the great eastern newspapers but also from as far away as the *Salt Lake Deseret News* and the *Lewiston* (Idaho) *Tribune*. Also from the *Dallas Times-Herald* and the *Chattanooga Times* and the *Mobile* (Alabama) *Press* and the *Providence Journal*. The *Washington Post* put it simply: Ritchie was the "greatest Governor

Maryland ever had." More than four decades and eight governors later, few would challenge that.

A certified hero, then, this masterful figure with his twinkling pince-nez and faintly distant manner. But what made Ritchie tick? Where arose his strength and, for he had some, his blind spots? How much did he simply luck into the mood of his times, how much did he embody political values durable, whether good or bad, before him and afterward? More important to the sad entanglements of Marvin Mandel: What political network leads largely unchanged through the Ritchie successors to surface, as of old, in the Mandel time? How come the winds of the 1920s waft one governor to a gleaming pedestal while, in the 1970s, a tempest leaves another governor shattered, disgraced, a near-tragic figure?

Today much of the Ritchie story seems transient, hence only glancingly pertinent to Mandel. But surprisingly much endures, or did endure, so a beginning of true understanding of the later man runs through the earlier man. Among other things, Ritchie furnishes Mandel perspective.

Fraud! cried Maryland Republicans in November, 1919, and called for a recount. H. L. Mencken tended to agree.

Harry W. Nice, Mencken said, "was probably hornswoggled out of the governorship."

What made Mencken think that? Well, Democratic election officials in Anne Arundel and Baltimore counties—both notorious for cockfighting, bootleggers, and creative vote-counting—turned up suspiciously late with their election returns. When the ballots were finally totted, Nice found himself second best. He lost by 165 votes in 224,000 cast.

And who was the hornswoggler?

He was Albert Cabell Ritchie, darling of Baltimore's finest, destined to write his name in history as Maryland's greatest governor and to wrestle for the presidency with the Champ. Evidence of hornswoggling was strictly circumstantial and, besides, things were tough all over.

The greater marvel may be that Ritchie won at all. Throughout 1919, most political signs flashed ugly omens to Democrats high and low. At the top Woodrow Wilson, trapped in the what-price-victory? disillusionment following World War I, was wrenched into hopeless embrace with a Republican majority in the Senate.

Harding would complete the Republican deluge twelve months later, sweeping Maryland by a record margin. In Annapolis, to universal astonishment, Republicans had two years earlier won control of the House of Delegates. That very spring, in the Democratic heartland of Baltimore City, voters coolly turned aside a confident Democrat and elected a Republican mayor. The weather hung menacingly Republican, and that wasn't the Democrats' only trouble.

Among themselves, they wandered all but leaderless. They stood bereft of their once-formidable machine: Gorman, the state leader, and Rasin, the Baltimore City leader, had died some dozen years earlier. No convincing replacement had arisen. Even Rasin's city heirs—John Mahon, of the "Royal Family," and Frank Kelly, "the Kelly"—had stiffly declined to speak to each other for the four years past. That it was a squabble over $10,000 in campaign money which split off boss from solemn boss demonstrated the rancid, riven mood of the Democrats. What's more, this clear-eyed young Ritchie didn't sound to such bosses as still functioned like their kind of governor at all. "I am going to do the controlling," Ritchie stiffly informed them early in his campaign. In annoyance the outgoing Democratic governor, Emerson C. Harrington, turned his eyes away. United States Senator John Walter Smith, an aging relic of the vanished Gorman machinery, cast about for a candidate less starchy, one more docile in the good old style. But the old style was the Gorman style, and Ritchie wasn't having it. Ritchie had a different idea.

Historically, Ritchie is sometimes hung with labels misleadingly shinier than the facts can justify. He was not, for example, a zealot reformer or even an early pioneer. Political reform had been in the field, though not in control, forty years before Ritchie was elected. He did become the first governor to convert the reformers' zeal from a sort of elitist evangelism, hence gusty and intermittent, to a hard movement, an organized political staple that was active election after election. He did outmaneuver all statewide challengers and gather to his own hand the parochial bosslets. Another step was creatively more important. Ritchie built up upon the shaken party foundation a largely new layer of men, new at least in a sense of freedom from the grasping old Gorman ways. These "Young Turks" and their descendants, both familial and political, were to color and sometimes to dominate Maryland politics for many years. One seed planted in the Ritchie years sprouted into the West Baltimore Democratic club that, fifty years later, first brought Marvin Mandel into political contention. Another Ritchie protégé, E. Brooke Lee, had already fathered an infant, Blair Lee III, who was destined to serve Mandel as lieutenant governor. In the 1920s, however, it was Ritchie and his works which overshadowed all else. As Louis Azrael wrote in the *Baltimore News*, he "bestrode the narrow world of Maryland public life like a colossus." The *Baltimore Sun*, which hated political organizations but quite fancied Ritchie, mused uneasily, "[Ritchie] is the organization."

One early if flickering beacon had showed Ritchie the way three years before he first reached public office as assistant city solicitor in Baltimore. Beginning in 1907 the Crothers administration in Annapolis had recognized that reform had become more than a rallying cry. Governor Austin Crothers, stung personally by charges of vote buying in his home Cecil County, hustled a batch of progessive steps into law. A corrupt practices act went on the books to stop the merchandising of votes. Then came a Public Service Commission to rein in monopolistic utilities. Also a Workmen's Compensation Commission, as well as a Roads Commission to rationalize highway building for that looming social force, the automobile. Out went the old boss-run convention system of party nominations; in came the direct primary. Young Albert Ritchie caught the spirit and, when raised to assistant counsel to the new Public Service Commission, he forced Baltimore's startled gas company to lower its rates. No one had done that before. Reform was finding not just a voice for crying out but the governmental tools to work with, and Ritchie became a recruit in a movement he did not invent. Following the Crothers four years, Governors Goldsborough (called "the Maryland gentleman") and Harrington lost reformist headway. So to Ritchie, coming along after, this fresh field was left invitingly open. Luck and a conjunction of events awarded him the chance to escort political reform to maturity in Maryland.

Certain exceptions to reform must be noted, exceptions that arose from Ritchie's philosophical distaste for national intrusion into what he considered a state's constitutional right to make its own governmental decisions, right or wrong. Most Marylanders went contentedly along. Prohibition of the national traffic in alcohol, for example, was bracketed by some with the fashionable new onwardness and upwardness. Not by Ritchie, not by the Marylanders he led. Prohibition laws went ostentatiously unenforced, Maryland ran openly with illegal liquor throughout this prim, maybe noble experiment. A Baltimore example: one rowdy young prizefighter shifted from the ring to highjacking bootleggers, made some money, wangled from a bemused Ritchie an appointment to the state boxing commission, opened a political storefront. Jack Pollack was in business (and Marvin Mandel would be his grandest, if ungrateful, product). Likewise to national calls for voting rights for women and blacks, Ritchie and Marylanders stood defiantly, anachronistically deaf. Until 1973 the state declined to ratify the Fifteenth Amendment enfranchising blacks. The Nineteenth Amendment, for women's voting, stands formally unratified in Maryland to date—although Ritchie, once ratification went through elsewhere, necessarily scrambled for the "lady vote" with the rest.

The significance is that Ritchie operated from principles no less compelling for being highly personal, even quirky. Central among his principles was state rights, and never mind that history which for nearly fifteen years made him its pet and a national figure rounded on him, near the end, and broke him. Still, principle in its national philosophical sense only rarely reaches down to electrify the humdrum housekeeping of workaday state government. Here is where Ritchie shone as a paragon of efficiency and economy, of importing new professional techniques to a field hitherto plagued by listless vagary at best and, at worst, by self-serving political calculation. He was the state's first full-time administrator, thereby laying down a tradition of competence followed with varying enthusiasm by his successors. Of these Marvin Mandel may have been the most skillful, leaving aside the ethical, apparently criminal, matters he fumbled.

Today the Ritchie innovations sound like administrative routine. A hiring system for state jobs which puts merit above patronage seems only natural. So does equalization money to help poor counties match rich-county schools. A central purchasing bureau is no more than common sense; fewer elections are obviously preferable to a statewide hodgepodge. Free-and-easy racetracks called out for the state regulation they got, no less than did vast expansion of the state roads system—and adoption of revenue bonds to pay for them. Routine, natural, obvious today; but boldly experimental in the 1920s and, as with racial integration of the University of Maryland professional schools, fiercely resisted. A Ritchie enterprise outright daring was his stern dispatch of the National Guard to quell a lynching uproar on the still-benighted, prickly Eastern Shore. When in the early 1930s the Depression began to bring queasy banks to their knees, Ritchie forestalled panic by ordering a Maryland bank holiday before Franklin Roosevelt got around to it for the rest of the nation.

Such was the body of the Ritchie governance, pragmatic and conservative, but enlightened too and studded at critical turning points with emphatic action. That he was Maryland's best governor seems beyond serious dispute; none who followed successfully claimed superiority. By 1932, midpoint in his fourth term, presidential lightning flickered excitingly about Ritchie's head. But Maryland was too small a state to generate significant steam against massive New York and driving Texas. Besides, the Depression had profoundly frightened many Americans, and the once-stirring Ritchie rhetoric about state rights seemed quaint, obsolete, ineffective. Franklin Roosevelt's aura of national urgency overbore a gallant band of Ritchie boosters at the Chicago convention and, in November, swept the country. As a national voice Ritchie's was heard but passed over as too little, too late.

Maryland, it soon turned out, began to tire of its seemingly perpetual governor. As one Republican challenger asked in a campaign slogan provoked by the Ritchie fifth-term campaign in 1934: "Ritchie forever?" And another: "King Albert the Fifth!" Most likely, as when the ancient Greeks rejected Aristides, it was a case of boredom at hearing him proclaimed over and over, for fifteen years, as "the just." Uncharacteristically, Ritchie failed to sense the omens or else, solidly in character, did sense them and brushed them aside: Who was this Harry Nice anyhow? Harry Nice was only a Republican, only the man Ritchie had bested four elections ago, only a man not noticeably invigorated by any fresh ideas acquired over the fifteen years since. But that fall Harry Nice funnelled his way Maryland's brimming discontent and dislodged the governor who had hauled the administration of Maryland out of the nineteenth century and deposited it, humming and successful, squarely inside the twentieth. Two years later Ritchie died, personally gloomy and unreconciled. Historically, he left a yardstick of performance against which all successive governors would be measured and, in most cases, be called short.

Besides this historical, almost monumental figure, realists will suspect, there existed another Ritchie, a Ritchie carved less in marble and more in flesh and frailty. It is this more human Ritchie, little documented as he was in those reticent decades, who offers special insights into Marvin Mandel, a man whose personal nonconformities drew—in his own view—an altogether unprecedented, undeserved flood of documentation from that wellspring of political vileness, the news media. Another parallel, maybe a perpendicular: Would a Ritchie resurrected in 1979, his state right beliefs sturdily intact, have discerned in the federal prosecution of Mandel Washington's ultimate intrusion into a sovereign Maryland, an intrusion Ritchie had long ago warned against? In principle Mandel certainly thought so, and in fact urgently argued as much in court. Ritchie might well have agreed, and if so a critical point emerges. Ritchie's own blind spot was his encrusted sense of invulnerability and his failure, consequently, to detect the philosophical ground moving beneath his feet. In Mandel's version of the same phenomenon, it was a change of ethics in midgame which threw him unfairly off-balance, a post-Watergate onset of popular suspicion directed at all holders of public office. The essence is the same in both cases. For different reasons and in different ways, each governor lost touch with that vapor which all political leaders must breathe as they breathe air: the public will. Ritchie did lose, Nice did win; the voters held command, as usual. Mandel was convicted, his appeals were dismissed; the law did prevail, also as usual.

Women seem not to have presented Ritchie with a serious problem, although well they might. He was a handsome man, affable, obviously destined for the heights. He was in effect a bachelor nearly all his life, a youthful marriage having early miscarried. So opportunity was present, and one instance is recorded, for what it's worth. A then-freshman member of the House of Delegates from Baltimore reports that, upon leaving a rousing session of the Ways and Means Committee in the spring of 1928, he was so excited he forgot to pick up his hat. It was a new hat and, after dinner elsewhere, he hurried back to the darkened committee room to get it, entering through a side door. He flicked a light switch: before his astonished gaze there sprang up from the committee chairman's desk the young woman secretary of the committee, half-dressed, her hair askew. But stop! Whose back was that bent over the secretary, that figure also largely undressed?

One flicker of the unmistakably black eyebrows, of the gubernatorial silver hair, told the Baltimore delegate more than he wanted to know. Instantly he snapped off the light switch and slid backward out the side door, new hat forgotten once again. The hat was still there when the committee session opened the next morning.

A piquant little story if a lonely one: no other specific Ritchie peccadillo bulges the tacit blanket spread upon the times, only a thoughtful glimmer in the eyes of men now in their eighties. Anyway, more than Victorian prudence may have shielded Ritchie. He installed his widowed mother as hostess and mansion keeper in Annapolis, hence as a sort of duenna or, more probably, a duennalike screen. Besides, the man's legs were knotted with varicose veins, apparently a source of personal embarrassment which denied him bathing beaches and cut off that source of temptation. So on the feminine flank the Ritchie facade stands publicly unsmirched, if reassuringly virile in private. Marvin Mandel was to have less luck when, after a decade of dalliance with a woman not his wife, his private screen was ripped away by a new public appetite for revelation of personal detail about public figures.

Two less gauzy, more substantial, aspects of the Ritchie era also reflect the realistic side of a governor whom convention tends to hold up as heroic. One of these is his almost dynastic establishment of political authority in Maryland, discernible threads of which both link and divide his successors for generations to come. Rated a progressive in his day, Ritchie knew what he wanted from state government; as a politician, he knew how to get it and, at the same time, survive. The second loosely associated Ritchie aspect is his attitude toward political corruption. Pertinent here is the always delicate relationship between political figures on the one hand and, on the other, business people who, politically inert themselves, are nevertheless willing and even eager to apply money as leverage to bend politics to their own profit or self-aggrandizement. This is not to suggest Ritchie was corrupted in the sense a jury said Mandel was corrupted; he was not. On the contrary, what follows is aimed at illuminating Mandel both by contrast and by comparison with Ritchie in the ways two Maryland governors, worlds apart, answered questions strikingly similar.

As a politician, Ritchie seems to have given no thought to

sowing seed for posterity to reap. That was a coincidence, unplanned. What he set out to do in 1919 was much simpler. It was to get himself elected, no light undertaking under the Republican skies then prevalent. Thereafter, in four successive campaigns, the Ritchie goal was to face down squads of challengers, Democratic as well as Republican, and stay governor in a state that up to then had rationed each governor only four years. Ritchie built an organization first to help him break through to the power levers, then to survive personally at the polls. As noted earlier, he found among the remnants of the Gorman-Rasin machine random cogs and gears in need of fitting together. Also he sensed rising in Baltimore City, long scorned by the old county squirearchy, fresh winds surging with political energy. Herbert R. O'Conor, Ritchie's last running mate for attorney general, represented the triumph of an Irish-Catholic breakthrough in the city. The political arrival of Thomas D'Alesandro, Jr., would do the same for Baltimore Italians. A new Jewish pride rode with Philip Perlman, closest of all men to the Ritchie throne.

A more personal, less institutional increment emerged from the "Ritchie Leagues," men mostly attuned to Ritchie's own gentrified rhythms and yet ambitious, as he was, to get on with bringing to Maryland a progressive and workable government. Of these a prominent handful were former army officers freshly discharged after World War I. Major General Milton A. Reckord and Lieutenant Colonel Millard E. Tydings turned up in Harford County as Ritchie admirers. Montgomery County preferred its latest—Colonel E. Brooke Lee—in a line long politically distinguished. A young major, W. Preston Lane, Jr., took up the Ritchie banner in Hagerstown, and Lieutenant Colonel Stuart S. Janney, a close Ritchie friend and law partner, led the Ritchie League in Baltimore. Despite appearances, the Ritchie movement was scarcely a military Putsch; it was simply that wartime dynamics had brought promising men to leadership more quickly than the customary political escalator and that, on their reentry as civilians, Ritchie turned them his way. Other civilians who came along, though up to then largely apolitical, included the leading Baltimore lawyers William L. Marbury and Eli Frank. B. Howell Griswold, the city's foremost investment banker, became at once a Ritchie friend and booster. Even Virginia seems to have had political cards to play in this Maryland unfolding. In 1925, homestate ties between Ritchie and two Virginia-born cousins, Howard and William Cabell Bruce, provoked from the *Baltimore Federationist* a stab at sardonic verse:

> Virginia's heel is on thy shore
> Maryland, my Maryland.
> Her blue-blood scions ruel [*sic*] o'er
> Maryland, my Maryland.

Such was the Ritchie circle or circles, widespread apart but still concentric and magnetized in a loyal matrix by the governor himself. They furnished the Ritchie regime its complex flavor, plus—in names like Lee and Lane, Tydings and Bruce, D'Alesandro and O'Conor—the foundations of political dynasties to come. Still Ritchie was no narrow establishmentarian, no parlor politician. He was a realist who picked up whatever came to hand and made the political most of it. In one or another way, the machine performed before, during, and after Ritchie.

Sample strands spanning the years tell the story. One durable legacy from the Gorman regime to Ritchie and his own heirs begins in the Baltimore City machine led with leathery aplomb by I. Freeman Rasin, generally called "Free." "Grim, cunning, unscrupulous and yet curiously sensitive to criticism," according to a contemporary account, Rasin had sprung from old Eastern Shore stock to operate by 1870 the most formidable machine the city knew before or after. It was wired together ward by ward, generally responded to Gorman's direction at the top, lasted thirty years and began falling apart before Rasin's death in 1907. Fractionalism occurred, plus an outburst—here, at a different level, the dynastic impulse again—of political procreation. For Rasin begat Mahon (appropriately called "Sonny") as city boss and Mahon begat Kelly, at which point Ritchie came onstage. Both Mahon and Kelly grudgingly acknowledged Ritchie's leadership but, backstage, the begetting went on uninterrupted. Kelly begat William Curran, called "Barefoot Billy," a masterful city boss in his own right but also a masterful begetter. Curran begat Herbert O'Conor, the first Democrat to succeed Ritchie as Governor, and also begat Jack Pollack, who in turn at least helped beget three separate governors: W. Preston Lane, J. Millard Tawes, and Marvin Mandel. This procreative process carried in it little romance or even affection. Gorman and Rasin were mutually suspicious, each with excellent reason. Mahon-Kelly relations were normally sulfurous. Curran, a political metronome, alternately fought and supported Ritchie. Pollack denounced Curran as "Machiavelli," Tawes as a liar, Lane and Mandel as ingrates—having first fed politically on all four.

It's a circuitous trail these leaders trod, but a trail nevertheless. By direct political descent, it led from Reconstruction to Watergate, from Rasin to Pollack, from Gorman to Mandel. It ran 100 years, and Ritchie, first elected 50 years from both beginning and end of the period, stands out at midpoint. He is both watershed and, if unwitting, the main architect of the second half, here pertinent as the political environment that produced Marvin Mandel.

Now the ground common to Ritchie and Mandel turns more specific. It is corruption, an intrusion most governors abhor and resist, Mandel no less than Ritchie. The trouble is, corruption whether pale pink or flaming scarlet finds its own toeholds for twining about governmental structures. Governors' salaries are notoriously stingy: Ritchie was paid $4,500, Mandel $25,000. True, housekeeping and entertainment expenses are thrown in. Juicy perquisites formally attached to the governor's office have run from a free mansion to live in, maintained at public expense, to annual dollops of entertainment money, to official limousines, to state troopers in constant attendance and even, gaudy bauble, to a lavish gubernatorial yacht. Still, how is a governor to pay income taxes, finance vacations, pay college tuitions, buy family clothes? So pressed financially, governors writhe, and some buckle. Commonly less inhibited are a governor's friends, who cling to the old spoilsman's rationalization: Someone has to get the juicy contracts and commissions—why feed the enemy? Why not feed political friends? Pressing down on both governor and his allies in the last few decades is the punishing cost of an election campaign: $3 million is the threshold price for winning nomination and election as governor of Maryland today, television time being the most voracious consumer of campaign funds.

Where the money goes in all categories is obvious. Where it comes from is kept scrupulously less obvious because essentially corrupting, but is no less a pivotal fact of political life. The fringe of the political world is richly peppered with businessmen and businesswomen whose financial survival hangs on governmental favors, on an inside connection to shortcut business competitors. To such people, the First Amendment offers an open door. An

American is entitled, isn't he, to express his political opinion? Notably, by giving money to the candidate of his choice, right? So runs the fat cats' creed, whereupon down come the flimsy laws against corruption, laws written by legislators who are themselves vulnerable at election time to the mercenary benevolence of encircling political money raisers. And gaily through the legal loopholes hustles an army of contractors and insurance men, engineers and architects, underwriters and entrepreneurs. All know the urgent pressure for money which afflicts people in public office. Each is willing to help alleviate such cruel pressure, the understanding being that the favor is returnable. Quid, as the Romans observed, pro quo.

Gorman had been dead thirteen years when Ritchie was elected, Rasin fourteen. Their cash-register ethics slid into a half-life, crippled and stripped of the old-time elan. Indeed, it was charges of corruption, as distinct from demonstrated corruption itself, which shadowed the relatively wholesome if not outright antiseptic Ritchie period. Still, the charges personally embarrassed Ritchie. Opportunities abounded for fast work in the political backrooms, and the bosses did what came naturally. Illegal slot machines and an infant numbers racket, then called "policy," offered pay for protection and apparently got it. National prohibition reigned and, while defiantly ignored in "Free State" Maryland, created a troublesome ambivalence about law enforcement. Two serious defalcations scarred Ritchie's State Roads Commission, and the Depression precipitated a flutter of bank failures in Maryland. There arose an outcry against bank management clumsy and worse. Personally, Ritchie escaped the mudslinging election time brought on, but challengers did force him to defend underlings publicly and, in one case, to sling back a handful of mud himself. A prudent man, Governor Ritchie had to do a little prudent winking.

Conowingo was the flash point. A name of melodious Indian origin, Conowingo rang out in distinctly unmelodious cacophony in the 1926, or third-term, Ritchie campaign. On one side stood an old villain, the electric power utilities; on the other, a Ritchie politico-financial angel. Talk of money in denominations then huge and hugely suspicious sounding broke the habitual Maryland tranquility. The project in hand at Conowingo, a convenient Maryland point on the Susquehanna riverbank, was to dam the great river's flow and convert it via sluicegates to electric current.

So far, so promising. Trouble arose when it turned out that a Philadelphia power company, not a Maryland concern, was to exploit this Maryland-based power. Worse, power was to be sold to Pennsylvanians and not Marylanders. More awkward still, one substantial contract for the dam's construction was held by the Arundel Company, whose dominant figure was Frank Furst, a key Ritchie political adviser and fund raiser. Millions of dollars changed hands, Marylanders were said to have been robbed of their birthright, political collusion was charged. All this ammunition fell into the understandably eager hands of William Milnes Maloy, Ritchie's challenger for the Democratic nomination in 1926. Maloy fired almost daily and with gusto.

A cautionary note: some excess of exuberance in Maloy's manner caught the cold blue eye of H. L. Mencken, who wrote him off as a "blood-sweating Methodist divine . . . rather worse, if anything, than the average." Maloy stood undaunted. "Flagrant corruption!" he said of the Conowingo affair. "Quid pro quo!" As Maloy saw it, the $3-million annual profit Philadelphia was to draw from Conowingo meant that "Ritchie bought a third-term nomination for $3 million." On and on Maloy went, pointing to the Arundel Company's "special interests" fattened on tremendous "slush funds" and "manipulating" the legislature. The *Baltimore Post* struck a sonorous gong: the "Conowingo scandal," it said, was "the most important since the question of secession half a century ago." A Republican candidate, Addison Mulliken, discerned behind Conowingo the "cunning hand" of Albert Ritchie. Others discerned something else. This was a hollow note in the outraged trumpeting: onlookers scoured the terrain for broken laws, damaged citizens, anything immoral or even untoward. They scoured in vain.

There was, to be sure, no grand jury investigation, no gratifying resolution of the issue laid apart soberly in court. The times offered two less meticulous substitutes for courtroom procedure. One was an exhaustive journalistic investigation which led the *Baltimore Sun* to pronounce the charges "baseless" as far as Ritchie was concerned; as for others than Ritchie, charges were probably pumped up by political exaggeration. Maryland voters seemed to agree. Ritchie was handily renominated and, on election day, ran up the handsomest majority of his three to date. Whether Marvin Mandel, similarly spared a federal investigation of the Marlboro Racetrack episode, then judged like Ritchie only by a friendly newspaper and voters instead of a jury, could also have faced down his accusers is debatable. Anyway, that's not the way it happened.

Other differences separated Ritchie's relationship to the Conowingo affair from Mandel's to Marlboro. Ritchie had family money: it was called "a modest personal fortune" by Frank R. Kent of the *Sun*, a friend and confidant. Mandel had little or no family money, earned little in his few years as a practicing lawyer. Ritchie had no wife to support, no children to educate, so little taste for costly vacations that, after his defeat in 1934, a trip to London was his first holiday in twenty years. Mandel married twice, the second time expensively, counting in divorce costs. He saw two children through college and law school and, for vacations, sampled garden spots in the United States and Europe, sometimes with his new wife's children as company. Ritchie's notion of recreation was a long evening of ample drinks and conversation—sometimes, a Victorian residue, literary readings—with his fellow establishmentarians in a paneled corner of the Maryland Club, Baltimore's most aloof. From working politicians he kept a discreet distance. Mandel surrounded himself with politico-businessmen, embracing in particular those whose careers it had long been to raise political money, to broker elections, to watch out for political investments that would, literally, pay them back. Ritchie was startlingly candid and enjoyed, consequently, excellent relations with most of the state's newspapers, the *Baltimore Sunpapers* embracing him almost too warmly for comfort. Mandel was close-mouthed, shy, and resentful of reporters' questions he considered overly personal or stupid. His news conferences tended to be duels, sterile to report and sterile to read about. He feared and distrusted the *Sunpapers* as anti-Mandel, maybe anti-Semitic.

The two personalities invite a curious symbiosis. Wouldn't Ritchie, the imperturbable patrician, dismiss Mandel as a political aberration, a raw arriviste? Wouldn't Mandel, proud product of the new urban ethnics, pronounce Ritchie obsolete, old, old, his trousers rolled? And yet just there runs revelation.

Ritchie and his world, because so distant in time and flavor, provide a prism through which the Mandel world is often glimpsed more clearly than it can be seen head-on, framed and wearily familiar in its own surroundings. Six governors intervene between the Ritchie and the Mandel worlds, each shedding his own ray of light. Strangely, the overall illumination moves inversely with the years. The closer we approach, the more the Mandel wood retreats, individual trees intrude. Yet approach we must, this being an attempt not at verse but at history. Ritchie offers the best vantage point, the sharpest focus on Mandel.

C rime often does pay. What's more, not a few
criminals continue to enjoy the fruits of.
their crimes, even after conviction, with all
the safety of any blue-eyed Bible salesman. In the United States,
one reason for this is that atavistic Americans, still spooked by
the shades of ancient kings, shrink from the oldest of mon-
archical abuses: confiscation. They dislike watching the government strip a man of his private property, including property
criminally amassed. But such powers exist, and the Mandel case
offers a look at government confiscation in its current, somewhat
crippled, state of the art.

To use confiscation on Marvin Mandel's friends was tempting
for two reasons. One was that millions in profits at best questionable swirled about, inviting a federal grab at the swag. Another
was that prosecutors were confident of winning a conviction,
were eager to establish a useful new precedent, and had armed
themselves in advance. In the original indictment, they included
two counts drawn under the anti-racketeering statute, a statute
that provides for confiscation. Dependence only on the central
mail-fraud statute, not equipped with confiscatory powers,
would have made confiscation virtually impossible. But the prosecution stood forearmed.

So the pot looked full, juicy, and beckoning. Ready at hand lay
the confiscatory net. Hungrily the feds seized their chance and

dipped. The haul, rich but incomplete, must be called rewarding, and not in money alone.

The first and potentially largest confiscation, however, eluded the federal reach. Three, probably four, defendants held shares in Security Investment, Inc., the company that owned the hugely profitable Social Security complex on the Baltimore outskirts leased to the federal government. Holdings here by Dale Hess and the two Rodgers brothers were worth, by their own estimate, more than a million dollars. Also, Marvin Mandel himself had been given nearly half of Hess's shares. Because this gift was labeled a criminal bribe—to pay off the Governor for his help in fattening up another Hess-Rodgers enterprise, Marlboro Racetrack—the prosecutors called for confiscation. They undertook to seize all the Security Investment holdings from Hess and the Rodgers brothers, arguing that these holdings were part of the crime. Also, because they suspected despite denials that he still owned it, they asked for confiscation of Marvin Mandel's share, too.

Perhaps the prosecutors were too eager. Perhaps the confiscation powers they flexed were still too new, not yet soundly enough proven in court to carry off this particular sally. Judge Taylor turned it aside. He noted that Security Investment, as an operating business, had not been central to the criminal action of which the Mandel circle had been convicted. Brushed by the action, yes; marginally used by it, yes; but central to it, no—and hence not subject to confiscation. So ruled the judge on a point closely argued. This rich cache of Security Investment wealth was left to dangle just beyond federal fingertips, still unretrieved from hands formally pronounced felonious.

Prosecutors were dismayed but hardly crushed. They planned another and different shot at confiscation, which, while it carried its own little puzzles, had the look of greater promise by far.

This lay at the heart of the case. It was the Marlboro Racetrack stock—secretly bought by the Mandel group, aggressively manipulated by them, and concealed and enriched and sold profitably by them, all as the nub in the fraud case the government had proved to the satisfaction of a federal jury. No weakness arose here by reason of remoteness from the main action: Marlboro was the main action itself. And all but Mandel, rewarded separately via a free chunk of Security Investment, held slices tucked away out of the public view.

Or did they? That lone question, seemingly simple, proved sufficiently sticky to gum up a smooth conclusion of the Mandel case for nearly seven years. The original verdict of guilt—of mail fraud, of racketeering—had been handed up in August, 1977. Confiscation proceedings dragged on into March, 1984.

The rub occurred with Irving Schwartz, called Tubby, holder on the record of 240,765 Marlboro shares worth more than $1 million. Never mind that, on the witness stand, Schwartz had displayed his own vast ignorance of nearly everything to do with Marlboro, that his records were suspiciously blotched with the fingerprints of Irvin Kovens. Never mind that earlier he had made a virtual career as a front man for Kovens, that by special verdict the jury had pronounced Kovens, not Schwartz, the true owner of Marlboro stock carried in Schwartz's name. Never mind that the other Marlboro owners—Hess, the Rodgers brothers, Ernest Cory—were quickly separated from their stock.

Not Schwartz, for Schwartz wouldn't surrender. He insisted on fighting to hold his stock, or someone insisted. And so long as he kept the fight alive the government was blocked from carrying off the confiscation proceedings. The Mandel case hung unresolved on a vital point: who was to pocket the loot?

The Schwartz position seemed fragile but, as things turned out, proved unexpectedly durable. Unlike the others, he argued in court, he had not been indicted for mail fraud and racketeering. He had not been convicted of anything. Tubby Schwartz stood there an innocent man, and whatever the jury had said about ownership the stock was written in his name. Consequently, the government was powerless to use its confiscation power on him, powerless to take away his Marlboro stock. Government lawyers tried first this tack, then that one: for nearly seven years, in court and out, Tubby Schwartz held fast. Eventually the impression grew in the U.S. attorney's office that Schwartz might well dodge about successfully for as many as five years more. Prudent questions occurred.

True, the government was sure to win eventually. Both the facts and the law were clear and clearly located on the government side. Still, was a clear victory worth carrying on indefinitely this very demanding struggle? Was it worth tying up federal courts, prosecutors, the attorney general's office in Washington, internal revenue agents, all as far as the eye could see? And what about the increasingly heavy tax consequences of a legal wrangle still further prolonged? As it was, someone was already sure to be hit heavily by taxes, whether of the income or of the capital-gains variety.

Government officials, confident of ultimate victory but worn down by attrition, came to a faintly painful conclusion. As an exercise of good judgment, they had better make a deal saving time and money. They had better give Schwartz—or wasn't it really Kovens?—just enough of a taste of winning to justify himself in calling off the fight. Then cut losses, wrap up the long-delayed Mandel case at last, and go on about more urgent business noisily hammering on prosecutors' doors.

Schwartz—Kovens?—was willing. He—they?—would settle for keeping 40 percent of the Marlboro holding; unhindered, the government would confiscate the remaining 60 percent. And so this Gordian knot was sliced apart, the government coming away with 10 percent more than half and, as these things are delicately figured, with its much-valued principle shaky but intact. Loss of the principle might have set up straw men of the future as a safe harbor for the parking of stolen goods. As to Schwartz/Kovens, they could boast a 40 percent victory for whatever that was worth, and the reality was that financially it was not worth 40 percent, not the $400,000 some thought. As noted, federal and state taxes hovered threateningly. The $400,000 salvaged would shrink again. Thereafter, confronted by legal fees, once-fat Marlboro profits might vanish altogether.

4.

New Light on
George Mahoney

D
emocrats proclaim themselves champions of the common man, of the hungry and the lame and the lost. What a surprise, then, to witness this egalitarian, no-nonsense party caught up and tortured in Maryland, just after World War II, on so dainty a tea-table point as a social snub. George P. Mahoney was the snub's victim. In revenge, Mahoney loosed a whirlwind into which Maryland politics was swept and out of which, later, climbed another man who felt himself snubbed, Marvin Mandel. Complacency was blamed, rebellion was urged. But corrosion as much as reform was the product.

Little on the surface connects George Mahoney to Marvin Mandel. They were men of different generations, disparate in public style, personally inimical. What would this snorting bull, Mahoney, find to chat about with an evasive fox like Mandel? Beneath the surface, at the level where political trends start and stop, Mahoney is as critical to the Mandel story as is Albert Ritchie. The two influences stand in sharp contrast. Where Ritchie built, or anyway rebuilt, a durable political organization, Mahoney constructed a career by ripping the organization apart. Yet these two men, considered together, largely shaped the stage on which Mandel performed.

Ritchie became in his four terms the embodiment of the status quo. Politically, he established the establishment that undid Mandel. Until Mahoney, Maryland Democrats had been reaching with some success for restoration of Ritchie-like orthodoxy to party

50

affairs. The trouble was, rebellion came in season, and rebellion was Mahoney's fuel. Others rebelled intermittently, but George Mahoney fired up a political uproar. For nearly forty years he alternately shattered the Democrats and purged them; contemporaries wrote him down as the personal symbol of political demolition.

Today's historians may consider a longer view. They begin to suspect that Mahoney also partook of a public mood deeper than the catcalls he customarily hollered out from Maryland's political ringside. Time may establish him as the unwitting leader, in his day, of a demand long gathering among voters to close Maryland gates to official corruption, a demand thitherto heard only in ineffective bursts, but heard since 1875. Mahoney also was largely ineffective against corruption; he was too much the hard-breathing self-seeker, too little the broad-based public leader, to leave a lasting personal imprint. Where he was extremely effective, in his venomous way, was against hidden corners of old Democratic pastures in which it was corruption's complacent habit to breed. There Mahoney pointed his blowtorch, there gushed up his wanton fire and smoke: precision cutting—say, by laser beam—was a refinement beyond him. If Mandel later failed to grasp the limitations of the earth scorched open to him, few doubted it was Mahoney who did the scorching.

A quite different destiny seemed to beckon to Mahoney when, it is told, Herbert O'Conor's mother dropped a suggestion on her son the governor. George Mahoney, Mrs. O'Conor said, had been such a good friend of the O'Conor family. Why not give him a lift out of the gritty world of paving contractors where, by rough and tumble, George had made some money and a name for abrasiveness? Why not ease him now into the more genteel layer of Irish-Americans which the O'Conors, as earlier arrivals, already occupied?

Dutifully Governor O'Conor responded. He elevated Mahoney to chairman of the state Racing Commission, a perch then redolent of silky social position, seemingly the very embodiment of old Maryland families and of establishment éclat. The Racing Commission was where you went to pick up polish you didn't have, or at least polished friends. Didn't the Maryland Club itself stand near the end of this softly gleaming path? Maybe even—undreamable dream—the Bachelors Cotillon?

George Mahoney tried hard. He seized upon what he took to be the requisite graces and spread them across a sandpaper personality more at home on Baltimore's vociferous east-side street corners. Noisily, he clapped the racing gentlemen on the back, teasingly he jollied their fair ladies. For a time some did respond to a genuine animal charm. But many more did not. These averted their eyes at too-eager Mahoney effusions, whispered behind his back. Mahoney stood spurned and hated it. None of these grandees could know—and few care if they did—what volcanic rumbles their casual slight would call up. This mind set hardened against Mahoney, first in the upper reaches of the racing world supposed to smooth him off, ultimately among leaders in the Democratic world where he turned in angry search of vengeance. He never quite made it upward to elective office. Instead he slid sidewise, sharp elbows windmilling, knees out-thrust.

The Mahoney reign as racing chairman proved short and tempestuous. The fuse it lit smoldered long; Governor W. Preston Lane, Jr., was only the first of seven prominent victims, the lingering core of Ritchie's heirs. By the time of Lane's inauguration in 1947, Mahoney had turned from cuddling racing's royals to tormenting them instead. Scorn him as an intruder, would they? Pariah, was he? Well, he'd pariah them—and he did. Racing's weedy backyard furnished him a rebel's gold mine. There he unearthed what came to sound like a scandal a day. Racehorses were said to be doped to run fast or slow, depending on how gamblers laid their bets. Jockeys were called crooked, trainers conniving, races fixed. Torture itself was alleged: horses were whipped with chains, stung by batteries, forced to gallop lame on legs numbed by ice. Higher and higher rang the Mahoney crescendo, and some truth underlay fevered exaggeration.

Racing rulers scoffed. Just invite Mahoney to dinner at your house, one of them advised Harry Parr, the fastidious president of Pimlico Racetrack; he'll eat off your hand like a kitten. Stiffly, Parr declined. Mahoney raged on, scoffing turned to embarrassment, finally to cold anger. Mahoney must go, the gentry said, the governor must discharge him. And so Governor Lane did, a step soon proved politically suicidal.

Lane, a sprig of the landed gentry, had shared the gentrified distaste for Mahoney's shrill outcries; as a lawyer, he had doubted the Mahoney judgment. And yet the deeper misjudgment was Lane's. What the governor failed to recognize was that Mahoney, in addition to enemies, had attracted admirers, the nucleus of a fervent personal following. These were the forgotten people of the racetracks, the railbirds and $2 bettors, faceless thousands eager to share the suspicion Mahoney raised about sinister goings-on along the backstretch, worse behind the horse barns. Such people had swung not against Mahoney but behind him: they discerned him as savior of their petty but cherished gambling, really of their way of life. A genuine call to little people had been sounded, and little people heard. Lane's careless stroke, consequently, did not obliterate a noisy nuisance as planned. Instead, it galvanized the Mahoney throng. It lifted Mahoney toward a public stature destined to bring shivers to a political generation. All that Lane obliterated, it turned out years down the road, was the remnants of the organization Ritchie had years earlier resurrected. For Lane, to his dismay, breathed life into Mahoney, and Mahoney brought rebellion into political focus.

As a political gambler himself, Lane might have known better. He might have recognized the long odds standing against politics as usual in the midst of post–World War II awakenings, especially against overloading a sleepy political machine asked to carry startling—and expensive—new enterprises. What he inherited from his 1946 election, along with Mahoney, was the residue of Herbert O'Conor's wartime administration. O'Conor had run a quiet and efficient government but, because of wartime restrictions, a prudently penny-pinching one under a modest head of political steam. Modesty was an idea Preston Lane could not easily comprehend: The war was over, wasn't it? Grand concepts, bold moves, abrupt flexing of political powers: that was the thing, and Lane seems not to have noticed that the powers he called up to flex were mostly aging Ritchieites gone perilously long in the tooth.

Chief among the large notions that moved Lane was the installation of a 2 percent sales tax to underwrite his soaring designs. Today a sales tax lifted to 5 percent and higher is rated a sound, even standard fiscal prop easily accepted in Maryland and across other states too. But not easily accepted then, not in Maryland or anywhere: it was certainly not an easy political dose. The sales tax seemed a people tax, a drip-drip torture tax, a cruel instrument for extracting money, penny by painful penny, from the poor.

Lane bulled the sales tax through his first legislative session, making deals, knocking heads together. Quickly storm clouds darkened the horizon. Pennies for Lane! shoppers grumbled, handing over the few cents extra at the cash register. At subsequent legislative sessions, bills proliferated to soften the sales tax, to repeal it, to make it somehow go away. It didn't. Lane stood stubborn, his eyes fixed on a glowing vision of what Maryland could become. One late summer day, at the state fair at Timonium Fairgrounds, someone flung a handful of pennies in the face of Dorothy Lane, the governor's shy wife. Instantly Pennies-for-Lane was institutionalized, brutalized, as a popular obsession: turn the governor out. George Mahoney, publicly unfrocked and smarting, caught the ring of opportunity.

Wasn't Lane, his nemesis, standing there bloodied and assailable? Why not seize advantage, shoot Lane down as Lane shot him? Convert Mahoney racetrack fans to ballot-box fans, himself to political governor-killer? Vengeance, it's wonderful! As Mahoney incantations against racetrack abuses had caught the little man's ear, so incantations against the sales tax must catch the same ear again. Never mind if the sales tax made good governing sense, if Mahoney himself was quite innocent of what to do instead. Never mind, no, never mind: repeal the sales tax! Turn the rascal out! Vote, oh yes, vote Mahoney!

Which they did, 191,000 to 173,000, in the Democratic primary test. The swells at Pimlico and Laurel, at Bowie and Havre de Grace, were sharply reproved for their original Mahoney snub. Lane, their hapless protector, lay crippled in the dust, his boss-heavy organization stunned and silent. Lane survived momentarily, spared by a vestigial quirk in Maryland's election law—later found unconstitutional—which put aside Mahoney's popular edge and gave Lane renomination, 84 to 68, on the overweighted unit vote then called decisive. It was a hollow victory. That fall Republican Theodore R. McKeldin administered the coup de grâce in the general election. But the promise on which McKeldin was elected, sales-tax repeal, was a warmed-over Mahoney promise that McKeldin, once safe in the governorship, quickly abandoned. The sales tax lived on, a sturdy joist to Maryland budgets.

More significant to the Mandel story, Mahoney having arrived also lived on. Against Lane his first little covey of railbirds swelled far beyond the racetrack to proportions, a loyal 100,000 voters, now politically formidable. Thereafter the Mahoney modus operandi would vary little through years to come. First, as with Lane in 1950, would arise one more darling of the organization—but always one with an exploitable flaw. Second would unroll the Mahoney attack, whether against taxes or against bosses, against "waste" or against black-voter demands. Hot words would ensue, the Mahoney target emerge bloody. Third, and finally, election day would elevate one more Republican, and Mahoney would retreat until opportunity beckoned again. The Mahoney hatchet flew afresh in 1952, 1954, 1956, 1958, 1966, and 1968. Democratic candidates for governor and for United States senator dropped wholesale. Only one Democratic candidate, J. Millard Tawes in 1962, survived November following a Mahoney primary. Twice Mahoney secured Democratic nomination, only to fall later in the general election. Small wonder Maryland Republicans openly counted Mahoney a most effective weapon, this man who single-handedly delivered candidates to high office their minority party could scarcely win by itself. Small wonder organization Democrats, excepting the occasional apostate, turned en masse against Mahoney.

Still, why did Mahoney fail each time to break through himself? His personal popularity surged regularly among voters drawn to political clarion calls: What inner weakness shone through with equal regularity to trip him up at the lip of success, to rob him forever of actual election? Cleverly he had caught the popular mood: turn the insiders out. Maybe that needed doing and, to a society going querulous, Mahoney looked good at doing it. But do what next? After the wreckage, where lay the path ahead?

Mahoney scarcely seemed to care. Never did he offer a convincing road map, never a governing program built to last beyond election day. His was a voice without message, he a prophet lacking prophecy: there wasn't any more there. A majority of voters seemed to sense an inner emptiness in Mahoney and, election year after election year, turned elsewhere for leadership. And yet, historically, he wins a place larger than perennial also-ran, larger than a thirty-year string of asterisks at the bottom of the page. Mahoney served as a turning point on which the political scene shifted. In the end he was a quixotic figure no more accepted in the new and restless scenery he helped produce than in the old scenery whence, by a twitch of the nostrils from the box-seat circle at Pimlico, he had been first thrust out seething. The Mahoney bequest was organizational turmoil, but turmoil carries its own creative rhythms.

Specifically, it was following departure to Washington by Spiro T. Agnew—last of Mahoney's Republican beneficiaries—that Marvin Mandel had to patch together from bits and pieces at hand a new Democratic organization of his own. Ritchie momentum had kept Democrats rolling for a half-century. By 1969, when Mandel's inheritance fell due, the old machine sagged ominously, as obsolete as a whiffletree. Three Democratic governors since Ritchie, at least two of them taunted by Mahoney, had used or abused it. Directly thanks to Mahoney, two Republican governors had undermined it, beaten it, humiliated it. Ritchie's old machine, if it could still be called that, shuddered up to Mandel's door and there collapsed, a horse and buggy astray on an expressway. As the new governor arriving by a constitutional side door, Mandel had no choice but to look around for some political conveyance more contemporary. The new rig he slapped together rode famously for a while, but only for a while. Built into it was a fast-moving form of obsolescence, an obsolescence not planned at all. Mahoney had called up political energies broader and deeper than he was himself.

Julius Caesar and George IV would have diagnosed the affliction as an excess of democracy, of pesky bubblings from below. For ferment is a political fixture: where Ritchie and his Young Turk movement started out somewhat rebellious, official power soon converted these Turks from Young to Old, indeed to Old Guard. As Ritchie faded, personal rivalries surfaced, hence cleavage, then battling factions. Lower down the organizational stairs, where loyal Democrats had been accustomed to march on signal, the once-venerable party banner began to lose its cohesive force and, some said, its sense of responsibility too. That was inside the machine.

Outside, among voters increasingly assertive of their own requirements, all manner of rebels roiled the scene. Sometimes, as noted, they were Republicans—in heavily Democratic Maryland, always a tribe rebellious by necessity. But sometimes they were Italian or Jewish or black, or Kennedyite reformers or George Wallaceite throwbacks or simply, in a constructive parochial spirit, mindful of their own neglected neighborhoods. Women called out for first-class citizenship, not second. Young people of the Vietnam generation insisted that whatever was, was wrong.

As always, money men worked the edges of this political push-pull, eyes sharp for make-a-buck leverage.

So buffeted inside and out, the Maryland pattern began to switch about midcentury from rigid and predictable to kaleidoscopic, mobile, elusive. An overriding result was descent of the center of political gravity—and, along with that, the power of political decision. Bosses stumbled, bosslets deserted, voters declared political independence. Raggedly and in disorder, leaders gave way to the led. If turbulence meant wrecking an aged machine, and it did, George Mahoney had been just the man. He strode forward to rule the wreckage.

Despite Mahoney, the Ritchie style gave ground grudgingly. Three Democratic successors who had watched Ritchie in action—O'Conor, Lane, and J. Millard Tawes—tried to reconstruct the once-triumphant old ways.

O'Conor was the first. He had achieved statewide recognition by election as attorney general in the same 1934 election which finally broke Ritchie. As a symbol during the four Republican years of Harry Nice, O'Conor quietly kept the Democratic flame alight, an American version of British shadow government waiting in the wings. Symbolically, too, O'Conor's elevation to Government House in 1938 brought reinstatement and then political enlargement of two men who had earlier caught Ritchie's eye. Each would provide historical linkage to the Mandel story. One was Howard Bruce, millionaire industrialist, party angel, wistful aspirant for party office himself: Bruce helped ease O'Conor's personal financial plight. The other was the brilliant William Curran, politically direct descendant from I. Freeman Rasin via Frank Kelly. In O'Conor's interest, Curran assembled a Baltimore-wide circle of district leaders, among them Thomas D'Alesandro, Jr., later Baltimore's mayor, and Jack Pollack, destined with D'Alesandro to preside twenty years later over the collapse of the city machine: its conqueror, an ad hoc circle about Mayor Harold Grady, would carry important seeds of the Mandel circle. Symbols and history, linkage and seeds: the O'Conor years illuminated the future.

A final illumination of a different sort was O'Conor's successful confrontation with what had been thought, at least, to be Maryland's insuperable bias against a religious ethnic in the governorship. Certainly Harry Nice, trying to hold on for a second term against the Roman Catholic O'Conor, thought bias was still worth a sly political prod. In his radio speeches, Nice commonly spoke of his Democratic challenger as "Herbert ROME-ulous O'Conor." It didn't work. O'Conor became the first Catholic resident of Government House. That bit of prejudice set at rest, others were emboldened to ask later, Why not the first Jew? Why not Marvin Mandel?

Preston Lane, like O'Conor, was a graduate of the Ritchie school. More purposefully even than O'Conor, he tried to reassemble the now-aging Ritchie princelings in a coalition to rule Maryland. So he did, but factional differences in Lane's 1946 primary produced the first, most profound post-Ritchie split. Lane men and O'Conor men scrabbled among themselves for power. Lane managed to extract from beneath O'Conor key parts of the Curran-led city machine: chief among these was Jack Pollack, ex-pugilist and ex-hijacker, Moses to Jewish politicians, launcher of Marvin Mandel. The Lane coalition discarded the O'Conor-Curran-Bruce layer of Ritchieites, yet it amounted to a bona fide recreation of the flower of the Ritchie regime. But for Lane's soaring imagination, marred by his inability to point out to others the stars he followed, he might well have established a pattern workable for years to come. Mahoney, Lane's gravest miscalculation, changed all that. McKeldin was the instant beneficiary, later Agnew, finally Mandel.

Lane's defeat in 1950 meant more than the failure of one man, more even that the collapse of a Democratic coalition. Out with Lane and his circle went the heart of the Ritchie revival. Scarcely more than thirty years had elapsed since Ritchie first stitched together in 1919 a new pattern from relics of the Gorman-Rasin machine, itself a creature of little more than thirty years vitality. Tugged between Lane and O'Conor, the old organization burst apart at the top. Mahoney exploited the rift, summoned up a largely personal force of his own, fell repeatedly, tantalizingly, short in the clutch. If he cleared the way for others, he left little foundation to build on.

That responsibility fell in the 1958 election to J. Millard Tawes, a governor by then able to show only superficial lineage reaching back to Ritchie. True, political genealogists can make pedigree points. O'Conor first brought Tawes forward as state comptroller; Curran tried, too early, to make Tawes governor. Lane subsequently reached across a factional split to raise Tawes to comptroller again, thus setting up the Tawes governorship for later. So much for political ancestry: Tawes sprang from Ritchie roots. To an extent significantly larger, Tawes became his own man sailing free of a Ritchie heritage largely eroded—call it Mahoneyized—into lifelessness. His eight years in Government House freshened several Democratic initiatives, not always to righteous applause in the editorial columns. And Millard Tawes lifted Marvin Mandel to Speaker of the House of Delegates, his direct springboard to the governor's chair.

Personally, Tawes was too disarming a man to fasten public attention upon his own leadership. He was the antithesis of the driving Lane, the sulfurous Mahoney. Instead, he gave off a gentle air of tentativeness, of being faintly ill at ease among throaty back-slappers astrut on marble statehouse stairs. Annapolis reporters nicknamed him "Mallard," after a plump duck shyly at home on its native marshes of the Eastern Shore. Yet the Tawes years proved pivotal. Whether because of the governor, in spite of him, or maybe no more than coincidentally, this last Democratic regime before Mandel left a fateful residue.

Tawes was an instinctive survivor, hence a realist. He strove for stable, mildly progressive government and produced it. State revenues held steady, legislators cooperated. Better roads and a new Chesapeake Bay Bridge were built. Needy counties won financial help, blacks gained a measure of white respect, worn-out oyster beds revived. Beneath this placid, Tawes-type surface, a disruptive mood prevailed: George Mahoney, now as usual, tried to play to it, as usual unsuccessfully.

Still, angry voices edged with rebellion loosed a tangled political turbulence, which Tawes, ever the cautious traditionalist, failed to understand and master. In one quarter flamed white racism, twice the destroyer at primary-election polls of Tawes's hopes to project his own quiet orthodoxy into a successor's hands. The governor had to watch one protégé, United States Senator Daniel B. Brewster, be cruelly clawed in 1964 by George Wallace's backlashing rednecks. Two years later, while reaching for the succession Tawes tendered him, Thomas B. Finan fell athwart Mahoney, who this time was wearing a Wallace face. With both Brewster and Finan badly singed by racist fires, the last shred of the Ritchie dynasty burned through. White racism soon retreated, but the old ways and old Democratic connections it destroyed yielded place to new and different ones.

Turbulence in the Tawes years was not limited to racism or to unrelieved destruction. Black Baltimoreans broke upon the scene, in counterpoint to Wallace-Mahoney thrusts. They overran Jack Pollack's once-invulnerable Jewish precincts in West Baltimore, then constructed a formal alliance with the Tawes administration. William Adams—still wearing the tag, Little Willie, of his numbers racket days—challenged the Mitchell family's long command of black Democrats. Newer still, if more diffuse, was a mushrooming of community organizations in the city and its suburban counties. Mostly opposed to politics in the patronage-grabbing sense, they helped replace vanishing local bosslets as watchdogs over neighborhood interests. Familiar walls were crumbling at the bottom.

Crumbling also, it began to seem, at or near the top. Of overriding significance to the Mandel story is the generation, during the Tawes years, of two forces. One force would elevate Mandel to power, a contrary force drag him down. The elevating force—elevating in the political sense, not the moral—had its origins in George Hocker, a sometime beer lobbyist converted by Tawes to politico-financial manipulator, or money raiser for Tawes's election campaigns. It's an old and often unsavory art, also a necessary one so long as political campaigns run on private money. Hocker brought this art nearly to a science in the form of the testimonial dinner: guests were contractors and insurance men, architects and engineers, bond floaters and aspirant judges. Upon these tickets were pushed, often in blocs, at $1,000 apiece. For the fat cats, it offered a handy way to tip hats to the patronage-dispensing power. For Tawes, Hocker & Co., it was the best way yet of raising campaign money. What's more, it was legal.

A fiscal refinement of still farther-reaching significance was another Hocker creation, Tidewater Insurance. Here was one more money machine but with a different twist: you didn't have to spend all the money on elections. Instead, you could put a lot of it in your pocket or, alternatively, buy expensive presents for needy friends who were in a position to return the favor in a different coin. Friends like an underpaid governor hard-up to finance a difficult divorce.

The Tidewater principle was scarcely new to politics in Maryland or elsewhere. You're a contractor, you want a contract with the state. By law you need insurance to get the contract: How about buying from Tidewater? Here's why: in addition to Harry

Rodgers and Hocker himself, well known as Tawes's money raiser, another Tidewater partner was Philip Tawes, the governor's son. And since presiding over the state Board of Public Works, source of the yearned-for contracts, was the governor, would-be contractors could scarcely miss the message. Tidewater had the inside connection. No wonder Tidewater's income soared from the outset, no wonder it leaped from nowhere to top rank among Maryland insurance purveyors. And precedent was ample. Howard Jackson, as mayor of Baltimore in the 1920s, fed into his own insurance company premiums not only from favor seekers but from the city's own insurance as well. Later, in the D'Alesandro mayoral days, Jack Pollack did the same. The Mandel circle, when its turn came, had only to pick up in Tidewater a relationship to political power long established. Via circle members it produced jewelry and clothes and vacation trips for the governor.

That it also produced up to six criminal convictions was a new and unwelcome wrinkle imposed by a changed public attitude. This was the second new force, the one Mandel would disastrously misread. It focused on the United States attorney's office, historically a politico-legal backwater. Federal prosecutors had been supposed to watch over federal laws, state prosecutors over state laws. In the 1960s Joseph Tydings, then the Kennedy-prodded inhabitant of the federal prosecutors office, took a different view. What provoked Tydings was an invasion of Maryland by non-Maryland schemers who, camouflaged behind local names, corruptly milked the Maryland savings and loan market. A number of innocent depositors were hurt or threatened; state prosecutors looked the other way. But federal laws too lay broken, and Tydings summoned up a federal grand jury. Wholesale convictions ensued, including those of a Maryland congressman, Thomas Johnson, and the Speaker of the Maryland House of Delegates.

Here was reform of the head-bashing variety, and Tydings undertook to spread his "shiny-bright" movement beyond the courtroom directly into state politics. He did win one United States Senate term for himself, badly jolting the Tawes regulars. But he failed, Mahoney being on the scene, to push through his Tydings-backed candidate to the governorship. If the Tydings political reform fizzled, its legal forerunner in the United States attorney's office flourished. Federal power had awakened in

Maryland, and it frowned on listless policing of the state's own front porch. A string of abuses larger by far awaited the federal purge that Tydings began and his successors carried on. Maryland's old repute for toleration could no longer be ballooned, by those of a too-enterprising spirit, to blimpish permissiveness— anything goes, anything at all. Instead, federal law would be keenly read, lawbreakers sternly prosecuted. This was profoundly different from the amiable indifference of the past. Not all state officials tuned in betimes to the change.

To the two dozen news reporters covering the trial, one of the most revealing moments in Governor Mandel's appearance on the witness stand arrived when he seemed to deny that his own telephone number was, indeed, his own telephone number. Let the courtroom exchange between Barnet Skolnik and Marvin Mandel relate the incident:

Skolnik—Governor, who [in the Governor's executive offices] had the phone number 267-5901?

Mandel—Mrs. Grace Donald.

Q.—And who else, sir?

A.—Mrs. Grace Donald.

Q.—Wasn't that your phone number, sir?

A.—No, sir, that was Mrs. Grace Donald's phone number listed to the executive office. That was her phone. That is the way she handled it. It was 5—

Q.—Let me show you—

A.—May I answer, Your Honor?

The Court—Yes, sir.

A.—It was 5901, -02, and -03.

Q.—Let me show you a directory for the State of Maryland Executive Offices, sir, and let me show you the highlighted numbers. Is it not a fact that 224 [sic], Marvin Mandel 5901, Grace Donald, and another secretary named Ethel Tigner—and aren't those the only three people in that office who had that phone number in those days, sir?

A.—No, that is not. There was one other person.

Q.—Who was that, sir?

A.—Those were on the desks of Mrs. Donald, Mrs. Tigner, and I think that same number was on the desk of Mrs. Hromadka who also had another number, and I think you will find her other number listed on there for her appointment-making arrangements. Those numbers were listed to three different people in the office. They were not my number. They were the office number for anyone calling from around the state.

Several pages later in the transcript, Skolnik spoke again to Governor Mandel:—Governor, 267-5901, I think we have agreed, was your telephone number in those days . . .

There was no further objection.

Skolnik had not simply been toying with Mandel over a small point of veracity. He was leading up to something more substantial, namely, the Governor's position about when he had learned that his friends at Tidewater Insurance had bought Marlboro Racetrack. Early knowledge suggested guilty connivance; late knowledge suggested innocence, as Marvin Mandel claimed. Skolnik produced telephone company records that, he would say, suggested early knowledge—and Mandel's guilt.

In the thirty months between mid-1971 and the end of 1973, the record showed sixty-two telephone calls placed from the offices of Tidewater Insurance to the Mandel telephone number in the State House. That was an average of two calls per month. Defense counsel objected that no evidence existed as to what these calls were about, that it was unproved whether or not there was any conversation at all, or even whether the caller had reached the Governor himself. Still, it was the pattern into which the calls fell, close to the pattern of telling events, which Skolnik emphasized. He concluded the testimony about telephone calls with a long question.

Skolnik—Governor, somebody picked up the telephone at Tidewater and called a phone number listed in the state directory to you, and Mrs. Donald, and Mrs. Tigner, and somebody picked up the phone at the other end in Annapolis, so that call was completed, and the toll call put on the Tidewater phone bill was as follows—calls like that occurred as follows: December 29,1971, the day the loan was approved for the purchase of the track; ten phone calls on December 30, the day before the track was purchased; two calls the day after Mr. Casey told the press he owned the track; calls back and forth between Weinberg & Green, Mr. Cory, Mr. Casey, and the men at Boca Tika [Florida] while you were down at Boca Tika; a call to you the day Mr. Cory wrote to the chairman of the Racing Commission, Mr. Brewer, a call the day the Racing Commission—the Racing Commission said that Marlboro could race at mile tracks; Mr. Hess breakfasted with you on the morning he went to New York to talk about merger, he called you from Florida right after the meetings about merger; there were four calls four days before the men at Tidewater sold their interest to Mr. Cory; there were three calls the day Mr. Cory talked to Mr. Hess and Rodgers about an annual meeting of Marlboro, and the day before the Racing Commission granted Marlboro the benefit that had almost been obtained through the consolidation bill, the transfer of the thirty-six days at the mile tracks—

Weiner—All right. Now I have my objection. He's throwing in again this business with the transfer of the racing days to build up to this argument. If there is a question mark at the end of this thing—

The Court—Let him finish his question, gentlemen. Let him finish his question, and the Governor can answer it, if he will.

Skolnik—Governor, in light of all that, is it still your testimony that you never knew until March of 1975 that Mr. Hess, Mr. Rodgers, and Mr. Kovens owned the Marlboro Racetrack?

Mandel—Absolutely, ... I never knew.

Skolnik—Your Honor, we have no further questions of this witness.

5.

Turning the Rascals Out—and In

A backward glance at the writhings of Maryland Democrats during the century following the Civil War reveals something scarcely perceptible in the ups and downs of individual contenders. This was the evolution of an answer to a question as old as politics itself: How do we prune the old to make way for the new? How do we adjust government leadership to fit changes in the requirements of the led? In the political ringside version: How do we turn the rascals out?

Just there the question turns involuted. For when is a rascal a certified rascal? When is he, instead, a good old boy doing a bad old thing? Slipperier still: As rules change for the better, what of politicians caught in transit? If new rules are made to apply, are old offenders unfairly indicted? But if old rules are let linger in a sort of legal ghost-life, can new rules ever gain footing?

Large concepts collide but, either way, it's the politics of purge, of cleaning government's house. Carrying off this essential operation and, at the same time, preserving a reasonably stable government is a delicate art at which democracy still fumbles but, withal, fumbles more effectively than rival persuasions. It was Marvin Mandel's historical misfortune and his own botched judgment of contemporary moods which conspired to bring him down.

To the complexities of this politics of purge, George Mahoney brought in his time an answer of sorts. He did pick off Old

Guardsmen gone complacent in office. He did help ventilate a Democratic party too ingrown for its own good and too inflexible for ready response as Maryland's needs shifted. Give Mahoney his due: if he was unhappily short of answers, or anyway of the right answers, the popular attention he excited did raise pertinent questions. Momentarily, in the late 1960s, the advent of the Joseph Tydings reformers suggested that a broad change was at hand in the Democratic party, only it foundered on a last-minute Mahoney torpedo. The essence of it is that Mahoney undertook a job too big for himself. He offered himself as a substitute for the two-party system, more specifically for a Maryland Republican party. He tried to fill a gap any one man might find daunting.

Behind the Mahoney phenomenon runs a question larger still: Whatever became of the Republicans as an all-weather party in Maryland? What of America's two-party system, the vaunted machinery in which challenge by the political outs is a vital cog? Why was Maryland denied this self-laundering device?

Republicans did manage in the post-Ritchie decades to loft up as many governors as the Democrats did, almost as many United States senators. For the most part, however, these were simply byproducts of the Mahoney era, candidates who climbed grate-fully through holes in the Democratic walls blasted open first by Mahoney. At lesser levels, where a political party draws suste-nance from the people—city and county office, the legislature, registered voters—Republicans made little discernible dent across the state. Consistently voter registration tilted one to three against them, in some places a hopeless one to five: a troop shortage meant hesitant leaders, small plans, narrow and even oddball philosophies. As a consequence, "two-party system" has been a misleading label in Maryland. One-and-a-half-party system is more like it, and this enduring imbalance leads us back to the Reconstruction period following the Civil War. There the frailty is rooted.

After Appomattox, Maryland Republicans had their greatest opportunity and blew it, never fully to recover. A second chance came their way thirty years later, but the promising Republican breakthrough in 1895 shortly closed tightly over. Again in 1950 and after, Mahoney populated high Maryland offices with more Republicans than the party itself ever did, but he was a force called up less by Republican strength than by Republican weakness. It was a weakness recognized by that time as inherent. In Maryland, it seemed, Republicans were snake-bit from birth.

What bit them was no snake but a profound misunderstanding of the ambivalence of Maryland voters. Democrats, as a party seasoned in Maryland long before the Civil War, understood the state's elusive sensibilities and played shrewdly to them. Republicans, all but unheard-of prior to Fort Sumter, did not. The party's new-risen leaders wrongly assumed that the Union's military victory could be converted to a governing mandate. In Maryland they thought voters left wobbly by their border-state geography wanted bracing up to the newly triumphant standard of the North. True, this program wasn't the harsh Reconstruction imposed on neighboring Virginia and its old Confederacy sisters to the south, for Maryland though tortured did not secede from the Union. But pronouncements from the radical or hard-line wing of Republicans chilled Marylanders of still-divided beliefs. Loyalty oaths were imposed on returning Maryland Confederates, black ex-slaves were given the vote. Southern sympathizers were frowned upon, and wartime memories of federal soldiers astride Federal Hill, their cannon intimidating Baltimore below, were awakened. Maryland stood loyal but not that loyal, principle be damned. Politically, Republican radicals overplayed the right hand in the wrong place.

Two postwar years wrapped them up. Maryland Republicans fractionalized, radicals hardening into the first nucleus of a state party, conservatives drifting across party lines into more tentative Democratic circles. By 1867, Democrats had taken command again as smoothly as they had before the war, striking a gentler keynote Marylanders could accept in comfort. There would be Reconstruction, yes, but self-Reconstruction—something short of the stern stuff Republican radicals brandished. Politically, Democrats were off on the right foot, Republicans on the wrong, and a proper two-party system stood flawed in Maryland for more than a century.

Republicans did not drop altogether dead there, as they did in the still-smoldering Deep South until the middle of the 1900s. They ran on in Maryland but, nearly always, ran lame. The Republican surge begun in 1895, momentarily greeted as genuine party resurrection, was soon unmasked as a thrust by Democratic reformers in disguise. True, Maryland voters turned fiercely on reigning Democrats, and the Gorman-Rasin machine crawled away broken or badly bent. True, too, that festering corruption was dragged up, that reform momentarily proved a viable political vehicle. Yet Republicans were unable as a party to hold ground won, let alone extend their turf. Soon back came the Democrats, a bit humbled, a bit less rancid, but once more commanding in a way Republicans couldn't manage. Not until 1934, when Albert Ritchie fell of his own four-term weight, and again at the beginning in 1950 of the Mahoney era, would Republicans present a convincing alternative. Even in those two instances, since both the catalysts—Ritchie and Mahoney—were Democrats, the Republicans scraped up cold comfort. For them the two-party system had become a sometime thing, a casual spoon to flip them scraps from the Democrats' table. Thomas D'Alesandro, Baltimore's mayor in the 1950s, summed up Democratic contentment: "Let Republicans have the two-party system, give the Democrats the political jobs."

In one sense the curious formula evolved in mid-century Maryland for political refreshment—an unfulfilled Mahoney plus unpartied Republicans—worked fairly well. Change was produced, fresh faces appeared, sometimes new ideas. Maryland government functioned satisfactorily if not brilliantly. But there was another, more troubled sense: How deep beneath the surface did these changes penetrate? Were the new faces truly new or, as with Ritchie and his admiring heirs, only the ever-blooming of entrenched political dynasties? Among new ideas, wasn't there one ineradicable old idea that a hopeful newcomer, to get along in Maryland politics, had to go along with some of its backstage practices? Deep-seated corruption infected high and low in both parties. The series of Mahoney-aided Republican turnovers, while agitating the landscape, left all but untouched the corruption beneath.

Here arises one of the knottiest puzzles in the case of Marvin Mandel, a puzzle that Mandel himself only knots tighter. Publicly, at least, Mandel holds to two points. One is that, despite his criminal conviction, he did nothing wrong. He says, second, that what he did do was no different from what a number of Maryland governors before him did. Leave aside a certain incongruity in the two points. Taken together, these points seem to draw an exonerating blanket not only over Mandel personally but also over his predecessors in the governor's chair. Whatever was, was right—and still is right, so argued Mandel. The difficulty here is that the argument is only half-stated, hence only half-true.

The demonstrably true half is that corruption stained Maryland politics, as it stained politics nearly everywhere, for at least as long a time as history records. The second half, more telling, is ignored in the Mandel position. It is the fact that history records along with corruption a rising tide of public impatience with corruption. By 1969, when Mandel took office, a new set of court opinions had stiffened old federal law against corruption. Whatever may earlier have been tolerable, it was now held, had been tolerable only in its own time. Thereafter, in a more mature time, the line separating right from wrong was more precisely drawn. Political corruption, always shadowy, took on a more discernible shape. The new law—sharply written, and insistently enforced—would try to determine the difference between right and wrong.

The process of change was not new, nor was it sudden. As it had been with earlier antisocial practices—slavery and racketeering, child labor and tax dodging—so it was with corruption in government. Private morality, long troubled, forced its way onto the public stage: a principle central to the democratic system simply asserted itself once again. The rules did indeed change, and for national government the Watergate affair is commonly cited as a turning point. In Maryland by that time both corruption, as Mandel would suggest later, and the public turn against corrupters and corrupted, although he disastrously ignored that part, had been long in the hatching.

The earlier corruption Mandel saw and seemed to cite in his own defense was undoubtedly there. And maybe it wasn't held in those years to be corruption. Examples abound, acceptable yesterday, flagrant today. During the Revolution, it was thought by many to be no more than a commonplace when John Randall, then quartermaster to the American forces, was court-martialed for jobbing Yankee uniforms. The Civil War too had its eminent profiteers: But was Johns Hopkins, then a Baltimore merchant anxious to preserve his national market, wrong or simply prudent to bribe legislators to hold Maryland in the Union?

Reconstruction set railroads booming, which in turn set off a political battle between the Baltimore & Ohio and the Pennsylvania over right of way into Washington. The B&O had right of way, the Pennsylvania didn't. Still, few but B&O officials snorted when Oden Bowie, after being boosted to the Maryland governorship by the Pennsylvania road, pulled from his pocket a secret charter opening to the Pennsylvania the crucial Washington right of way. And, as noted, Arthur Gorman was similarly entwined with transportation a few years later. He used leverage at Annapolis—legislators and governors alike—to boost C&O Canal interests against the rival B&O. Gorman flourished politically. Both canal and railroad began to fall apart.

Reaction was insignificant. Nearly parallel to Gorman's rise, and possibly more telling for things to come, was the rise within the Democratic party of a relatively new and certainly contrary force. Composed partly of routine political dissidents, partly of outraged independents, an anti-Gorman sally had taken formal shape as early as 1875. This was the Citizens Reform party, an uplift movement destined to crest first in the great breakthrough twenty years later and, less dramatically but with gathering conviction, to color Maryland politics for a century. Not that reform achieved instant, steady progress. Rather its rhythm was a tidal rhythm, ebb and flow, washing away at Maryland's encrusted cynicism about politics. Slowly it built instead the idea that public office is a public trust, not a license to feed on the body politic. Despite Gorman's collapse at the end of the nineteenth century there was still much reformist washing to be done.

That an official's personal interests, private and public, should not conflict or even seem to was a lesson hard to teach. Besides, a governor wasn't really expected to live on a governor's $4,500 annual salary, was he? Edwin Warfield, when elected in 1903, didn't think so. As governor he held tight to the presidency of the Fidelity and Deposit Company and, the next year, threw gubernatorial weight against a bill providing state examination of trust companies—one of which, as it happened, the governor himself was in the process of founding. That Isador Rayner apparently bought his way to the United States Senate—I. Freeman Rasin, commander of the legislative votes then necessary, had them for sale—occasioned no public outcry. No more so than did the concession by Austin L. Crothers, the otherwise progressive governor elected in 1907, that he had once been so forgetful as to tilt the ballot box his way in Cecil County. And Albert Ritchie's first election in 1919 hung, as noted, on the thin margin of 165 not-unquestioned votes.

More pointedly, and more personally, what would be recognized later as the Mandel problem began to take shape. This was the dilemma forced upon a poor or anyway nonrich governor supposed by the legislature to live and support his family on an annual salary of $25,000. Perquisites notwithstanding, after income taxes, to which governors are as vulnerable as anyone, $25,000 looked cruelly pockmarked to Marvin Mandel. Ritchie and Lane, among modern governors, held moderate to considerable private fortunes. They went untroubled by financial pinch. Others did not.

For Herbert O'Conor and Theodore McKeldin (who, like Mandel, were lawyers but lifelong holders of public office) little legal practice had been established, no private nest egg laid. Yet each had a family to maintain, indeed each managed to acquire a substantial family house in a glossy Baltimore neighborhood, O'Conor in Guilford, McKeldin in Homeland. All this, on $4,500 a year? How? Few today can be sure, but a partial answer seems to involve a sort of unpublicized noblesse oblige: rich admirers undertook privately to keep the O'Conor and McKeldin families financially content. One O'Conor patron was Howard Bruce, the Maryland member in O'Conor's day of the Democratic National Committee: among other favors Bruce helped secure for O'Conor, when his elective days were over, a comfortable legal retainer. One McKeldin patron was M. William Adelson, a Baltimore lawyer who partook profitably of bond counsel fees then customarily passed out as political patronage; privately, McKeldin and Adelson shared legal offices. A McKeldin innovation appeared at his annual birthday party. Rich friends were invited on the understanding that a birthday present of at least $200 was expected, in cash or as an addition to the McKeldin rare-coin collection. Embarrassment spread when one such McKeldin in-gathering broke into a newspaper column, calling public attention to legal prohibitions. McKeldin, grumbling, gave most of the gifts back.

Other, darker, talk was heard of more substantial charity, some of it linked to political quid pro quo or, bluntly, bribery. Little was proven until the 1970s when, as a follow-up on its earlier savings and loan exposé, the United States attorney's office began digging into kickback corruption throughout the Baltimore area. Foremost among those to fall was Spiro T. Agnew, then vice-president but tripped up by money transactions—Agnew, too, was without his own financial backlog—left over from his days as governor and earlier.

Here was the turn of mood, Maryland's own Watergate, which Marvin Mandel failed to detect in time. When belatedly he did detect it, the new mood was already mature, firm, formidable. Immediately prior to the opening of the Mandel administration, warning lights flashed with particular intensity. The same federal investigation that would lead to Mandel was upending two county executives in the Baltimore area—Dale Anderson, in Baltimore County, and Joseph W. Alton, Jr., in Anne Arundel County—and in a third case had already upended Jesse S. Baggett, then chairman of the Prince Georges County Commission.

The Baggett case held particularly pertinent pointers for anyone who happened to be looking. Prosecutors argued that, although they could not point to any single action taken by the chairman, an overall pattern of favors was intended to—and did—influence Baggett to tilt his zoning decisions to favor Ralph D. Rocks, a developer. Both Baggett and Rocks were convicted on federal charges, despite imprecise links between the quid, the pro, and the quo.

So one important dimension of the case that would later tie Mandel to his uncommonly generous friends was apparent in ample time to warn them. That none seemed to notice the oncoming hazard, let alone to deactivate the conspiracy, is a sign probably partly of careless arrogance, partly of being in too deep to crawl out. They knew the risks, took them, and lost.

Certainly by the time Mandel was convicted in 1977, the rules were no longer new. They had been changing in Maryland since the Reform Party had been born in 1875. They were a century old, plus two years.

H is second term as governor having been cut short by court action, Marvin Mandel quit Maryland's stately governor's mansion with his wife, Jeanne, forever early in October, 1977. Ugly questions arose:

Did the Mandels, as they would angrily maintain, take with them from the mansion only what was rightfully, legally, their own property? Were vindictive lies told about them? Was cash wrongly pocketed by servants?

Or did they instead, as the state maintained in court, make off with at least $23,800 worth of mansion property clearly documented as owned by the state?

This unseemly quarrel sputtered grudgingly for five years. In late 1983, more than three years after the state sued to recover furniture it claimed was wrongly taken, Mandel agreed to pay $9,250. To the end, as he had in his earlier conviction for mail fraud, he insisted he had done nothing wrong.

Where lay the truth? What sort of light does this grabby little byplay throw on the Mandels' personal veracity, on their sense of public decorum?

Conflicting evidence rolled fog across some of the facts. Was this antique chair really brought to Annapolis from Jeanne's former residence in Leonardtown, or was it purchased later, with state money? One way, it was hers to keep; the other way, it belonged to the state. How free a hand were the Mandels permitted in the disposition of a $40,000 household fund earmarked for official entertainment? Rules seemed obscure and rubbery.

Other circumstances, less befogged, put the Mandel-Maryland dispute into perspective.

The Mandels had rented a small, comfortable estate just north of Annapolis, which they occupied upon leaving the governor's mansion. In the sixteen days before they moved, Jeanne Mandel put in four separate orders to Giant Food, Inc. Orders were made chargeable to the state in the last quarter of 1977, payable after the Mandels had left. The items ordered are revealing. The quantities are more so. In Jeanne Mandel's handwriting the following list appears:

> 2 cases tuna fish
> 6 cases dog food [later valued at $489]
> 4 doz. pkgs. bacon
> 1 doz. National Hebrew [sic] salami
> 1 case tomatoe [sic] soup

Other Mandel purchases in this sixteen-day period, according to the Giant Food clerk who handled orders for the mansion, included:

> 48 cans, 12 oz. each, Bumble Bee Tuna
> 1 case, of 24 Hunt's tomato sauce
> 12 bottles Heinz Tomato Ketchup
> 12 cans Crisco
> 36 boxes Duncan Hines Cake Mix
> 3 10-lb. bags Domino Sugar
> 2 cases, 24 each, Sanka and Maxwell House coffee, both
>   regular grind
> 24 tubes Crest 7 oz. toothpaste
> 12 bottles Scope

The above is only a sample. A sixteen-day intake of food and toiletries to a total of $1,544.58 stands documented in mansion accounts, in Giant Food invoices, or in both.

There was more. Some forty-three full cases of household supplies ranging from toilet paper to cleaning fluid to furniture polish were requisitioned, late in September, 1977, from the state's building and grounds warehouse. Value was set at

$517.01. Also 350 bottles of liquor, valued at $1,750, were found to be missing from mansion closets. In all, these categories accounted for $9,080.01 in goods the investigators claimed was left owing the state in the wake of the departed Mandels.

The key question was obvious: Were these commodities illegally packed off to their private estate to help subsidize the Mandels in beginning their new, postgubernatorial life together? Not at all, they said, not at all.

Jeanne Mandel denied taking anything not hers. Asked by state investigators about the large quantities ordered just before she left Annapolis—notably, the twenty-four tubes of Crest 7 oz. toothpaste, the dozen Hebrew National salami—Mrs. Mandel said she was thinking of the incoming governor, Blair Lee. Indeed, she went on, she sent inquiries about what he liked and didn't like. She was stocking the mansion, she said, for him.

Asked later to verify such inquiries Judy McClure, Lee's Secretary, said no one asked her anything like that. Blair Lee said nobody mentioned toothpaste to him, let alone salami. To the contrary, what did turn up were vouchers showing that a great deal was missing or unaccounted for. Shortly after the Mandels left it, $2,131.77 of the mansion's household fund was spent by the Lees to replenish food supplies there. Then $1,157.40 went to put the usual liquor stock back in place.

So much for the mansion's consumables, at best an elusive category, hard to put a finger on. Mansion furniture is different: it is durable, more readily identified and appraised, less subject to mysterious disappearance. Nevertheless, it was over furniture that controversy turned hottest in the aftermath of the Mandel departure.

As many as eighty-seven separate items were challenged by the state. Furniture under direct question ranged from a five-piece bedroom suite to an assortment of Waterford crystal to a set of redwood patio furniture, from a collection of spoons and plates put out by the Franklin mint to a kitchen full of cookware and flatware to two historic wooden sculptures. These sculptures had been chopped from a pair of carved doors once gracing the front of the mansion. Remounted, they were found hung in the Mandel house.

A formal evaluation of $10,812.71 was put on the lot, all

paid for by the state. The missing items, said the state, were held illegally.

The Mandel version differed. Some items were said to have come from the previous Mandel house in Baltimore, some from Jeanne's house in Leonardtown. Four items, they said, went out by accident and would be returned. The Mandels wanted to keep nine other articles, bought with state money. But Marvin Mandel tendered a check for $3,100 to pay for them.

That should square things, shouldn't it? Everything straightforward and aboveboard, right?

Wrong, said state investigators. They hesitated momentarily, however, to reach out for what they were convinced was state property. No wonder.

In the background flew a dead-cat barrage of accusations by both sides. Inventories of furniture, it was said, had been tampered with and "whitewashed." Protests were lodged, then overridden. Invoices were called "doctored," private furniture was repaired at public expense, state-paid purchases were called wedding gifts. So one side cried out.

Oh, no! cried the other. There was in the mansion "an internal problem," a not-so-delicate charge of stealing by the mansion staff: cash was said to have been put up to cover Mandel-made purchases, then privately pocketed and the state made to pay anyway. And all that talk about liquor: why, bottle after bottle had been given to the Mandels by personal friends. It was their own liquor to take, not the state's to keep.

For three dutiful years, state investigators picked their way through this unlovely scene. What emerged were three circumstances that, taken together, could not help but provoke puzzlement at the very least.

One circumstance was the absence from the mansion, after the Mandels left it, of quantities of furniture hitherto recorded—if somewhat chaotically—in several earlier mansion inventories. Second was the physical presence in the Mandel house of article after article that, despite elaborate Mandel denials, looked to investigators very much like the very furniture found to be missing from the mansion. A third circumstance did little to diffuse suspicion: dated vouchers suggested that between September 26 and October 9, some fifteen men using four moving vans transported ten to twelve truckloads of boxes and furniture from the mansion to the Mandel residence.

Nor was that all. Several servants diverted from regular duties at the mansion spent a number of days—some on overtime, all paid by the state—cleaning up the house prior to the Mandels' arrival. Jeanne Mandel apparently oversaw the packing, cleaning, and moving operation. She took charge, witnesses reported, in person.

That autumn of 1977, when he formally took over as governor, Blair Lee immediately heard staff complaints. He took no action. Personally ambivalent about the Mandels, and heavily dependent anyway on Mandel political lieutenants for help in his own election campaign in the year then just ahead, the new governor turned an ear philosophically deaf. At election time, he did not win.

Harry Hughes, elected governor on a reform platform in 1978, brought with him no such inhibitions. He was openly outraged at the Mandels. More, he resolved to enforce state law. What he did early in 1979 was alert Maryland Attorney General Stephen H. Sachs—also freshly elected, also a reformer—to the situation a Hughes aide had uncovered in the mansion.

This situation, in a masterpiece of diplomatic language, was as follows: "[An] uncertainty or a difference of opinion [exists] between some personnel of Government House [the mansion] and the Mandels with respect to the removal, ownership and/or value of items purchased by General Services, and also questions relating to the legal status and ownership of items purchased from the Government House housekeeping account."

Painstakingly, slowly, Attorney General Sachs's subordinates researched the evidence. They found it heavily documented against the Mandels. They also found Marvin Mandel's settlement offer—$3,100 and call it square—grossly inadequate to meet the sums involved, not to mention myriad violations of law.

The state resolved on a civil suit, not criminal. In January, 1980, it asked: Return of fifty-seven pieces of mansion furniture (originally the state claimed eighty-seven pieces, of which the Mandels returned twenty-two but kept the rest) and payment of $23,811 in compensatory and punitive damages.

The day before, Marvin Mandel had sued the state asking the

court to declare him the owner of thirty-eight of the disputed items. He also asked the return of eighteen items he said he had left behind in the mansion.

Before the cases, joined as one, could be brought to trial, Marvin Mandel reported to federal prison at Eglin Air Force Base, Florida. Trial was deferred, pending his release. In the spring of 1983 the attorney general's office and a lawyer for the former governor opened negotiations. They made a deal to avoid further court action.

Marvin Mandel was to pay $9,250, return some furniture, and keep the rest. A handful of personal items he had left behind in the mansion, but that had been impounded by the state, was to be returned to him.

6.

Cherchez la Blonde: Exit Bootsie, Enter Jeanne

B uddy "in love"? No!
In love with that woman? No! That Jeanne Dorsey, that . . . that . . . No!

Buddy going "to marry her"? Her own Buddy Mandel, her Buddy of thirty-two years? It was crazy, something was wrong . . . No! No! No!

It was July 3, 1973, and Bootsie Mandel couldn't take in what she was hearing. Yet there it was, right there on the evening television. Very formal, very official, icy cold . . . "release by the Governor's office . . . press room . . . State House . . . Annapolis." Bootsie fought off the freezing words.

Fought off, too, a word unmentioned in the official message, a word that hung silent in the air, a word that blacked out the television screen, the whole room around her. Divorce, yes *divorce*. DIVORCE. At that hideous word Bootsie Mandel's world shattered. In pieces lay the life that, with Buddy at her side, she had struggled piece by piece to put together for the two of them . . . No!

Governor Mandel, still "Buddy" to his family, had a different thought. For him a brave new world was opening. Out of the shadows at last, it seemed, into a radiant sunlight he had never known before. So it was, in one way. But the price he would pay for this midlife leap from old wife to new—really, from old life to new—would help shatter him too. At that moment, however, this new world looked golden. Golden as Jeanne's sparkling hair.

80

There ensued, of course, a meantime. It was Bootsie's to play out, and she played it for five and a half months. Played it, too, in costs to Mandel, for several hundred thousand dollars he didn't have. Some say that's where this narrative begins.

Yes, Bootsie had heard rumors about another woman. No, she hadn't believed them—at least not that they would come to this. She herself was a worldly woman, not some pink-cheeked choir girl. Men, even governors, played sly games—but men got over them, governors kept them hidden. Didn't they?

True, Buddy *had* begun to seem strange to her, remote and somehow distant. She'd first noticed it after he'd hurt his head in that automobile accident two and a half years earlier: now he ought to see a psychiatrist. And yet . . . did she really believe that? Or was she, she wondered, privately manufacturing for her own comfort another explanation, one less painful than the one leaping at her throat off the television screen?

Bootsie didn't know, didn't know. Still, ever since the accident he hadn't been the Marvin Mandel she first knew at 15 years old, she had married and whose two children she had borne, she had helped up the long ladder to governor of Maryland. This new man she didn't know, this man whose words (His own words? Or, really, words that Jeanne put in his mouth?) some television announcer was reading into her sister-in-law's place in Baltimore. No, she kept saying, she didn't know this Buddy Mandel at all.

What Bootsie did know was who *she* was. Once she could think again clearly, after that ghastly July evening, she remembered. She was still First Lady of Maryland. (Later she would say about Jeanne: How can she be First Lady when she isn't even a lady first?) It was a proud title but also, deftly managed, the title of a position of tactical value. Also again—why not?—of value financially. So divorce was imminent, was it? Bootsie's instincts, instincts born of a lifetime of political maneuver, were aroused.

Buddy had moved first. After casually ascertaining she would be out of Annapolis for the day, he had quietly extracted a suitcaseful of clothes from the mansion and transferred them to the Annapolis Hilton, a few blocks away. Bootsie settled on a counter move: it was quick, defiant, passionate. No, she wouldn't creep away sobbing in the night. What she would do instead was stay rooted in the mansion, the most tangible symbol of the power and prestige which the governorship, and the first ladyship, commanded. Now she would command it, alone if necessary, or at least until Buddy came to his senses. Besides, it was Bootsie's suspicion that it was the mansion for which Jeanne hungered . . . that Jeanne!

Well, they would see about that. All Maryland would see about that, including Maryland voters due to speak out election day next year. When the reporters finally reached her on the telephone in her sister-in-law's apartment, Bootsie was tremulous but ready.

One reporter, to get things going, read her a line from the governor's official statement: his wife was "completely aware" of his new love for Jeanne, Marvin had said. Also aware of his intentions about remarriage. All very dispassionate, rational, civilized. Marvin "working something out." Was it, the reporter wanted to know, all worked out with Bootsie?

Hardly. Bootsie's opening shot boomed across Marvin's bow: "We've shared the same bed for thirty-two years. As a matter of fact, we got out of the same bed this morning. I am absolutely amazed at this."

Yes, well. What about the "numerous discussions" about Jeanne Marvin said they had had?

That one Bootsie sidestepped. Her response raised instead the question of Marvin's mental condition: "The pressure of this job must have gone to his head . . . I hope he gets some treatment."

Still, what were her own intentions? What would she do now?

Off went the secret weapon, Bootsie's surprise defense: "I intend to remain in the mansion. I intend to remain Mrs. Marvin Mandel."

Which is just what she did from the crucial July to the following December, when divorce lawyers finally wrestled out a settlement.

A woman scorned and defiant, a man trapped: a scenario not unfamiliar. What lifted this renewal of a sad old sequence to the extraordinary was that the man was the Governor of Maryland, that the woman was First Lady, that the mansion he deserted and she retained carried with it the aura at least of a state's ultimate political power. Because much of this was played out openly before a startled public audience—in the Washington newspapers, the Mandel-Mandel contretemps rode higher on Page One than Elizabeth Taylor's discard that same day of Richard Burton— readings were many and varied.

Bootsie's position was either admirable or ridiculous, totally justified or transparently scheming. Marvin was (1) a bold romantic or (2) a helpless football, be-scrimmaged between two forceful women. And Jeanne, to some an electric blonde worth any sacrifice, to others a brazen home-wrecker twice running. Because you could write in your own adjectives, many did. But to divorce lawyers teamed up on both sides emotional colorings were beside the point.

The point was, Marvin Mandel could scarcely ask Maryland voters for re-election in 1974, not if still awkwardly a-swing on a trapeze between one wife and another. Voters dislike airy spectacles in public men, so the lawyers asked simply: How much? How much money must Marvin pay to entice Bootsie from her captive mansion? In transfer charges, how much to exchange wives, to finalize a trade-in of one life on another?

No final figure was announced, but partial revelations turned up at trial more than three years later. A common estimate of the divorce settlement was $250,000; in addition, lawyers' fees were thought to drive the cost to Mandel above $400,000. He had no such money. Indeed, to judge by his own remarks still later at sentencing, he was by then a virtual pauper. Onlookers were quick to point to a financial coincidence. A $400,000 price tag on his divorce would stand strikingly close, adding proven benefits together, to the bribe a federal jury convicted him of taking. Hence a temptation to balance one $400,000 against the other $400,000, a temptation easy for analysts—and irresistible to male chauvinists.

The temptation was to trace the roots of Marvin Mandel's downfall to his divorce, specifically to two women, one pushing him, one pulling him into a financial desperation with which he could not cope. Mary McGrory put it succinctly in the *Washington Star*: "He loved beyond his means." Or steelier and less romantic: cherchez la femme, woman is man's hidden motivation. Just enough truth sustains this wistful version to keep it alive at the center of a swelling Mandel legendry. Yet as sober analysis it seems only a part of the truth and a misleading part at that.

The whole truth runs larger and deeper, less open to glib labels. Childhood days—as when young Buddy Mandel, the newsboy, hustled late editions against scrappy competitors near home at Pimlico Racetrack—carry in them seeds for the future. Important too is social environment. As a malleable teenager Buddy Mandel discovered that a "Polish" Jew, in the then sternly stratified Baltimore of the 1930s, was unwelcome among better-established "Germans" and still less welcome in the Christian community dominant at the time in school, college, law school.

Law? The ethnic elevator? When the big prestige-encrusted law firms found no place for him—ethnicity, in the 1940s, was not yet the Baltimore style—he turned for clients to family connections in the city's grungy, tinseled Block.

How about politics as a path to a better life? Mandel's formative years fell by necessity into the massive, brine-soaked but diamond-studded hands of the old prizefighter, Jack Pollack. As political boss of Baltimore's west-side Jews Pollack did proudly shove the brightest young lawyers on stage as candidates. Behind the scenery, he humiliated them by relentless deal making, job scrounging, insurance hawking and, always, money making. Jack Pollack blasted out of the ghetto that once fenced in Baltimore Jews, made himself a million doubtful dollars, and first hoisted Marvin Mandel, now richly marinated in street-battle wisdom, toward a then seemingly impossible pinnacle: Maryland's first Jewish governorship. But, mainly, there had been Bootsie.

Most important of all—thin days and thick, through Marvin's climb to the top—there had been this sturdy woman named Barbara, called "Bootsie." This was a marriage all right, solid, loyal, two-way trusting, wholesomely conventional. But it was more than a marriage; Marvin and Bootsie were a working partnership. Politics sustained them, and some thought Bootsie made the better politician of the two. Marvin had the brains, the quick insights, the nice sense of legislative balance, an engrossment with the social machinery by which masses of people manage to live together. He was good at governing, always studying it, often teaching it. The brains needed to lead, yes. The no less vital brass was something else.

For Marvin Mandel, though the leader, tended to shrink personally from those he led. He had qualms even at the entry level that faces the would-be professional politician. He could not easily shake a stranger's hand, he recoiled from asking a campaign contribution. Kiss a baby? Slap a back? Marvin Mandel tended to look the other way.

Bootsie was put together differently. Bootsie shrank from no one. So outgoing was she, so cheerfully objective about nudging Marvin upward into the limelight—"I knew I had a smart husband"—that she seemed to spark the elementary political warmth Marvin lacked. Marvin dissected political anatomy, arranged workable solutions: his hedged suggestion, "maybe we can work something out," was often, often mistakenly, taken in the State House as a promise. Bootsie tended to other matters. It was not simply that handshaking came easily to her, that she used as a model one contemporary who, she said in wonder, "could shake hands with a snake." More than that, she increasingly took charge in their home neighborhood of the basic machinery that ground out the product vital to Marvin's advancement: votes.

From Pimlico to Pikesville, the stretch of political turf they trod together, it was Bootsie who stepped out front, Marvin a step behind. She worked the precincts, enlisted helpers, on election day hustled out Mandel voters. Overall she spread a sociability strongly contrasting with Marvin's cool reserve. In time she stood close to the center of a Jewish matriarchy once incautiously labeled by a State House aide "those yentas in Pikesville." What a clucking that let loose!

Jack Pollack knew better. As organization boss, he suggested once that Bootsie, not Marvin, had better run the precincts. Bootsie admired Pollack's sagacity: so did Marvin, up to a point. But he also flinched at Pollack's hard-handed ways and, when the aging Pollack became an elective drag, Marvin Mandel deserted him for political backers more subtle if not notably more virtuous. Loyally, Bootsie went along.

Five years as First Lady furnished Bootsie her reward for all the earlier struggles, the hard decisions, the personal obscurity that is the lot of a legislator's wife. It was a reward the more relished because largely unexpected. As late as 1968 Marvin, though an effective Speaker of the House, had given little thought to running for governor. Being a Baltimore Jew, he suspected, was a handicap probably insuperable: Would suburban politicians take a chance on supporting him? Would rural areas—notably, benighted pockets on the Eastern Shore—vote for him? Doubtfully, Marvin and Bootsie talked this over. They put it aside as unlikely: as cautious Jews had for millenia, they decided to leave the proscenium out front to others, but to pull the telling strings backstage. They settled in for a long, satisfying home in the speakership, the site of Marvin's growing legislative virtuosity.

Larger, destabilizing forces intervened. When in November of 1968, Spiro Agnew was suddenly elevated from governor to vice-president, his discarded Maryland office was left empty for filling in 1969. Abruptly the spotlight swung to Mandel: 1969 being a nonelection year, extraordinary machinery was called into play— machinery peculiarly adapted to Mandel strengths and Mandel weaknesses. Ordinary voters, under the Maryland Constitution, would not choose the new governor: anticity and ethnic preju- dices were thus short-circuited. Instead, Agnew's replacement would be determined in the very spot where Mandel stood out the commanding figure: the legislature.

Not every single legislator was persuaded. Mandel carried faint scars of the old Pollack days, also of newer and shadowy associ- ates: he was not a member of the small reformist circle reaching for power and, indeed, he scorned it. These reformers were badly out-gunned. Their token candidate was smothered in a rush of votes by legislative regulars, by delegates and state senators who knew Marvin, trusted Marvin, wanted Marvin up front where they could do business with him. They were not to be deterred.

So the Speaker became the Governor, his lady became First: the Mandels had arrived, somewhat to their own surprise. For Bootsie a dream she had dared not dream had come true. Signs that it would crumble to nightmare five years later broke the gleam- ing surface nowhere. And yet this surface, this trusty Bootsie- Buddy union, was almost too seamlessly all-American for easy credibility.

They had met in high school in the 1930s. Each was the New World offspring of an Old World immigrant: Marvin's grandfather from Poland, Bootsie's father and mother from Russia. The Ober- felds, Bootsie's family, had made out somewhat better than the Mandels. A blacksmith by trade, Oberfeld started a trucking com- pany that prospered modestly. He raised seven children. Marvin's father learned to be a cutter in a clothing factory; later, after a heart attack, he opened a small liquor store in a West Baltimore ghetto sliding from Jewish to black. Both families were hard- working, unpretentious, orthodox—but not too orthodox to resist when Marvin and Bootsie took a quite unorthodox step. They got married in 1941, an entire year before he finished law school at the University of Maryland.

Still, their romance twinkled with no whirlwind courtship, no runaway elopement. It was more a boy/girl next-door convention, a thoughtful drifting together of two young people, each essentially clear-eyed, prudent, upwardly mobile. High school for Marvin was City College, the proud "Castle on the Hill" across town to the northeast. As student, he was good enough to pass. As athlete, he was better. Though small, he was lean and wiry: he played snappy baseball and boxed with the best of his weight. Socially, he was so quiet and retiring that many of his classmates of 1937 found it difficult, later, to place him in memory. The City College yearbook of 1937 shows no record of him whatever. What is remembered is that at graduation time, in June, his date for the prom in the lofty ballroom of the Lord Baltimore hotel was a pink-and-gold Bootsie. They didn't rush things. It took them the next four years to pick a wedding date.

One reason was a mutual understanding that, to break out above the hard-scrabble level their parents had endured, a dose of higher education was vital. Marvin's mother, a purposeful woman, insisted on a law degree; Marvin would be the first of his family to attend even college, yet alone law school. Bootsie's impulse was less pointed: she was pretty and petite, blonde and gray-eyed. (In Jeanne, many years later, gossips would note similar coloring: Did Jeanne somehow represent for Marvin, they asked, a younger version of Bootsie?) About her in school Bootsie's hearty vivacity drew a dozen sorority friends destined to furnish the core of the Mandels' circle for thirty years ahead. But Bootsie was no playgirl.

It was she who, to save expenses while Marvin finished law school, moved into her in-laws' house. When the army took him for a year's training in Texarkana, Texas, Bootsie trudged dutifully along. A heart ailment made it difficult for her father-in-law to keep his liquor store open: Bootsie, joined by Marvin after law-office hours, put in long evenings behind the family counter. That wasn't anything special to her. It was what members of close families did. For added closeness, Bootsie prevailed on Marvin to shift their religious affiliation from orthodox to conservative, from sitting in temple separated by gender to sitting together as a family. Not that they were religious activists: big fund-raising campaigns by which others made a place in the community were left to those with more time and money to spare. Later, in Annapolis, Jewish leaders often looked past Marvin for help on special Jewish interests.

This togetherness of Bootsie's was strengthened instead of weakened, at least for a while, by the usually centrifugal pressures of politics. A Democratic club meeting? A legislative session in Annapolis? Bootsie stuck close to Buddy's side. Unlike wives who quickly wearied of the political drone—and whose husbands' searches for more responsive female company enlivened many an Annapolis evening—Bootsie found the legislative grist rich and flavorful. She studied the issues, watched bills come and go, easily cemented the friendships that Marvin found uneasy. She steadied the ladder up which he climbed.

Upon reaching in 1969 the position of First Lady of Maryland, Bootsie stood in full bloom. Hardly the remote homebody, she emerged as almost equal partner with her newly gubernatorial husband, a resolute teammate as seasoned politically as he was himself. Bootsie's friends believed she had earned her way to the top and that Marvin's chances without her would have been, at best, reduced. And yet she was paying a price she could not see. Overbusied with counting ladder rungs leading upward, she forgot to watch out behind her for the approach of the very hazard she was sure married tranquility had sealed out. For Marvin, at first perhaps unaware himself, was turning bored.

Boredom didn't show on the surface. What did show was the increasing confidence of a man who after early unsure struggles finds in his middle years a solid personal success. Marvin Mandel at 50 exuded a new assurance bordering on complacency. He was a year into the governorship, he had easily mastered its challenges, the next election held no terrors. His marriage to Bootsie, so far as most people could tell, seemed at least as soundly buttressed as his political position. That was the surface: serene, cool, unflappable. A midnight occurrence in December of 1970 was the first scratch in the surface, which, it turned out, hid interesting layers beneath.

Immediate reports were elementary, credible. A pedestrian had been killed, the Governor injured somewhat in an automobile accident on the road leading from Southern Maryland. A state trooper was driving the Governor, but he seemed not to blame. Bootsie hurried to the Annapolis hospital where governor and trooper had been taken. Both Mandels were calm, police routine took over. Only a small detail dangled.

Where in Southern Maryland had the Governor been coming from? Why at that early morning hour? The press was puzzled. Quickly, almost casually, the State House staff moved in with an answer. Oh some little meeting in Prince Georges County. Political? Sure. Where? Well . . . I'll find out . . . get back to you. And so the accident passed off as a misfortune, regrettable but not unlikely. Was the little scratch in the surface smoothed over?

Not quite. Not later, when no one in Prince Georges County could recall any political meeting, none anyway with the Governor on hand. Apparently, it turned out, there hadn't been any meeting: the Governor was coming from somewhere else. This report, as it unfolded and hardened into fact, found at least a handful of upper-level State House officials profoundly unsurprised. To them Marvin Mandel's disappearances had become a weekly phenomenon. Thursday afternoons he would slip quietly out of the Governor's office: no destination was recorded in his engagement book. Friday mornings, he would show up, the customary gray shadows beneath his eyes gone a shade deeper. How long had this been going on? Some said two years, some six. Backstairs gossip filled in the rest.

Documentable facts about Marvin Mandel's romance with Jeanne Dorsey are scarce because neither chooses to discuss it. Others do. The essential point to emerge is that Jeanne's marriage to Walter Dorsey was disintegrating, that disintegrating with it was the place in the power structure she liked and cultivated. She met Marvin, just then coming into his political own as Speaker of the House of Delegates. Beneath his wariness she discerned a vulnerability—his marriage gone stale, his children grown, his private life progressively less absorbing than his more-vibrant public life. Why else those endless evening hours he spent in the Speaker's office shuffling reports, amendments, budgets? Jeanne sensed Marvin knew nothing more exciting to do. She did.

She encircled him. Tempted, yet inherently cautious, he resisted. Slowly their affair budded, flowered—but always studiously fenced in by Marvin's sense of personal propriety, also his fear of political repercussions. Clandestine meetings multiplied, intimacy ensued. Inevitably with his rise to the governorship rumors, quenchable earlier, began to flare up.

Came January 1970 and the automobile accident. Just where had Marvin been, anyway? Bootsie sniffed something on the wind—and by one version, was handed a diamond bracelet to quiet her. Delightedly sniffing too was folksy Leonardtown, Jeanne's home community and the waterside scene of the Thursday rendezvous. Knowing sniffs came from Marvin's staff in the State House, soon from legislators and the press.

For Jeanne the personal strain was turning intolerable. She demanded a decision, doubtless set deadlines. Marvin stalled, evaded. He was famed for his legislative compromises; why couldn't they work out something here too?

Jeanne was adamant. She had her man, or anyway part of him. She wanted the rest: Marvin's open acceptance, marriage, the power and the glory of the Governor's mansion. No! Here was one deal where Marvin couldn't work something out. Jeanne—this assertive bundle of tempestuousness—wasn't settling for mouse-like hole-in-corner seclusion. A public man's private plaything? Hell! Jeanne wanted to be First Lady of Maryland. Let all flags fly, damn the consequences. Damn Bootsie too.

Maybe ten years after they first met, three and a half years after the automobile accident began to strip away the camouflage, Marvin's resistance crumpled. Surrender was complete and publicly announced. He would divorce Bootsie, who, he said, had agreed. He would marry Jeanne, whom he said he loved. A year after the announcement, less than an hour after his divorce was final, Marvin married Jeanne—then hurried off to attend a funeral. Bittersweetly, a fat divorce settlement in hand, Bootsie wished the newlyweds "all the happiness they deserve." Jeanne had won hands down. Her victory would prove Pyrrhic.

Love? Apparently so. He was 53, the father of two, she 35, the mother of four.

Love a shade middle-aged, perhaps. Love's blossom a bit too wilted on both sides to invite notions of a dewy springtime idyll. But love nevertheless, love proven all the more urgent by obstacles overcome, obstacles both of convention and of politics. Love between Marvin and Jeanne can be disparaged. It can hardly be argued away.

Of the two, Jeanne's part seems more readily understandable. She had little to lose taking on Marvin, a glittering big world to gain. Her branch of the Blackistone family, though venerable even in ancient, ancestor-ridden St. Mary's county, was a branch largely unblessed with worldly goods. Her father was a waterman and penurious. County schools sufficed for Jeanne's education; no silky private school finished her, no college broadened her.

A country girl, but she was pretty and bright and determined. A contemporary Becky Sharp, alert for opportunity.

After school she hired on as secretary in the law office of Walter Dorsey, himself the scion of an old county family. But the Dorseys were better fixed: they ran St. Mary's Democratic machine, a genteel throwback still capable of churning out votes and jobs for its rulers. Walter's father, Philip Dorsey, presided both as machine boss and as county judge. Walter would become a state senator, as had his father before him. For Jeanne, to marry Walter was to marry her way upward.

Marriage meant money and position, new dresses, gaiety. It was a large step up from the drab prospects otherwise open to a struggling waterman's daughter, no matter how pretty and captivating or how venerable the lineage. She married him, achieving powerful new friends in the political and slot-machine circles then profitably cogged into the Dorsey machine.

Jeanne had arrived. A radiant ornament on the arm of her handsome senatorial husband, she began exploring the headier world of Annapolis. She made a quick hit.

And yet among Jeanne's new-found splendors lurked a nagging gloom: it was Walter. Handsome and physically imposing, bright and aggressive, Walter seemed to hold the political world in his hands. Why not governor? St. Mary's friends asked, then found out why not. Walter Dorsey was difficult. Friends edged away, vistas shrank, his political base wobbled. Quarreling is how Leonardtown friends best knew Jeanne and Walter. They watched the pair drift into cold isolation, then virtual separation, while continuing to live stonily in the same Leonardtown house. Now when Jeanne visited Annapolis—as she continued to do, having found the legislative whirl lively—she traveled without Walter. With young women friends from Leonardtown, a sort of county Democratic club, she became a familiar figure in the joyous drinking rooms of the Maryland Inn, a gracefully restored waterhole then favored by legislators on the lookout for postsession relaxation.

Precisely who introduced Jeanne Dorsey to Marvin Mandel is hazy. Two more general points are clear. One is that after-hours Annapolis offers a number of jolly options, that young legislators feel free to put aside home ties and join the frolic. Clear too is that

Majority Leader Mandel, by then a budding father figure in the State House, stood firm against the tide of bibulous womanizing. He would drink, but sparingly: one Old Grand-Dad, with water. He would talk to a woman, but about bills, bills, bills. Bootsie spent up to three nights a week at his side.

Legislative junkets to other state capitals laid open larger opportunities, smaller reasons for inhibition. But Bootsie commonly went along, whereupon Marvin turned stiffer still. Together they formed an island of senior restraint in a sophomoric sea. What neither of them seems to have reckoned on was the magnetic force of Jeanne Dorsey, and Marvin's vulnerability.

Let a close observer, long on the scene, give a blunt appraisal: "Bootsie is not an unattractive woman. She likes fun, kidding around, earthy—but stable, so stable. And very loyal to Marvin. Always saying Buddy did this, Buddy did that. A Jewish momma. Now Jeanne is something else. Shrewd, vivacious, bubbly. Also blonde, gentile, and eighteen years younger than Bootsie. Mainly, she's a woman who knows how to make you feel good, if she likes you. Makes you look good too, when you're with her. A showpiece."

Anne Tyler, a Baltimore novelist writing in the Sun, is more eloquent: "So here comes this blonde, divorced, from an Old Southern Maryland family. (Ah, her family. It's the combination that gets him, we feel. Her brassy, glittering hair, levitating about her head and then dripping in well-modulated scrolls, coupled with that Anglo-Saxon lineage . . .) She wears the sort of breezy, silken clothes that seem designed for lunch beside the golf course. She's irresistible."

Almost imperceptibly Mandel, the workaholic Speaker of the House of Delegates, began spending less time burning the midnight oil. But an occasional hour or two talking politics with the boys at the Maryland Inn was work, wasn't it? Few marked the entrance to these little Mandel-centered gatherings by the women up from St. Mary's county, by Jeanne Dorsey of the glittering hair.

The episode of the missing gloves was, at first, a joke. One night the St. Mary's club needed a ride home from Annapolis, two hours by car. Could Marvin help? Yes, Marvin could—maybe (cautious second thought) with a couple of legislative friends along as company. Next morning, one of the friends reported his gloves missing: Left in his car? Left in Jeanne's Leonardtown house, where they'd paused for one for the road? The friend allowed uneasily he wasn't going back to the house to look, not with Walter maybe upstairs there, maybe mean as hell. So getting the gloves became an excuse for someone to go back later, when Walter wasn't there. When it was Marvin who volunteered to go— Marvin the hitherto prim, Marvin the always wary—the friends looked at one another thoughtfully. But that was in the 1960s, a couple of years before Jeanne divorced Walter, a couple more years before Marvin got around to separating himself from Bootsie. Headlong speed, apparently, was not built into this romance.

Still, matters progressed. A legislators' junket aboard the state yacht, *Maryland Lady*, dropped by to investigate Leonardtown's watermen. Jeanne, screened by her friends, turned up to greet the Annapolis team. Other trips, other meetings. In restaurants in Leonardtown, in Annapolis, in Washington. Came Jeanne's divorce from Walter, which was contested and bitter. Came Marvin's election to governor, inviting at once a new freedom and a new caution.

Marvin, his constituency now extended to the whole state, could more readily leave behind Bootsie to her delighted First Ladying in Annapolis. The cover of friends melted away on both sides: the informal Jeanne-Marvin affair turned formal, even earnest. Still, a governor's movements catch attention, in this case unwelcome attention. Jeanne and Marvin did their best to keep the lid on.

Conveniently, Walter had moved out of the Dorsey house at the watery edge of Leonardtown. Jeanne stayed on, so this became the rendezvous—a pleasant waterfront hideaway with swimming pool. Beginning with Thursday evenings, Marvin and Jeanne made the most of the privacy. They kept to the house, avoided restaurants and parties, invited few people in. Leonardtown is too intimate a village to be deceived. Soon stories began to rustle in courthouse corridors: Guess what turned up last night at the bottom of the hill, at Breton Bay Drive? A big black car! In eating places like Duke's and Bailey's: Why was that trooper—Gibson?—drinking coffee cup after cup for hours at the state police barracks? Someone reported a state chopper buzzing down noisily on a dusty field nearby. Someone else told of seeing through the Dorsey shrubbery, early one morning, a golfer practicing chip shots on the Dorsey front lawn. It was a man, the observer said, who looked like Governor Mandel.

Some believed, some did not. Stories flew regardless, and

Leonardtown absorbed the situation with various degrees of relish. Variations tended to a political slant. Those of the pro-Dorsey persuasion—Jeanne was still counted a member of the Dorsey faction, despite divorce—tended to approve. Anti-Dorsey groups snickered. But Leonardtown though folksy is a tolerant town and, besides, the affair held respectably to shadow. Not a few felt the village gained a certain style from the Governor's moonlit comings and goings.

Leonardtown was not permitted for long to hug to itself its Marvin-Jeanne affair. An immediate problem was Walter Dorsey, by now all but publicly humiliated. Also resentful: alimony requirements went largely unheeded; a suit was filed, unsuccessfully, for custody of the youngest Dorsey child, later formally adopted by Mandel. If Walter was still a trouble point, how could trouble be minimized? Jeanne, increasingly desperate, had no answer. Marvin did.

What Walter needed was a face-saver, a ribbon to pin on his coat, really something to get him off Jeanne's back. After the divorce as before, life had gone hard for Walter. Job after good job—state's attorney, state senator, assistant attorney general— had slipped through his fingers. Couldn't Marvin, now stripping him in addition of wife and child, make some gesture to mute ominous rumbles? Couldn't Marvin soothe the tremulous—and determined—Jeanne?

Characteristically, Marvin thought he could work something out. Assistant public defender over in Howard County wasn't a flashy job, maybe, but it would put Walter safely out to pasture. Put him, too, comfortably out of Leonardtown into Ellicott City until Marvin and Jeanne, still using his house as a trysting spot, could sort themselves out elsewhere. Later, Walter would drop Marvin's patronage handout for private practice. He would return to his Leonardtown house with a new wife, his experience put aside if not forgotten. So much for Walter Dorsey: something had been worked out.

Disposing of Joseph Weiner wasn't so easy but Jeanne, again, was insistent. She owed much to Weiner, a county lawyer long politically connected to the Dorsey faction. He had guided her decisions, eased the turbulent Walter, advised Marvin, furnished tips on the divorce. In return, Weiner wanted a judgeship— which, as it happened, was Marvin's to bestow. The judicial vacancy had opened, ironically, upon retirement from the bench by Walter's father, the now aging Philip Dorsey. Why not me? Weiner wanted to know.

One reason why not was that Dorsey-minded lawyers, stripped of their judge, were politically obsolescent in the county. A stronger reason was that opposition to Weiner had crystallized around John Hanson Briscoe—a man popular in St. Mary's, strong in the legislature, a personal friend both of Jeanne and of Marvin. A secret ballot among local lawyers rated Briscoe for judge well ahead of Weiner. So the quandary, with its special personal twist, landed on the Governor's desk.

What to do?

Appoint Weiner, thereby repaying personal obligations and quieting Jeanne's demands, but inviting resentment from Briscoe admirers both in St. Mary's and in the legislature? Or instead appoint Briscoe, flattering county judgment and winning points among legislators, but defying Jeanne as well as the Dorsey political loyalists?

Mandel, agonized, left the vacancy unfilled for ten months. In the end he turned to Weiner, Jeanne's choice. Weiner's tenure as judge, however, was cut short at the end of six months. St. Mary's voters had followed all this closely. Queried at the polls about a full judicial term for Weiner, they firmly said no: they rejected Weiner in nearly every county district, replacing him with Joseph Mattingly. John Briscoe, meanwhile, took himself out of the running for judge and went on instead to become Speaker of the House of Delegates. It was not the last time Jeanne's hand would be felt in gubernatorial matters, not the last time Marvin's hand would be forced into the fire.

H e bore the starchy name of Alford R. Carey, Jr., but everyone called him Skip and, on the whole, rather liked him for his early work with handicapped children. Later, Skip Carey changed faces and lifestyles. He became a forger, an embezzler, a briber, and an extortionist. Also a lot of other things, according to state prosecutors, who said they couldn't quite document them all.

The most titillating question about Skip Carey is left dangling to this day: At bottom, was he really no more than a feckless cat's-paw cruelly exploited by the Mandel circle? Did he, as he said he had, grudgingly furnish still another smudged screen behind which Marvin Mandel and the boys from Tidewater Insurance hid the pickup of an extra $25,000?

Or was that confession, as Marvin Mandel pronounced it from his temporary residence in the federal prison at Eglin Air Force Base, Florida, "The most outrageous lie I have ever heard in all my years in office. . . . I'm going to have to check into this."

Prosecutors tended to agree with Skip Carey, but no outsider was to know for sure. By 1981, when Carey finally opened up all the way, the pertinent statutes of limitations had run out: prosecutors were left powerless to prosecute. It scarcely mattered, as a matter of justice. Both men by that time were convicted felons, destined to live out their years indelibly stained.

Still, the Skip Carey episode lays open a rare aperture, quite separate from Marlboro Racetrack and Security Investment and all that. Through this aperture a glimpse may be caught of the Mandel circle in actual operation.

Unlike Marvin Mandel, Skip Carey pleaded guilty. He had reached his pinnacle as chief of Maryland's $1.1-billion program to build public schools, one of the proudest ornaments of the Mandel administration. Like Mandel, Carey fell in love with a woman not his wife. Expenses mounted: he forged a school contractor's invoice to extract from the state a check, then cashed the check to pocket $22,105 not rightfully his to pocket. Hence forgery, plus false pretenses.

So Skip Carey confessed early in 1976, after being indicted by a county grand jury. A sad story, not uncommon. Three years later, under new charges of bribery and extortion, Carey was convicted again. This time, pressed for information implicating the Mandel circle, he explicitly denied its members were involved.

By 1981, however, Skip Carey was having second thoughts. ("To save his own neck": Mandel). At a court hearing on possible reduction of his second three-year prison sentence, Carey swore to these points: A North Carolina company building portable schoolrooms for the state faltered in the early 1970s in its performance. Skip Carey, about to drop the company from the state program, was dissuaded by Dale Hess. Tidewater Insurance had an interest in the construction company's success. Carey, Hess told him, stood to make himself $20,000 in cash by keeping the contract alive. Then-Governor Mandel, according to Carey, was present when the bribe offer was made.

The bribe money was never paid. On the contrary, Mandel had used Carey's credit card to run up a number of expenses, including a vacation trip to Aruba and a "fur coat for his girlfriend." The boys from Tidewater had also used the Carey credit card "under circumstances in which they did not wish their identity revealed." Carey's creditors pressed him for money.

When Carey in turn pressed Hess for payment late in 1973, Hess said that was now impossibly dangerous. Federal agents were poking about embarrassingly in Tidewater's affairs. But Hess suggested an alternative: Why not embezzle the money from the portable classroom funds at Carey's command? Hess gave him some pointers. Carey proceeded to swindle the state of $22,105.

In addition, and separately, he extorted from the same construction company $3,000 to help finance Mandel's 1974 reelection campaign. It was this which brought Carey his second conviction.

So the embezzled $22,105 went to pay bills at least partly incurred by others using Carey's credit card. And the extorted $3,000 went to fatten the Mandel war chest. A news reporter once counted seven pictures of Mandel in Carey's office.

"I realized no financial gain from this embezzlement," Carey said in a formal statement in court.

Was all that true or false? If true, why had Carey waited so long to tell his whole story? Why demur until time had lifted Marvin Mandel and his friends safely beyond the reach of state law?

A deputy attorney general said much of Carey's information was substantiated by independent investigation. Would charges have been brought against anyone, he was asked, if Carey had told his full story at his second trial in 1978?

"Possibly," was the answer.

7.

When the
Bell Tolled

Governor Willie Stark, a character in *All the King's Men*, laid his hand on an old political verity when he talked about goodness and badness, about what's taken as right and what's taken as wrong. His words illuminate the corrupt shadows of public life, which are called its practical side. Here arises one of the most troublesome aspects of Marvin Mandel's run-in with the law. This is the belief, held by others in addition to the Mandel defendants, that the line between right and wrong was shifted against them—and shifted unfairly. Shifted, it surely was. Shifted unfairly is not so clear, hence a source of contention.

Governor Stark, ruminating on his own troubles, put it this way: "What folks claim is right is always just a couple of jumps short of what they need to do business. Now, an individual, one fellow, he will stop doing business because he's got a notion of what is right, and he is a hero. But folks in general, which is society, Doc, is never going to stop doing business. Society is just going to cook up a new notion of what is right. Society is sure not ever going to commit suicide. At least, not that way and not of a purpose."

Stark's distaste for some individual's "notion of what is right" is apparent. A self-protective society, he concludes comfortably, will shortly smother each reformist sally. And yet these reformist notions keep popping up: Stark acknowledges as much, then grudgingly stops a couple of jumps short of the other, less seamy side of political reality. This is the fact that not all such notions

99

succumb to smotheration. Many do, but here and there one sticks in place and survives, whereupon society broadens to accommodate it. Once cogged into the social machinery, that new notion hardens to a standard. A standard soon becomes law. By such means society long ago lifted itself out of the jungle and, thus enlightened, today pursues a more or less constant program of self-refreshment.

Translated to politics, the process is called government reform, a simple bettering of the arrangements by which people contrive to live together. Otherwise, society stagnates, government stands locked in its own rust. Blacks would lie still enslaved, sweatshops still harbor child labor. Women would continue voteless, air polluters flourish uninhibited. That is not what happens. Instead society moves forward, if at an erratic pace well short of headlong. To refine Stark's conclusion: society is sure not ever going to commit suicide, at least not that way.

So Marvin Mandel's perception seems unquestionable to this extent: the rules do change, the law changes with them. Both changes, it should be added, are commonly in the general welfare. Yet for many the puzzle remains pesky: In this case, were rules changed too abruptly and without fair warning? Was Marvin Mandel, as a result, blind-sided by the sudden application of a new and drastically sterner rule to which others before him were not held to account? From a long line of Maryland politicians gaily "doing business," was Mandel singled out unfairly for punishment?

In one way the question has its almost frivolous side, as if no more were at stake than a debatable new rule in a game of checkers—suddenly a checker king is told it can't jump forward, only backward: consternation! In a much truer way, profound values of ethics and government, of crime and punishment, are touched. But frivolous or profound, the question of whether Marvin Mandel and his friends were somehow jobbed nags at the conscience of many objective onlookers.

Essentially, this probably comes down to a question of timing. Public impatience with political corruption in Maryland had been a century in the rising; as law, the process crested in the mid-1960s. But were the alarm bells sufficiently sounded? As a matter of fairness, was the Mandel circle given reason to heed the warning and so to scamper back across the right-wrong line? Did they get the warning in time?

The fall of Spiro Agnew offers only an unsatisfactory answer. It was a warning all right but, strictly speaking, that bell rang too late to alert Marvin Mandel. Agnew did get caught with his hand in the Maryland till and did have to resign the vice-presidency under federal pressure. Go quietly, Nixon had Agnew told, or else. But Agnew's resignation came in 1973, four years after the Mandel term began. And to judge by evidence later offered in the Mandel trial, operations that led to the Mandel conviction closely followed his inauguration. That was in 1969, again four years before Agnew went out pleading nolo contendere.

So in 1969, as Mandel took office, Agnew still rode high as vice-president. No Agnew warning sobered those exultant at the Mandel inauguration. Because it was belated, the Agnew lesson went untaught, unlearned. And yet much that was instructive already lay clear on the record.

As a mood short of clear-cut the fashion for change had been gathering in Maryland as early as the Citizens Reform party of 1875. There followed the anti-Gorman blow-off twenty years later, then the hopeful curbs on boodling written by Governors Crothers and Ritchie into state law during the first third of the twentieth century. George P. Mahoney with his outcry against old-style Democratic bosses and the swampy miasma they imposed upon public life in Maryland carried the mood into the 1950s and beyond. That boss-baiting Mahoney would later ally himself with boss Jack Pollack—"Have you heard of the famous wedding?" Representative Clarence Long would ask. "St. George has married the dragon."—showed the fashion had not yet matured. Instead, the Mahoney-Pollack nuptials put neatly into perspective the chronic ambivalence that still characterized Maryland's perceptions of its own political ethics.

Still, change was in the air. By the 1960s what some called reform—Brooke Lee, with a sniff, called it "the uplift"—was fast losing its capricious nature. Up to then, reform while long present had as long been crippled by lack of steady focus and worse, by lack of political leverage. Reformers seldom agreed where they were going. When they did agree on a destination, they didn't know how to get there.

So reform as a cause had no staying power: Realistically, how expect state law enforcement agencies, themselves creatures of state politics, to poke about inquisitively among their own political roots? They didn't—and Maryland's failure, from the Civil War forward, to sprout an all-weather Republican party robbed reformists of the cathartic machinery at least offered by a credible two-party system.

What began to change all that was intrusion by a fresh force from outside. This force, while essentially political itself, nevertheless ran free of entwining traps set by, and to protect, local political hierarchies. It was the federal government, specifically a cocky young band of prosecutors who showed up in the office of the United States attorney.

Here was an unfolding redolent of the Kennedy era, an era that in its exuberance, its daring and faintly tigerish righteousness, put up the backs of old-guard Democratic machines like Maryland's. Traditional Democrats centered in the administration of J. Millard Tawes, then governor, fought the Kennedys at every turn. Against white-collar crime, the long-missing leverage was supplied by Robert Kennedy as his presidential brother's attorney general. Nationally, Kennedy vowed to catch up at last with the defiant criminality of James Hoffa and his Teamsters. In Maryland, the Kennedy extension of federal power installed Joseph Tydings as United States attorney. To the Kennedy leverage, Tydings added a second vital element: focus. He pointed this new weapon straight into the forgiving, old-boy murk that for nearly a century had shielded sticky fingers attached to holders of state and local office.

Beginning with Tydings, early in the 1960s, reform put aside its historic flickering. It achieved a flame steady enough at least to expose its hitherto elusive antagonist, political corruption, and at most to give politicians an instructive singe. Here chronology reveals something important to appraisal of the Mandel case, specifically of the much-discussed change in rules.

As noted, the ways of governors and others before Marvin Mandel were not all ethically sanitized. A little something going profitably on the side had been the rule and widely accepted as such. But the complaint that the rule was unfairly changed for Mandel carries a chronological mistake. The rule was changed—in favor of reform, against corruption—but not just for Mandel, not just at the beginning of his time as governor. Nor was the warning rung by the Agnew case—too late, probably, to catch the Mandel ear— the first or only warning. The rule change took effect with Tydings nearly a decade earlier, ample time for the Mandel defendants to hear and to beware. They were not the first to fall; they would not be the last. They fell as part of a new pattern of justice, a pattern clearly discernible and firmly established before their arrival at power in 1969.

That Joseph Tydings was to define anything so far-reaching as a new and enduring pattern of justice was not immediately apparent with his elevation to federal prosecutor in 1961. What was apparent was that he was off to a fast start and that he meant business in a way few if any of his gentler predecessors had managed. One unique advantage was his: as stepson of a venerable United States senator, Millard E. Tydings, he bore a name that guaranteed him instant political recognition and a happy send-off. To that he added, via Kennedy sponsors, a restlessness with things as they were in Maryland—meaning the cozy complacence entrenched in the Democratic organization. George Mahoney's roundhouse swings had bruised the old-boss system grievously in the 1950s, but the organization regrouped amoeba-like in the governorship of J. Millard Tawes and lumbered on.

Joseph Tydings—younger than Mahoney, better connected, more politically sophisticated—presented a threat far sharper. Besides, as United States attorney, he carried a weapon beyond Mahoney's grasp: the federal law, freshly honed. Nonadmirers, discerning a touch of brutality, labeled Tydings "the killer shark." Others heard the deeper drumbeat of rebellion, maybe bloody but generally enlightened.

In the end Tydings failed to carry off a full-fledged revolution in Maryland, later losing his way politically—and his Senate seat—amid Washington elegancies. His true legacy was the establishment of critical momentum in the federal prosecutor's office. With him a new menace entered Maryland politics on the right, or legal, side. Things would not soon be the same again.

Tydings detected corruption at or before his ascension to the prosecutor's chair. The thrust had come from outside Maryland but, in the easygoing Maryland way, it was soon hospitably embraced by midlevel local politicians. These, while receptive to a hustled dollar, thought they knew a thing or two about cover-ups they didn't know. What they aimed to produce was a refined swindle, an action hidden in the sleepy bosom of a respected neighborhood institution: the savings and loan market.

On the surface, advertising broke forth glittering and seductive. A newly chartered set of savings and loan companies offered investors enticements far beyond Maryland and far beyond the old-time prudence: dividends offered were sharply higher, "gifts" handsomer, share conversions to cash easier. Beneath the surface ran the swindle: the safety noisily "guaranteed" to depositors—a protective insurance essential to all thrift institutions—was in fact no insurance at all. Beguiled, Marylanders and non-Marylanders flocked to invest their savings, unaware that the safety net supposedly underlying their investments was, in large part, airily rhetorical rather than solidly financial.

A downward lurch in the financial markets upset this fragile, unprotected craft. Maryland institutions wavered, frightened investors cried out. Tydings moved in, federal indictments flew. The catch was impressive. In 1963 two United States congressmen, Thomas F. Johnson from Maryland and Frank W. Boykin from Alabama, were convicted of influence peddling, or attempted cover-up. Mail fraud charges hooked the originators, from Illinois and Utah, of the savings and loan scheme. When still another Marylander, A. Gordon Boone, Speaker of the House of Delegates, fell to the Tydings prosecutors, the law touched the inner machinery of the J. Millard Tawes administration at Annapolis. A coincidental byproduct: Boone's successor as Speaker of the House, and the Tawes-chosen candidate, was Marvin Mandel, direct heir to a political vacancy pried open by the tough new rules Tydings established. At this point, the new rules worked not against Mandel but materially for him. No Mandel protests were heard.

Tydings had more than made his mark personally. Such was the vigor he injected into the once-languid prosecutor's office, so astute his choice of keen young assistants, that the momentum he created survived his own departure. Tydings himself went on as a political independent to the United States Senate in 1964, striking Mahoney-like at the boss-run Maryland establishment as successfully at the polling places as he had earlier in the courtroom. This fresh political impulse would sag when, six years later, Tydings lost out for reelection, the victim, in part, of machinations within the Nixon White House. More pertinent to purging Maryland politics, Tydings successors as prosecutor picked up smartly. If then unrecognized, even by its own leaders, the federal march toward Marvin Mandel was underway.

First among these, and a Tydings protégé, was Stephen H. Sachs. To Sachs fell prosecution of United States Senator Daniel

WEDDING DAY. Marvin Mandel and Jeanne Dorsey, August 13, 1974.

THE BOSSES. State boss Gorman takes charge of city boss Rasin, October, 1905.

ARTHUR PUE GORMAN. To some, a powerful member of the United States Senate. To others, the epitome of political corruption in nineteenth-century Maryland. (Gorman Papers, MS. 706, Manuscripts Division, Maryland Historical Society Library)

Wide World Photos

ALBERT C. RITCHIE. Four times governor, between 1919 and 1935, he was called Maryland's best. But he tried in vain in June, 1932, for the presidential nomination at the Democratic National Convention in Chicago.

106

ROSES ALL THE WAY. Still a fresh governor, Marvin Mandel addresses a joint session of the legislature. His predecessor, Vice-President Spiro T. Agnew, looks on. At this time, April 14, 1970, the future looked rosy for both men.

Baltimore Sun

Baltimore Sun

THREE BENEATH THE SEAL. One sitting governor, Marvin Mandel, and two destined to be governor later, Blair Lee III and Harry Hughes (*background left and right*), are caught in this September, 1970, photograph with United States Senator Joseph M. Tydings. Above them, partially obscured, hangs the ancient seal of Maryland.

Baltimore Sun

GEORGE P. MAHONEY. Here presenting signatures for his campaign as an independent candidate for the United States Senate in July, 1968. He ran and ran and ran. He never won elective office.

107

Baltimore Evening Sun—Mike Lane

Baltimore Evening Sun—Mike Lane

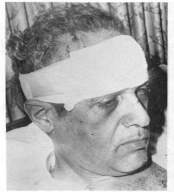

MORNING AFTER. Returning from a then-undisclosed spot in Southern Maryland, Governor Mandel was injured in an automobile accident late one December night in 1970. Shortly thereafter, word of his affair with Jeanne Dorsey spread.

MARVIN AND JEANNE MANDEL are shown leaving the Court House after the presentencing report, September 1, 1977.

BARBARA O. MANDEL. After her divorce from Marvin Mandel, she kept up her interest in Democratic party affairs, as here in October, 1978.

TEN DAYS TO GO. Governor Mandel denied, at a news conference held on November 14, 1975, that he had done anything wrong. Ten days later, along with five others, he was indicted.

W. DALE HESS. He managed the legislators.

IRVIN KOVENS. He managed the racetracks.

110

Baltimore Sun

ERNEST N. CORY, JR. He managed the dummy stockholders.

Baltimore Sun

HARRY W. RODGERS III. He managed the insurance company.

Baltimore Sun

WILLIAM A. RODGERS. He "drove the getaway car."

IRVING T. ("TUBBY") SCHWARTZ. He said he controlled Marlboro Race-track. A federal jury said no, he was only a front for Irvin Kovens, who really did.

Baltimore Sun

Wide World Photos

"MANDELNIKS." *From left*, Ron Schreiber, Frank Harris, and Maurice Wyatt. They served Marvin Mandel as persuaders on the floors of the legislature.

March 22, 1968

The Honorable Marvin Mandel
506 Equitable Building
Baltimore, Maryland 21202

Dear Marvin:

Since meeting you at your office the other day, I
have given considerable thought to what would be a
fair amount to pay for legal services that you have
rendered to me personally and to various companies
in which I am involved. I wish you would have been
kind enough to set your own fees so I would not have
to suggest an amount to you. Since you did not,
thinking back over the number of years that you have
been advising me on legal matters, I am suggesting
that we arrive at a figure of $17,000.

As you know, I am not financially in a position to
pay you for your past services at this time. However,
as I discussed with you, I am willing to give you the
right to participate in the Edwiness Venture which I
feel would be of value to you at this time of approxi-
mately $2,000. I am enclosing a letter to you giving
you this right. If you accept same, then it is my
understanding that legal fees will be reduced from the
$17,000 which I have suggested to $15,000 still owed
to you. You can rest assured that as soon as I have
money available, I will start making payments on the
unpaid balance.

I certainly hope that this meets with your approval.

Sincerely,

W. Dale Hess

WDH:ahm

Enclosure

WHAT ALICE'S SLIP SHOWED. Dale Hess was badly frightened by May, 1974. A
federal grand jury was after him, and what would it find? That the Governor was
secretly on the Hess payroll. It must be somehow explained away. Hess had his
secretary, Alice Riley, write the Governor a letter saying Hess owed him "legal
fees." As a cover the letter was dated March 22, 1968—before Mandel became
governor. A change in Alice Riley's typing style over the six years intervening
gave the letter away as false.

113

Cu Hess, Cory —
Mandel has skotched coming
clean —
Hess' desire to report as
per Cory feder —
Concerned about audit by
E+E

NO, COVER IT UP: M.M. In December, 1972, their lawyer, Richard J. Himelfarb, strongly urged Dale Hess and the Rodgers brothers to admit publicly to the ownership of Marlboro Racetrack. Hess wasn't sure. He said he must first telephone the Governor. After the Hess call—according to careful notes kept by Himelfarb—Hess's report was: "Mandel has skotched coming clean." Publicly, at that time, the Governor was denying any knowledge that his benefactors owned Marlboro.

Phone: SAratoga 7-2729

Alper & Meyers

CLOTHES MADE TO MEASURE
327 W. BALTIMORE STREET
Baltimore 1, Md., _12-20-69_ __19

Sold To _Charlestown Race Track_

N° 276

6	Uniforms C 62 ⁵⁰			375 00

"MADE TO MEASURE." "Go buy some new clothes," Irvin Kovens told Marvin Mandel, just chosen governor in 1969. Mandel got the clothes but did not pay. Instead, Charlestown Racetrack, mostly owned by Kovens, paid $375 for "6 uniforms," supposedly for track guards. More expensive clothes were later to come Mandel's way, also paid for by others.

114

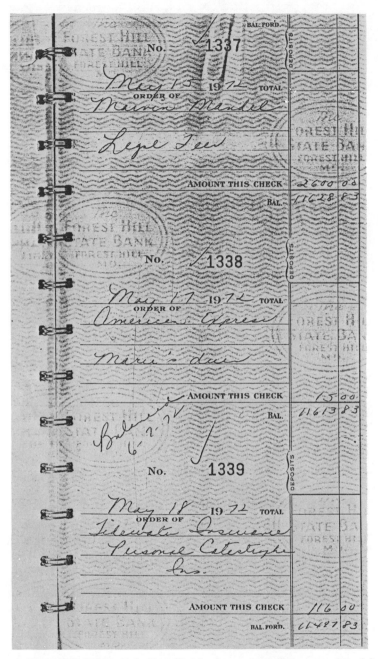

A SMUDGED STUB. Dale Hess first began paying off Governor Mandel on May 15, 1972, with a check for $2,600. On the Hess check stub the label "Sec Inv"—for Security Investment, their mutual holding—was originally entered. When the federal heat went on, "Sec Inv" was erased. "Legal fees" was written in, but the erasure was still visible.

THE FIRST INSTALLMENT on what the government called a bribe.

Baltimore Evening Sun—Mike Lane

116

THE "CZAR" UNCODED. Who was this "Czar" or "Zar" or simply "Z"? In Ernest Cory's notes the name occurred in company with other names, obviously coded—"Country Boy" for Dale Hess, "City Boys" for the Rodgers brothers. What's more, "Z" seemed to own "60%" of something, probably Marlboro Racetrack, a secret the legislature was desperate to unravel. The reverse side of Cory's business card held the answer. Beside "Dale," Cory had written Dale Hess's telephone number. Beside "Z," he had written a telephone number listed in the name of Irvin Kovens.

117

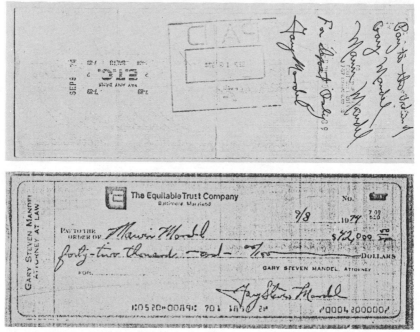

SIDE-DOOR ALIMONY. Marvin Mandel was too hard up to pay his former wife, Barbara, the $42,000 in alimony he owed her, due in September, 1974. His usual patrons found in William H. May a useful go-between. A motorcycle salesman, May had never met Mandel, but others gave him the money, the understanding being that the Pallottine Fathers would later repay all donors. So May wrote a $42,000 check to Mandel. Marvin Mandel endorsed the May check to his son, Gary Mandel, who in return gave his father his own check for $42,000, dated the same day. Prosecutors said the check was thus laundered to avoid awkward questions about why May was paying Mandel $42,000.

JUDGE ROBERT L. TAYLOR. Gently but firmly, he presided over the trial where the Mandel Six were convicted. He was reversed, but only temporarily, when the defendants appealed.

ARNOLD M. WEINER. He represented Marvin Mandel and was the lead lawyer for the defense. Judge Taylor pronounced him one of the best criminal lawyers in the country.

BARNET D. SKOLNIK. He was the assistant United States attorney in charge of the prosecuting teams that ran down three county leaders—Dale Anderson, Joseph W. Alton, Jr., and Jesse S. Baggett—as well as one governor, Marvin Mandel, and one vice-president, Spiro T. Agnew.

Baltimore Evening Sun—Mike Lane

Baltimore Evening Sun—Mike Lane

Baltimore News American

"VINDICATED." In January, 1979, Marvin Mandel won a reversal, temporarily, of his conviction on charges of mail fraud and racketeering.

RETURN TO OWNER. Former Governor Mandel sent back items that state officials said, in December, 1979, he had improperly taken from Government House. Four years later, under legal pressure, he agreed to pay the state $9,250 for the other items taken from the mansion.

121

Baltimore Sun

WELCOME HOME. A public reception at Baltimore-Washington International Airport on December 4, 1981, welcomed Marvin Mandel home after nineteen months in prison.

Baltimore Sun

AT EGLIN. One of the former governor's jobs, while he was in prison at Eglin Air Force Base, Florida, was sorting the laundry.

B. Brewster. A dismaying episode. Schoolboy leader, Marine hero, Brewster had become the darling of the Maryland hierarchy. Some regarded him as a potential rallying point for the oncoming generation of Democrats minded, in contrast to the rebellious Tydings, not to fight the organization but to go along with it. This golden boy proved more boy than golden.

What tripped up Brewster was an inability to master the adult world as his juvenile performance had suggested he might. As a grown-up he failed and took refuge from failure in liquor. His judgment of right and wrong faltered. In the pits, he accepted up to $20,000 (figures vary) he shouldn't have accepted from a giant mail-order house threatened by a postal rate change then before a Senate committee of which Brewster was a member. Brewster voted "right," meaning wrong. Sachs as federal prosecutor pounced, charging in effect bribery.

Court action became convoluted. Defense lawyers cited Brewster's alcoholism, argued congressional immunity. Conviction was followed by reversal, then retrial. In 1975 the exhausted Brewster surrendered on a plea of no contest to accepting an illegal gratuity, a plea commonly taken as guilty. From Sachs's success, two turning points emerged, interlinked. First was the final fraying out, with Brewster, of the last hierarchial strand traceable fifty years backward to the Democratic heyday presided over by Albert Ritchie. New faces backed up by new forces rose to fill the Democratic vacuum, including the makings of a new circle of power soon centered on Marvin Mandel. But such claimants bore a different stripe, a contrasting frame of reference. Brewster's fall meant more than the fall of a single Democratic faction. Because he had seemed to symbolize the future of the whole Democratic order, still momentarily clustered about Governor Tawes, the order seemed to end with him. It would not instantly rise afresh.

The obverse side of the failed Brewster symbolism was at least as important, maybe more so. It was embodied in the continued and indeed gathering strength, via Stephen Sachs, of the vigorous tradition first set afoot by Joseph Tydings in the United States attorney's office. Reformism as a cause had betrayed its inconstancy in the past by a roller-coaster pattern: an exultant do-gooder up, followed inevitably by a somnolent, politics-as-usual down. Politically, reform had little solidarity, hence little appeal, for politicians in search of a platform built to survive the flutter of popular whimsy. The arrival of Sachs, by history's lesson, should have led to a relieved outburst of good-old-boy winks, to revival as of old of corruption seeping inward from the fringes.

Sachs, consequently, shook the traditionalist prophecy badly. He not only pursued the once-blessed Brewster to collapse; he also undertook to crack a far tougher nut in Victor Frenkil, a legendary Baltimore contractor long half-glimpsed, money bags in hand, roving the cloudy outskirts of the McKeldin and Tawes regimes. Frenkil managed to evade Sachs but only with his tail-feathers frighteningly burned. Post-Sachs, both Brewster and Frenkil turned to good works, or anyway better ones.

Tydings started it, then came Sachs to prove Tydings more than a one-shot phenomenon. Sachs put white-collar criminals, political or otherwise, on notice that federal justice had entered the Maryland scenario with a momentum unslackened by a change of leaders. Here and there, constitutional lawyers grumbled quietly that federal power was being pushed unwisely deep into affairs historically reserved for the state. One of these lawyers, the late H. Vernon Eney, found "nothing basically wrong." What troubled Eney was philosophy. As a matter of public responsibility, he said, a state ought to "handle its own dirty linen" and "in due course" would be able to do so. Philosophy aside, the fact is that at the time of the Mandel case and before no state prosecutor's office existed. County prosecutors did exist but lacked resources to meet so complex a challenge. It was federal action or, as in the past, no action at all. And Eney-like grumbles have yet to draw Supreme Court support.

Anyway, neither Tydings nor Sachs was diverted. The immediate result of their pioneering was dramatic: the flexible old rules by which Maryland politicians had played were shoved aside—firmly, unmistakably, and, so far, indefinitely. Instead, values held for years to be politically vaporous—ethics, morality, reform—finally achieved a steady, even insistent thrust. They took on a knifelike edge of their own.

The entry of George Beall to the United States attorney's office in 1970 provided the Mandel investigation an overture. There emerged a warning so tingling with new-rule electricity that Marvin Mandel—then governor, then renowned for possessing acute political antennae—could scarcely have overlooked omens. Yet he did, or seemed to, and two possibilities arise. One is that he dismissed the Beall warning, and the Tydings-Sachs warning earlier, as many another long-seasoned politician dismissed them: Here, no doubt, was the latest flutter by transient do-gooders. As before, this would blow over, wouldn't it? In the second possibility Marvin Mandel's sense of personal security betrayed him: fresh from a triumphant election in 1970, he felt himself too smart to be caught, his maneuvers too cleverly disguised for detection. His gubernatorial presence was too successful, too overpowering to yield to a thirty-five-year old upstart in the federal prosecutor's office—a Republican, at that.

Either way, or both ways, Marvin Mandel held defiantly on course. He had given Maryland good government, hadn't he? Yes. He hadn't done anything wrong, had he, that others before him hadn't done? Perhaps not; that's a matter of degree and of public attitude. At the end, over and over, came the Mandel refrain. The rules had changed, had changed unfairly. Many Marylanders would agree, but that was a later phase.

At the outset of investigations in January, 1973, George Beall had little inkling he might discover Marvin Mandel himself at the end of the road he was traveling. In fact, he didn't. What caught Beall's nose early were aromatic rumors billowing out of the Baltimore County courthouse. County contracts were bought and sold, it was said, with county officials cheerfully extorting kickbacks in the good old county way. County prosecutors, bound politically, stood motionless. So did the state attorney general's office, inhibited by state law. Beall's federals barged in, calling up once again the tradition laid down by Tydings, renewed by Sachs.

With a little pressure, a handful of key witnesses cracked. The game fell into Beall's hands. Engineers and architects, contractors and consultants and bureaucrats, bribers and bribed alike, scurried to skin-saving confession. Down crashed the entire county edifice propped up by the Baltimore County executive, Dale Anderson, briskly convicted and jailed. Oh, and something to help clarify the tone of public life in the county: conviction of the county prosecutor himself, said by the state to have extracted intimate favors from a woman who, by demurring, would have invited prosecution. The singular charge: "carnal bribery."

Other findings produced in the investigation, if less salacious, leaped county lines. A lesser, almost routine follow-up ensnared Joseph Alton, the Anne Arundel County executive, to whom cash bribes were customarily passed along in demure white envelopes. Beall's flashiest catch was Agnew, by then swept off to the vice-presidency but a man whose notions of official rectitude had early seeded themselves in Baltimore County, then flowered in the state. Agnew was Maryland governor immediately before Marvin Mandel.

Beall's pursuit of Agnew instantly assumed national dimensions. By itself, proximity of the White House transfixed onlookers. To that was added the spectacle of Richard Nixon's ambivalence toward the thrashing Agnew, the president's growing determination to jettison the vice-president as a hazard to his personal security in the face of Watergate whisperings. Nixon at that point simply couldn't afford to embrace a stained Agnew at his side, so let him—with an icy push from Alexander Haig, then the Nixon chief of staff—drift off to his baying Maryland pursuers. Agnew succumbed with a grudge but without a trial: four witnesses, each in deep trouble, had pointed accusing fingers. A broken Agnew yielded up a frilled version of the same no contest plea offered earlier by Daniel Brewster. He's guilty was the common interpretation.

Inevitably, presidential complexities surrounding the Agnew case obscured in the public eye the comparatively simple mechanics of Agnew's actual offense. He admitted bribe taking, but not as part of some exquisite White House shell game. What enfolded him were petty extortions left over from his days on the humdrum if rancid soil of Baltimore County, Maryland. For Agnew this began while he was county executive and continued while he was governor. He demanded payoffs from and through businessmen, took money directly in cash, handed out rich contracts in reward. Here, as Agnew correctly noted, was little more than continuation of a custom that had flourished before and that had been tolerated in Maryland. So it had been except that, as Agnew ignored, and as Mandel would ignore later, Maryland tolerance was wearing thin.

From Agnew we may now leave aside the Nixon-related exotica, amply documented by Jules Witcover and Richard M. Cohen in *A Heartbeat Away* and mostly extraneous, anyway, to the Mandel case. To the long story of Maryland corruption, Agnew's fall was deeply symbolic, and in a sense broader than a debatably too-late warning to his successor. Until Agnew no high Maryland politician was so plainly pinned to corruption, none convicted. Certainly Arthur Gorman had brushed aside all complaints about political manipulation of the Chesapeake and Ohio Canal Co.; Gorman was never punished at all. No more had Edwin Warfield, while governor, acknowledged any public interest conflict with his private banking interests. Mayor Howard Jackson and Boss Jack Pollack had seen nothing wrong with tipping the city's insurance pot their way. No questions were publicly asked Governors O'Conor and McKeldin about certain pocketings, there were no public answers.

It wasn't that doubtful doings were unknown or at least not soundly suspected. It was simply that, known or suspected, "doing business" on the side was accepted by Maryland society. If the standard was ambiguous, it was the standard of the day. History records them all as honorable men, not in all cases totally honest men. If the distinction between honorable and honest was thought to be real, as it then was, it became with Agnew a distinction too delicate to survive the harsher eye of less muddled, more objective, times suddenly at hand.

Agnew's public admissions obliterated the old ambiguity, an ambiguity that by tilting toward "doing business" had served to shelter corruption. Now the cat was out of the bag, openly standing there on all fours, altogether too visible a cat for the most forgiving to ignore. Corruption was demonstrably not limited to petty finaglers at the county and city levels; it infected the very root of governmental authority itself, the governorship. What's more, and even more revealing, there arose reluctantly from the other, or bribing, side of the white-envelope table businessmen, engineers, and bankers with hands now called no cleaner than Agnew's own.

At this display, public attitudes tilted the other way. Now another old Maryland folkway came forcefully into its own. Long only intermittently effective, this was a popular yearning for government free of "doing business." The Agnew case dramatized the arrival of a different fashion, one from which public office corruption, if only for the moment, was being drummed out.

The second revelation of the Agnew fall was newer, indeed, pivotal. It was the demonstration that a federal capacity now existed which was competent to reach beyond mouselike nibblings at political underlings. Here came a force to cut through political cocoons inside which the highest officials, with justified composure, once encased themselves.

For Spiro Agnew, not even the White House was a defensible hiding place. For Marvin Mandel, later, the State House would prove a haven no more secure. Common morality, sharpened into law, had achieved something close to parity with those out to flout it.

Ⓐll six defendants in the Mandel case—Mandel and Kovens and Hess, the two Rodgers and Cory—were called liars by federal prosecutors. All were convicted. Lying, however, evidently did not stop with the Mandel circle. Four other men were also publicly accused of lies, lies told on the fringes in a cover-up of the bribery being carried out at the center. Yet none of these four was even charged with perjury, let alone convicted or sentenced.

Why not? Answers to the natural question furnish an insight into one part of the prosecution's strategy.

In his closing speech to the jury, Barnet Skolnik singled out by name these men who he said had told lies:

Eugene Casey, a racetrack tycoon, told the Senate Finance Committee and all Marylanders, via a news conference, that it was he who had bought Marlboro. Skolnik: Casey lied. Twice.

Herbert Alpert said he hadn't known that the tailoring of Mandel's suits he had charged as "guards' uniforms" to Charlestown Racetrack had been arranged by Kovens, owner of Charlestown. Skolnik: Alpert lied.

State Senator Roy Staten denied that he had passed the word from Mandel to fellow senators that the then-governor, despite his earlier veto of a bill to enrich Marlboro, would not now object to his veto being overridden. Skolnik: Staten lied.

Irving T. "Tubby" Schwartz testified that it was he, not

Kovens, who owned the largest share of Marlboro Racetrack. Skolnik: Schwartz lied.

As alleged liars, close to the defendants, why were these four not punished for their part in the Mandel cover-up? How did the government distinguish here between six guilty and four not guilty?

It did not distinguish. Perjury charges were seriously discussed, but, for two different reasons, prosecutors never followed through.

Casey and Alpert were relatively unimportant to the main game. Besides, their lies were too transparent to require belaboring. Casey admitted his lie; documentary evidence against Alpert was strong. Jurors needed no more convincing. So why stir up embers in a complex, difficult case already safely won on other grounds? For trivial points, why risk a dangerous blowback from changed testimony, from an unsettling judicial quirk, from some unforeseen new precedent? Although tempted to initiate follow-up trials, prosecutors put aside that course as imprudent.

Staten and Schwartz, on the other hand, were central to the main case. Some of the same prosecutorial prudence hindered further pursuit of them. But here a larger, even delicate, tactical gamble was also afoot. It was the calculation, always tricky, that testimony by Staten and Schwartz would boomerang. Wouldn't they prove grossly unbelievable in the witness chair? Wouldn't they actually hurt the defendants they thought they were helping, then help the prosecution they thought they were hurting? Wouldn't their own lies, conversely, tell the jury the truth? It was a daring maneuver, the prosecutors reasoned, but worth it.

Roy Staten, a gregarious senator long used by Governor Mandel as a legislative mouthpiece, had opened his proxy mouth wider than, later, he liked to admit. He talked, first, to a handful of senators who remembered what he said. He talked, second and more significantly, to a seasoned legislative correspondent who wrote down Staten's words and then printed them.

"I guess it had been decided," Staten was quoted by Edward Walsh in the Washington Post, "that the Governor didn't have any objection to his veto being overridden . . . the policy of the administration was that if you want to override, go ahead."

In court, this was terribly damaging stuff. In effect, the over-

ride would enrich the Marlboro owners, Mandel's friends, so
Mandel himself seemed drawn into complicity. Staten furiously
denied saying it. The trouble was, the Walsh report in the Post
laid solid support under the memory of senators to whom Staten
had talked earlier. Staten might still have walked away from the
witness chair half-believed but for the emergence of a personal
motive easily recognizable as ulterior.

Prosecutors learned, and pointedly put out the word, that
Staten had been angling for a juicy state job. It was a job as secretary of the Department of Licensing and Regulation and paid
$42,000 annually. Appointment to the job lay in the hands of
Governor Mandel, already irritable and now having to watch his
cover-up ripped apart by Staten's words. Would the Governor
punish his talkative floor leader, angrily strike him off the
patronage list? Or, instead, reward him for blind loyalty? It was
obvious to Skolnik that Staten had lied in his own self-interest.
Why press the obvious? Why draw up the explosive, unpredicta-
ble gun of a separate perjury proceeding? The jury understood.

Testimony by Tubby Schwartz carried in it an odd quality,
invaluable to the prosecution, of reversibility. His words on the
witness stand—betrayed, as often as not, by a nervous habit of
waggling his knees—seemed to turn backward the very meaning
he was hoping to put forward. For Schwartz was ordered in as a
role player, an undertaking for which he was transparently
unequipped. He was to pose as Irv Kovens, as the true owner of
Marlboro, as Kovens the shrewd, tough manipulator of racetrack
management and finance. Often before he had fronted for
Kovens. This time proved one time too many.

At trial a critical issue was whether Kovens or Schwartz was
furnishing periodic interest payments on a $2-million bank loan
made to buy Marlboro. If it was Schwartz, the implication was
that Schwartz was indeed Marlboro's majority owner, just as he
said he was. If instead it was Kovens, then Kovens looked like the
big owner, whereupon Mandel, as Kovens's close friend, seemed
ominously connected. That Kovens money was flying toward
Schwartz at more than $10,000 a clip was apparent from both
men's check stubs. But were these payments innocent loans to
Schwartz, which Schwartz paid back? Or were they really transfer checks, cover-up devices where Kovens paid the bank interest

in fact, then simply camouflaged that fact by passing the checks through Schwartz's checking account?

When prosecutors discovered that Schwartz held a $50,000 bank balance at a time when Kovens was said to be helping him through a cash squeeze, they began to smell a rat. In a rare move, Ron Liebman called Tubby Schwartz to testify as witness, not for the defense, but for the prosecution of his own patron and benefactor, Irv Kovens.

Liebman question: And when you look at your bank statement, do you see any indication that that money came from Mr. Kovens? Look at the top and see whether it says "IK, exchange check." Do you see that, sir?

Schwartz answer: Right here? That is the check.

Q. — Does it not say "IK, exchange check?"

A. — I wrote it that way. I wrote it wrong.

Q. — You wrote it wrong?

A. — I borrowed the money, deposited it in the bank, and I gave a check out for it.

Q. — So that is your testimony; if you wrote exchange check, that was wrong?

A. — I just made a mistake, yes, sir.

One mistake, then another check.

Q. — Just read us the penciled-in words.

A. — "Exchange check."

Q. — That was written by you, and that was in your handwriting?

A. — I would say.

Q. — Now, is it your testimony that when you wrote "exchange" that was another error on your part?

A. — I would say so.

Next came a letter to Cory in which Schwartz said he owned a majority of the stock in Marlboro.

Schwartz — Yes, well that is a mistake.

Then arose a puzzle about interest on a $200,000 loan Kovens in fact made to Harry Rodgers to help buy Marlboro. Someone had to collect this interest, had to report it for federal income tax. Why Schwartz?

Schwartz — I reported it unconsciously. It was done by mistake, for my part. Someone else made a mistake.

Four Schwartz "mistakes," and that wasn't all. In April, 1974, when the Senate Finance Committee was looking suspiciously into Marlboro's ownership, Tubby Schwartz made two more statements. One was that Dale Hess never owned any stock in the track at all. The other was that he alone, Tubby Schwartz, owned 192,000 shares. These two "mistakes," both admitted, brought the Schwartz total to six.

It was too much for the jury to swallow. In a special verdict, it discarded Schwartz's testimony completely. Irvin Kovens, jurors found, owned the lion's share of Marlboro Racetrack.

Four men, all called liars, none prosecuted for perjury. Yet each contributed first to the Mandel cover-up, then to peeling the cover back.

8.

"Mandel Has Skotched Coming Clean"

Two questions arose about Richard Nixon's personal involvement when the Watergate scandal first bubbled up. What did Nixon know? And, more important, when did he know it? The same questions arose about Marvin Mandel's part in the manipulation of Marlboro Racetrack. In Nixon's case, the answers would determine whether he could continue in office as president. The point with Mandel was sharper. If he truly did not know about Marlboro, as he insisted to the end and beyond he didn't, he would be an innocent man, a man cruelly used by his closest friends. But if he did know and lied about it, as the federal government said he did, he was guilty at least of gross deceit. Probably guilty too of bribery, of mail fraud, of racketeering. Prison as a prospect took on an icy reality.

So knowledge was the question, Marvin Mandel's knowledge, and whether or not in 1971 and after his knowledge could properly be called guilty knowledge. That question began to take shape publicly early in 1975. The *Washington Post* reported that Marlboro's owners in 1972 and 1973 were Dale Hess and Harry Rodgers. Because both were known to be close personally and politically to the Governor, questions were unavoidable: Did Mandel know Hess and Rodgers had secretly bought the racetrack? If so, did he know it at the time he took official action that had the effect, also in secret, of doubling his friends' substantial investment? Was there criminal collusion?

134

The *Post* story appeared February 5, shortly after federal investigators learned of Hess's and Rodgers's purchase. The next day the Governor held a news conference that told little about the facts but a good deal about Marvin Mandel. A second news conference more richly laden with atmosphere and nuances came shortly afterward. Key passages follow.

Edward Walsh of the *Post* started questioning Mandel: Governor, [do] you now or have you ever had knowledge of any financial interests Mr. Hess and Mr. Rodgers have had in Maryland racetracks?

A.—No, I have not.

Q.—Have they ever told you that they do have any interest?

A.—I think that question was asked at another press conference a long time ago and I answered it very clearly. I said that I have no knowledge of any interest nor have I been informed of any nor have they ever told me of any nor has anyone ever told me of any. I don't know of any.

James B. Rowland of the *Washington Star* continued: Governor, did Mr. Hess or Mr. Rodgers ever tell you or did you ever ask them if they had an interest in an organization called Marlboro Associates [the firm that owned the track]?

A.—No, I didn't. I have never asked that question and I don't intend to.

Q.—Have they ever volunteered?

A.—No, sir.

Q.—Why wouldn't you ask them?

A.—I'll tell you why. Because I'm not getting involved. I am not involved. I have never been involved, and I don't intend to get involved in any phase of any of that . . .

So that was February 6. Nearly two months later, a *Post* reporter in an interview found the Governor in a different frame of mind. His story, printed April 3, reported Mandel as now saying, yes, he had known before the first news conference that Hess and Rodgers had had an interest in Marlboro Racetrack. They told him, he said, after they had sold it.

At another news conference that April third afternoon John Aubuchon of WTOP radio opened the questioning of Mandel: When did you discover that you had made a mistake or a misstatement . . .

A.—Now just let me correct that—wait a minute. Before you go any further I didn't make a mistake nor did I make any misstatement, let me make that clear. When a reporter came to me and asked me yesterday some questions which I said I would be very happy to answer, he came to me because I had said that if someone would just ask me the right questions I could answer them. And he did ask the right questions and I answered them. And what I said was that some time ago—and I don't even remember when, and I am not going to try to tell you that I do—I haven't reversed my stand. I haven't changed it.

The questions that were always directed at me were did I know of any financial interest that was had in Marlboro Associates or Bowie Racetrack and . . . I have constantly said no because I know of no interest . . .

All I know is that after some questions were asked me by reporters, I called [Hess and Rodgers] and I said, "Do you have any involvement in Bowie Racetrack or any involvement in this Marlboro Associates?" and they said, "Absolutely not." I said, "Were you ever involved?" They said to me, "We had gotten into that, but we got out and we have no involvement." And I said, "Well, that's good; I'm glad to hear it." That's all I know about it.

Edward Walsh of the *Post* went on: Last February you were asked . . . whether you knew . . . of any financial interest that Hess and Rodgers had in any Maryland racetrack and you answered no, was your answer based on the fact that the question included the phrase "financial interest"?

A.—That's right. I don't know of any financial interest they had or do have or ever had. I don't know . . .

Q.—Well, Governor, for future reference, should we work on the assumption that unless we phrase these types of questions precisely right as you interpret them, we can't trust the answers?

A.—No, no, and you know that's not true, but I think a direct question ought to be asked and not try to go around the mulberry bush.

It's hard to miss the Governor's gathering panic, his sense that the hounds have picked up the trail. By then he knew that federal investigators were doggedly in pursuit of Hess and Rodgers, that scrutiny of their subpoenaed papers had revealed their ownership of Marlboro. But had they yet picked up footprints traceable to Mandel himself?

No, he keeps saying, no. He didn't know Hess and Rodgers had bought the track. They never told him, not until later. And then when reporters asked him about that they asked the wrong question. He's not to blame, he couldn't answer. He didn't know.

A wispy logic holds together this Mandel-didn't-know scenario. Hess and Rodgers didn't tell him they had bought Marlboro. Why? For fear of adverse political reaction. Legislators, press, everyone, would holler conspiracy! fix! cheating! So they would holler, indeed so they did holler when the *Post* finally drew back the covers. Hence it had been simply political prudence that had kept Mandel in the dark, not some evil conspiracy. He didn't know about Marlboro. He wasn't involved. No bribe took place, no mail fraud. The defense rests uneasily, for a moment.

The credible moment is short-lived. It begins to dissolve at the point where it stretches from a moment of not knowing to a period running more than four years long. Besides, Hess and Rodgers were not simply casual political acquaintances of Marvin Mandel. They had raised nearly $2 million to put him in office and keep him there. They had included him in two real estate deals. As Barnet Skolnik would put it later, the Marlboro buyers "expect this [Marlboro expansion] of him [Mandel] and want this of him, and in the way they look at things, in sort of a sad sense, are entitled to this from him. Is that why he pushed that bill so hard?"

The relationship had another dimension. The three were close personal friends. Members of the Mandel circle never denied their closeness. They emphasized it. When the U.S. attorney's office began asking questions about the gifts lavished on the Governor, the routine response was that they were gifts, friend to friend. This is the way friends as close as these treat one another, free of calculation, innocent of guile. On this ground, close friendship, the defense chose to stand, thereby committing what may have been its greatest bumble in logic.

For the government, a gate swung invitingly open. Prosecutors asked: Would such close friends and generous patrons of the Governor set out, in all friendship, to deceive him? Would close friend maneuver close friend into an ethical and political trap, a trap likely to snap shut at any moment—as it did—and snare them all together? Or, from the other side, was it probable that a governor as shrewd as Marvin Mandel, a seasoned politician for whom no sparrow fell unheard, stood deaf to the sound of his closest friends rattling about slyly in his own gubernatorial backyard?

That Mandel "didn't know" of their Marlboro operation from 1971, when it began, until 1975, when he read of it in the newspapers?

"That strains the imagination," said one lawyer close to the defendants.

This lapse in credulity was the chasm over which, in court, the defense found it hardest to leap convincingly. For ordinary non-legal onlookers, the suspicion wouldn't down that the Governor knew full well what his friends were doing with Marlboro. And that, when he said repeatedly he didn't know, only to retreat afterward on a sidewise slant, he was trying to conceal the real truth. Also, finally, that the truth carried in it urgent reason for concealment. On such skeletal suspicion, fleshed out by corroborative documents laboriously gathered, the indictment for mail fraud was drawn.

Marvin Mandel's news conference performance that spring of 1975 offered the first public confirmation of something peculiar in the handling of Marlboro Racetrack. It seemed to be something involving the Governor, something clandestine. It sounded a keynote for the whole Marlboro operation. Conceal everything, then conceal the concealment. It was a keynote certain to invite suspicion, and it did. But not right away, not for five years.

The fact is, as artful dodges go, Marlboro was a minor masterpiece. It disdained the white envelopes that, sullied by cash enclosures, had betrayed Spiro Agnew. No mean extortion in the Dale Anderson/Joseph Alton mode turned up. No kickbacks stained Marlboro, no politicized bond counsel, no judgeship bought and sold. Instead Marlboro aspired to an uncommon grandeur of design, original and free of petty criminal cliché. It was an elaborate trompe l'oeil, a creation only later recognizable as mail fraud.

In its bare bones, the Marlboro transaction is quickly recounted: Late in 1971 the racetrack stood old and staggering. Four men, close personal and political friends of the Governor, bought it cheap. Twelve days later, early in 1972, action by the legislature doubled the track's value: the Governor, delicately detached, seemed to turn his back. Weeks later, this time with open Mandel pressure, a still bolder fattening of Marlboro's fortunes would have succeeded but for a midnight legislative rebellion. A few months after that, the legislative rebels were by-passed when Marlboro smoothly merged with a larger track, now gaining extra value undreamed-of by those who had sold out to the Mandel circle a year earlier. The Racing Commission approved, so did the legislature. The Marlboro coup stood complete, its operators' profit substantially if temporarily enlarged.

From this profit, Mandel personally was paid nothing. Instead, he turned up with a number of lucrative new holdings including, notably, a $300,000 share in a federal building lease owned by partners in Tidewater Insurance. This last was the triumphantly elusive touch. Not a straightforward piece of the action, at least not of the central Marlboro action. So what? And where hidden? It lay squirreled away beneath quite another action, a gross manipulation of Dale Hess's check records. This second action was the one which Dale Hess's secretary, in an innocent quest for stenographic smartness, innocently fumbled, bared. In the longer view, Alice Riley's mistake seems no more than a betraying detail, a circumstantial fluke. In the design itself, otherwise skillful, where did the Mandel circle miscalculate? What was their overriding failure?

One theory holds—and theories in this case are plentiful, most of them undemonstrable—that the Marlboro arrangement came unstuck on a lack of bravura, an unwillingness frankly to hoist aloft the pirate's Jolly Roger. Leave aside legal refinements. What Hess and Rodgers and Rodgers and Kovens and Mandel did was wrong, a flagrant abuse of the public power entrusted to Mandel, then loaned out to others. Cory trotted along.

But were Marylanders irreversibly shocked by this wrongdoing to the point of abhorrence? Or could Mandel & Co., by openly conceding the shabby but scarcely unprecedented facts, have carried off their venture? Despite a hail of empty beer cans, could they have nevertheless survived an honest, contrite confession?

History can only raise the question, not answer it. But Ol' Earl Long, when caught as governor of Louisiana in an impossible self-contradiction, said endearingly "I lied"—and got away with it. Richard Nixon dumped Watergate blame on his subordinates and, if trailing a fishy aroma, contrived for himself a backdoor escape. The Mandel people, on the contrary, clung to their Marlboro version to the end. Mandel didn't know, public power was not abused, and so on. And down they went, the lot of them, clutching to their chests a set of facts which if grubby stopped short of outright repulsive. Confession, while humiliating them, might also have saved them.

An odder view is that it was their own sense of righteousness which betrayed them. Theirs was a singular species of righteousness which did not demand the presence of actual right itself; to them wrong seemed to do as well, or better. Where they put their trust was in their own endless public proclamations of right which they had come, in the delusion of power, to mistake for the genuine article. In this analysis it was hypocrisy that did them in, a hollow sort of political pretension they never convincingly mastered, hence flubbed to their own undoing.

So much for the outline of the Marlboro undertaking, so much for speculation as to how so clever a design went astray. More telling are the facts, notably the tentlike structure the Mandel circle built to block off from the public view what it had in hand. Mandel's own news conferences were no more than the pennant tacked fluttering at the peak of the tent. Woven elsewhere into the enveloping fabric was an array of evasion and deception, of half-truth and lie, of straw men, of altered checks, of all manner of sand in the eyes.

Deception stood present at the birth of the Marlboro venture including, exquisitely, a deceptive explanation of why deception was necessary and even proper. Deception took a nervous spurt under the prod, suddenly sensed, of the federal investigation. Finally, it was the federal dismantling of deception, piece by piece, which exposed Marlboro as the suspicious centerpiece in a larger design carefully crafted to divert the casual gaze.

The victims, a federal jury would find, were the swindled citizens of Maryland. Arguably, what citizens were swindled of was their right, also arguable, to honest government, to be treated as employers of responsible servants. This was a right rather newly perceived in the law, hence a right still imperfectly defined in the 1970s amid a whirl of earlier judicial rulings more or less parallel to the Mandel case. Still, law is seldom graven in stone. It is not dead but alive, evolving as human civilization moves forward from one consensus to another. Appellate judges would agonize over subtleties of legal concept and of procedure: that was at a different and higher level. About the stony facts of the Mandel case, notably its massive and studied design to deceive, little judicial debate was heard. Here through the evidence ran a torrent of what prosecutors call, with professional relish, marks of guilty knowledge.

As to Marlboro Racetrack, a question first became germane early in 1972. A knot of state senators, nonadmirers of the Governor, demanded to know who had bought up the old track late in 1971. So did the state Racing Commission, which, being mostly Mandel appointees, inquired more politely. So did the Thoroughbred Racing Protective Bureau, a respected national guardian against gangster meddlings. So did the state attorney general's office and a Baltimore attorney representing a private client. Most noisily of all, so did the always suspicious media, notably the *Washington Post*, already charged up over Watergate, and the *Baltimore Sunpapers*, eager to confront the *Post* in a disputed circulation area. Even the *Maryland Horse*, a magazine reflecting horsemen's views, poked hopefully into the shadows. Nearly everyone caught a whiff of manipulation, secret strings pulled by hidden hands. None could identify the source, and no wonder.

So who owned Marlboro?

First, up spoke Eugene B. Casey, a man of formidable wealth who collected racetracks as other rich men collect Matisse. I have taken over Marlboro, Casey announced publicly in January of 1972, then proceeded to crack around as if he actually had. But was that really so? Something improbably Napoleonic about Casey raised doubts. Soon the Casey pose began to fade.

How about Irving T. Schwartz, in April the next public claimant to Marlboro command? Not likely as a leader, was the common reading, but nicely provocative as a screen. A man called "Tubby" for reasons of personal contour, Schwartz had twice earlier acted as front man for another. This other was Irvin Kovens, who, whenever he was not personally comfortable in the spotlight, had found the shade behind Schwartz more agreeable. So was Kovens the hidden owner of Marlboro? If so, why hidden? If hidden, where hidden behind him moved Kovens's best friend, Governor Mandel?

Or maybe the pattern was more convoluted still. Maybe the real power was Ernest N. Cory, Jr., sometime fox-hunting socialite, sometime politico-lawyer once accused as fixer—along with the Governor's son Gary—in a Frederick bank scandal. ("I don't practice law," Cory was once quoted. "I practice influence.") Certainly Cory had strewn the trail with misleading clues. In one manifestation he was lawyer for the track; in another, owner; in still another, a discharged and aggrieved employee. Barrel of puzzles that he was, Cory caught investigators' eye as central to something larger than himself.

Cory was thus the turning point, the first catch of the year 1975 for federal investigators. It was he who—inadvertently, unwillingly, surely unhappily—linked an iron chain of evidence to the men who constituted the inner circle about Marvin Mandel. With Cory's evidence, investigators lifted their eighteen-month focus beyond Hess and the Rodgers brothers and their sharp doings at Tidewater Insurance. They looked beyond, and there square in the federal sights appeared the Governor himself.

Once again, as with Cory, it was a lawyer representing Hess and the Rodgers brothers who pointed his finger in the Mandel direction. Richard J. Himelfarb—protesting, overruled by the court—furnished his own meticulous notes of a consultation in which he repeatedly urged his clients as early as December, 1972, to put aside the secrecy in which they had enveloped their Marlboro holdings. Hess, according to Himelfarb, said he must first clear any such revelation with the Governor. After Hess made a telephone call, Himelfarb's notes recounted, the lawyer was given Hess's reply: "Mandel has skotched coming clean."

Protests would erupt in court from defense lawyers, but jurors could scarcely mistake the message emerging from Himelfarb's notes. A massive, deliberate deception had been underway about who owned Marlboro Racetrack. Not only did Marvin Mandel know, at least three years before the news conferences of 1975, who the real owners were and how their names were covered up, but when asked to let these owners "come clean," it was the Governor himself who "skotched" it. No, he told Dale Hess. No, keep the cover on.

As things turned out legally, the cover itself became a part of the government's assertion that a crime had been committed. Here was the interwoven series of devices to blind the Racing Commission, to blind the legislature, and, through them, to blind the citizens of Maryland. Here was the element of fraud of which the Mandel circle would be convicted. But why concealment? What was the motive? Instead of criminal, was it simply an act of routine political prudence, a dash of innocent eyewash employed to ease the passage of a difficult but legitimate bit of legislation?

So the defendants argued. The government took a more somber view.

Two things were not concealed because they could not be. One was the friendship long linking Mandel and Kovens, Mandel and Hess, and, via Hess, Mandel and the Rodgers brothers. Nearly everyone knew about that. The second thing nearly everyone knew was that the new owners of Marlboro Racetrack, twelve days after their purchase, found the value of their investment at least doubled. Also that, two months thereafter, this same investment nearly won a multiplier still higher. The scene of Marlboro's sudden, astonishing good fortune was the legislature, a body commonly responsive to the will of Governor Mandel. Whispers were heard, but whispers are always heard in legislative season. Onlookers shrugged off news reports from Annapolis, in part because two other factors, both critical, remained missing.

The first was proof that Mandel's friends—Hess, the Rodgers brothers, Kovens—had actually acquired Marlboro behind the scenes. The second was that Mandel, sponsor and promoter of Marlboro's phenomenal legislative luck, was a hidden partner of the owners. The Governor was drawing monthly checks from Hess and had a six-figure bond settlement from Kovens. These secret aspects—the Hess-Rodgers-Kovens ownership, plus the rich financial flow to Mandel—transformed the situation.

What on the surface had seemed unremarkable if puzzling became, upon deeper revelation, suspicious and maybe scandalous. Government investigators went further. They discerned a conspiracy to bribe the Governor and to pervert his official power, then fraudulently to conceal the bribe. It was a case of linking together the known and unknown, thus converting a provocative innocence to an indictable crime. Linkage was the device, and Barney Skolnik would later remember the moment of linking, hence of discovery, as "a light bulb going on" in the darkness.

It wasn't for lack of probing by suspicious legislators that Marlboro's new owners had been unknown. The legislature, insistent on knowing, declined to be put off. In 1973, a senate committee started official investigations. In 1974, a new law was enacted. The old custom winked at by the Racing Commission—a racetrack could put forward straw men or "dummies" as owners—was gone: now legislators were to be furnished the names of actual owners, those who stood to gain or lose on the ups or downs of a track's profits. No one doubted which track had sharpened the legislators' interest. It was Marlboro, the one track that, to judge by its zooming good fortune at Annapolis, enjoyed a powerful political influence, maddeningly hidden. Legislators felt they had to find out whose pockets, by boosting Marlboro, they in blindness had been induced to line.

Here arose a concrete instance of a midstream change in the law, a change that defendants would complain later was used unfairly to charge them with a crime not then recognized as crime. The fact is, straw men had long been permitted as substitutes in name only for actual owners. Other corporations do the same, commonly for legitimate corporate reasons. But the key word here is legitimate: corporations using this practice are not generally out to deceive, then by deception to lure their victims into actions, perhaps criminal, they would refuse to take if the actual names were known. Honest businessmen use straw men for honest corporate reasons, not to defraud outsiders.

What the Marlboro circle was up to was quite something else. The something else came in two versions, one innocent, one otherwise.

As perceived by the defendants, straw men were used to defuse the political electricity certain to be generated when it was known publicly that the Governor's friends had bought the track. Not only was the general public, including legislators, not to know. So too was Marvin Mandel himself to be kept in ignorance of what his best friends were doing. Why this great secret separating friend from friend?

Because if Mandel had known, the friends insisted, he would have dutifully reported the truth at his news conference—whereupon, the secret would be out, an uproar loosed, Marlboro imperiled. Worse, the Governor would have ordered his friends to abandon the project. Either way, so this argument ran, Marlboro as a perfectly legitimate enterprise would have suffered blows grave and probably fatal. But they were innocent, the friends said, and no less entitled to innocent privacy in business affairs than anyone else. Hence the straw men, hence the cover, both innocent.

Beguiling to some, this privacy rationale skipped nimbly past the overriding fact. This was that the Marlboro matter had its roots planted not in a private business venture but, instead, squarely in the state government machinery answerable to Maryland citizens. This was public business, not private. Marlboro's expansion, which is what was at stake, was doomed without the backing of the Governor and then acceptance by the legislature. Private, it wasn't; public, it was, and even that didn't reflect Marlboro's essential coloring.

As the defense put it, straw men were employed as a form of antipolitical tidiness, of keeping the politicians wholesomely silent in the dark. Silent, yes, said the prosecution, and certainly (except Mandel) in the dark. But wholesome? There was nothing wholesome about it. To the contrary, the objective as the prosecution saw it was deliberately to rob the legislature of facts it needed to know if it was to make an informed decision in the public interest. The short word was fraud.

Legislators had sensed deception. It wasn't simply a species of prurient curiosity that led them to try to lift the covers on this bed full of Mandel cronies. There was instead a responsible interest in their close Mandel connection, a connection riveted tight since his election in 1969 by political favors large and small. The array of favors was known to run from the friends to Mandel. Now, three and four years later, had the favors begun to run the other way in return? From Mandel back to Mandel's friends?

Small wonder legislators reasoned that if the time had come for the Governor to pay back his friends, they had better know the nature of the coin demanded. Was it his help in getting their Marlboro stake doubled, then redoubled? Was Marlboro an honest venture? Or a political payoff?

The Racing Commission didn't know either. Dutifully its secretary, James A. Callahan, telephoned Ernest Cory, who seemed to be speaking for Marlboro. Who owns the track? The senators, Callahan said, want to know. Back from Cory came a list. A few on it owned token shares, a few no shares at all. A few had not even authorized use of their names as dummies. No mention was made of the true owners: of Hess, of Rodgers, of Kovens. Without comment, maybe unknowingly, Callahan transmitted Cory's list by letter to the senate committee. The committee was unconvinced. Lacking facts, operating on suspicion alone, senators managed to outmaneuver a massive, almost feverish thrust that Mandel operatives built behind the expansion bill. It fell dead—or almost. Later it was resurrected elsewhere.

The flow of disinformation from Ernest Cory had only begun. When two months later the Racing Commission asked him again—Who owns Marlboro?—Cory switched his ground. He announced that he himself held 175,000 of 200,000 existing shares as lawyer for clients; he cited lawyer-client confidence in declining to name them. The commission persisted; Cory in July took a step deeper into cover—Daniel J. Hurson, for the prosecution, called this "perhaps one of the biggest frauds in the whole case"—when he submitted still a different list of supposed stockholders in Marlboro. This time, every single name was a dummy. No one on the list owned a single share of Marlboro stock.

Carl Jackson, a member of the commission, was puzzled. Was this at last, he asked Cory face to face, the real list everyone had been asking for? "That's it," Cory said. Jackson, for one, believed him. That fall, it was still 1972, the action changed again. Now the Marlboro owners, blocked in the senate in April, arranged to bypass the entire legislature and get what they wanted another way. They arranged as a private business matter to merge their half-mile track with still a different mile track, Bowie, and thus achieve profits happily multiplied by Bowie's far larger attendance. As a capital venture, the new Marlboro owners had improved the value of their original investment, some $2 million, by as much as $2 million more within the first year or less. Greater profits still were confidently awaited.

For this merger phase, the Marlboro owners emplaced new ownership scenery to match the new action. Still faceless and nameless, they christened themselves "Marlboro Associates." As usual no Hess, no Rodgers, no Kovens protruded from the new package . . . this time, apparently, because the Governor himself "skotched" coming clean. It was at this point in December, 1972, according to Daniel Hurson in his own analysis, that Mandel shifted from passive to active participant. Indeed, Hurson said, Mandel personally "was taking charge of the cover-up" at Marlboro Racetrack. No, don't let the truth out. Don't let the legislature know. The leader was taking the lead.

Six months after came the clincher. In June, 1973, the Marlboro deal was wrapped up officially, supposedly safely, and put on ice for the next five years. The Racing Commission officially approved the transfer to Bowie: Marlboro's thirty-six days would be exploited at the mile track, thus rejoicing in the greater patronage—and profits—generated there. And who, now, turned up as the newest, surprise owner of Marlboro's Bowie stock?

Here came Ernest Cory, hitherto only the lawyer for Hess and Rodgers, wearing more impressive costume. Cory reported he had bought out his clients' stock even though, in reality, he hadn't. What Cory's letter to the Racing Commission omitted in this case was not just the names of his clients. Left out too were the facts that he paid nothing for the stock and that, in five years, he would have to give the stock back to Hess and the Rodgers brothers. These were details that Cory, probably under instruction, found unnecessary to mention.

That five-year delay, if known, would have struck a particularly revealing note. It had the effect of maintaining the cover into 1978, the year Mandel's second and last term as governor would be complete. Thereafter, the cover would be no longer necessary, and his friends might safely emerge from their closet of namelessness. Everyone would be home free and a couple of million dollars richer, thanks to the Marlboro maneuver, than they had begun. As it was, the cover held and the legislature if by now twitching with suspicion was unable to pierce through to the full facts. In 1974, it tamely ratified Marlboro's transfer to Bowie. The rebellious bang of two years earlier had diminished to a whimper.

Still, the whimper persisted, gathered new force, took legal shape. In annoyance legislators at that same 1974 session put through the new disclosure act upon which Marlboro's cover was soon caught up and raveled. Early in 1975, as a byproduct of the Hess-Rodgers investigation, rumors of their Marlboro connection rose anew with a clatter. In the spring, frightened by the new law, Cory began to buckle. The day after he was questioned by U.S. investigators, he cracked.

In a final letter to the Racing Commission, he withdrew in effect as inoperative—which is to say, as lies—his previous stream of letters, oral statements, personal appearances. Marlboro's real owners, Cory admitted, included as principals Hess and the two Rodgers brothers. Kovens, alias Schwartz, he left under cover, there to await a day when the federal jury formally installed the still-protesting Kovens among the leading owners of Marlboro.

That would not occur until the federal mail fraud convictions of 1977 or, more ponderously, Armageddon. But by March, 1975, the cover-up was slipping perilously. Truth of many sorts came tumbling out.

L ate in 1975, indictment was unquestionably in the air. Governor Mandel, fuming, dispatched a long letter of complaint about the United States attorney's office in Baltimore. The letter was private. It was addressed to Richard L. Thornburgh, Assistant Attorney General, Criminal Division, Justice Department, Washington. It was dated November 7.

First on the Governor's list was "leaks" to the media. These, he said, amounted to a five-year effort "to undermine me politically, to destroy my rights as a citizen, and to poison the minds of those who elected me. These acts have been directed against me in violation of every judicial and legal standard which you and I as attorneys are sworn to uphold."

Marvin Mandel continued: ". . . The press has been a deadly weapon against me through a scheme of calculated, well-planned and systematic leaks. . . . It has become almost a commonplace occurrence for stories to appear about testimony given to the grand jury and about the United States attorney's plans and strategies. The appearance of these stories could only benefit those who wish me harm."

Who was guilty of such terrible leaks?

"It has been evident to me for some time," the Governor wrote, "that the prosecutors have been divulging this information to the press as a part of a campaign to portray me publicly as evil and corrupt, so as to enlist the support of the Justice Department in their proposed prosecution and to poison the public atmosphere in the event of a trial. . . .''

So stood the charge. Then came one more leak.

The first week in December, a few days after the indictment had progressed beyond recall, the Mandel letter to Justice began appearing in the Baltimore and Washington newspapers. On its face, here was scarcely a thrust that "could only benefit those who would wish [Marvin Mandel] harm." This was an attack on his attackers.

So who leaked?

Internal evidence strongly suggested that the letter had not been released by Richard Thornburgh. Even more unlikely as leaker was the letter's target, the Baltimore prosecutor. The most prominent beneficiary was Governor Mandel himself, acknowledged master of political manipulation.

News reporters, of course, knew that leaks had long turned up regularly from both sides, depending. Sometimes a helpful word came from sources revolving, tantalizingly, in the middle. Just who leaked the Mandel-Thornburgh letter, however, it would not benefit reporters to say. Tomorrow always brings another day, another leak.

9.

Dark Victory at Marlboro

The Marlboro cover-up was ingeniously opaque, if not quite impenetrable. What began to emerge as federal investigators pulled back layer from ambiguous layer was a pattern of subtle camouflage, a wonder of political foxiness. It's better not to deny a cover-up outright, the tactic seemed in several cases to say. Instead, give an innocent explanation. That will blur the first explanation that meets the eye, the not-so-innocent one.

You had dummy stockholders in Marlboro Racetrack?

Well, yes—but that wasn't to conceal a fraud on the public. It was simply a routine, temporary device to get an honest bill past a legislature unfortunately peppered with members of morbidly political mind.

His own friends deceived the Governor?

Sure, but only to shield him from personal embarrassment, or from innocently blurting out the facts—the legitimate facts—before a bunch of hostile reporters long resolved on his personal humiliation.

The Governor's lies to the press?

Those weren't lies. The Governor simply stated what he really thought was true at the time. Besides, the reporters asked him the wrong questions. It wasn't his fault, was it, if they got the wrong answers?

Ruses de guerre. Fancy footwork to divert the unwary, and for a time even the outright suspicious were successfully kept at bay. Then the game spun faster. Instead of public relations dodges and

150

outwitted reporters—both rated acceptable political conventions—gross political manipulation edged into view. Following hard on that came a telltale flicker of money and painstaking efforts to conceal it, which suggested that concealment was urgent. Fraud glinted in the shadows. So did bribery.

What was being concealed was the heart of the matter, the act itself. For here lay connivance between Marlboro's new owners, on one hand, and Governor Mandel, on the other, to pervert the power of government. The object, as indicated, was financial. The means was legislative: it was to induce legislators to furnish Marlboro first extra racing days, hence extra profits, and then expanded patronage at a larger track, hence expanded profits per day. The legislature was Governor Mandel's political vehicle. It was to be the chosen instrument: its service—really, Mandel's fee for steering legislators toward the enrichment of Marlboro—was repayable elsewhere and in other coin.

In both directions, this payoff was substantial. Track owners, the Governor's friends, would instantly convert their $2-million outlay to $4 million at least. None of the increase would be creditable to business acumen, all of it rested on legislative manipulation. Because the Governor held a legislative majority in his palm, he was the pivotal point. To him the reward, presented in myriad forms, ranged from his own partial ownership in a rich federal lease to an underwritten divorce. Estimates of the Governor's personal take ranged as high as $500,000.

Whether as a prosecutor's indictment all this was legally pinned down, i's dotted and t's crossed, is a separate matter dealt with later. Still, twelve federal jurors wrangled for 113 hours, then convicted six men. Eight appellate judges, while split and tortured, let all convictions stand. Finally the Supreme Court declined to review the case. The consequence was that a complex political maneuver of many sides went formally into history as a criminal violation of federal law.

Was justice done?

Informal samplings suggest Maryland onlookers were divided. Laypersons tended to the view that something large and illegal had taken place, that conviction was proper. At the same time, many shrugged off Marlboro as little more than an extension— alas, ho hum—of Maryland's long, spotty record of political corruption. Lawyers and judges were more troubled, citing what they called questionable extensions of earlier law and a dismaying judicial tangle that darkened the case at the appellate level. At the U.S. attorney's office, it was conceded that a disappointing 25 percent of Marylanders remained unconvinced by the case presented. Among Mandel admirers, the percentage of doubtful was reckoned far higher. A brief examination of certain key circumstances may furnish a little illumination.

About two episodes, more or less separate, the Marlboro intrigue revolved. The first was a decision by the legislature to override Governor Mandel's veto of a bill that had previously passed. The bill aimed to increase Marlboro's allotted number of racing days from eighteen to thirty-six. Procedurally, Marlboro was obliged to buy the extra eighteen days from another small and struggling track at Hagerstown, Maryland, then to secure the legislature's approval for the purchase. That was the first episode, provocative but not so clear-cut as the second episode.

In this one, the scenery and action were unambiguous: later, so was intent, and intent is the prime ingredient in a fraud trial. Here the early stage was an open push by Governor Mandel for a new bill, different from the one vetoed, which would expand Marlboro's racing operations by a factor as large as four. Expansion would be sudden and dramatic, consolidating Marlboro with two far larger tracks, Pimlico and Laurel.

Of the two episodes, overriding the Governor's veto caught more popular attention as singular, even freakish. The consolidation bill was more telling. It carried in it a demonstrable fact: the bloat of Marlboro's profits, hence its value to Marlboro's owners. Inevitably it provoked a furious outrage from legislators, elbowed and confused and snuffing up the sulfurous air of a midnight hustle. The consolidation bill produced the first public outcry that fraud was suspected.

At the time, early in the 1972 session of the legislature, the veto override drew little more than quizzical interest. Why would a governor as assertive as Marvin Mandel had long shown himself to be, especially on ticklish racetrack questions, accept with quite uncharacteristic aplomb this bolt of defiance from a legislature hitherto serenely docile? Why sit still and unprotesting while his own act of considered judgment—he had called the bill "unconstitutional" on technical grounds, then vetoed it—was abruptly reversed and the bill restored as by magic to life?

No big issue seemed at stake but because political inertness had never been the Mandel way, a question was put to the Governor's floor leader in the senate. What, Senator Roy N. Staten was asked, was up? Why this change?

Staten's response was that the Governor would not object if his veto was overridden.

That was odd in itself. How come Mandel wouldn't object? Override? Why go ahead? Staten never explained, indeed denied later he had said it. Odder still, and undeniable, was the spectacle of seven Mandel loyalists in the senate, fed by Staten "the word" from above, reversing the stand they had taken no fewer than eight months previously. As recently as April, 1971, the Mandel-prodded bloc had voted solidly against expanding Marlboro—meaning, against the track's then-owners. Despite that, the bill passed, whereupon Mandel vetoed it in May.

Then came the switch. In January, 1972, in the teeth of Mandel's May veto, the Mandel seven swung around 180 degrees. Seven battleships on course, bowing to the Admiral's signal, shifted direction without question from due east to due west. This time they voted, again en bloc, to override the veto in favor of the bill—meaning, in favor of the Marlboro owners. As first ordered, they went one way. As second ordered, they went the opposite. But the bill itself was unchanged, except for being tagged with the Governor's official rejection.

So was this some kind of rebellion against the Governor? That was one explanation, if hard to accept by those long familiar with this bloc's poodlelike adherence to Mandel's heel.

Another version was that "the word" from the Governor had changed, in private, from no to yes. If that was the case, was it the change in ownership at Marlboro—the sale had occurred just twelve days earlier—which explained the change in direction on the legislative floors of Annapolis? Surface puzzles suggested unseen currents swirling elsewhere. Out back, old track owner changed to new track owner; out front, red light flicked to green. Few failed to make a connection.

If the override of the Mandel veto raised questions in January, what followed that April raised open suspicion, then furious tempers. A belated rush brought to Annapolis a bill richly festooned with racetrack riches: of these, the most glittering by far were firmly earmarked for once-starveling little Marlboro. In attendance and in racing days, in prospective revenue hence in ultimate value, Marlboro was to be escalated overnight. A snap of the legislative fingers would transform this struggling half-miler, this dowdy Cinderella of Maryland racing, to equality with the sleek, urbanized mile tracks, Pimlico and Laurel.

Consider the dimensions of Marlboro's startling good fortune that far. It had started the legislative season with a meager allotment of eighteen racing days per year, then watched the override double those to thirty-six. On top of that came this new bill suddenly, astoundingly—no reason was given—tacking on no fewer than fifty-eight days more. That made a royal total of ninety-four days, the longest, richest racing season ever conferred on a racetrack in Maryland history. Nor was that all. Marlboro was also given the power to transfer its bulging, ninety-four-day season away from its own scantily attended oval and financially exploit it, instead, via the much juicier betting pools and patronage at the big mile tracks, Pimlico or Laurel. It was trading in a rusted-out Chevrolet on a sparkling new Cadillac. Incredibly, the trade-in was free.

Free, except for politics, which instantly exploded in Fourth of July vigor. Because the bill arrived too late to meet legislative rules, the House of Delegates slammed its door. The senate, with a gulp, slipped the bill in—then immediately began to fill the air with epithets flung between factions, quickly formed. Here the battle of Marlboro was fought to a narrow finish, but an illuminating one.

At one side ranged a potent mix of backers of the consolidation bill, of racetrack lobbyists and Mandel loyalists and gubernatorial arm twisters. The Governor, standing behind the whole wriggling package, solemnly invoked the principle of racetrack consolidation. Few disputed consolidation as a worthwhile objective: Maryland horseracing had long been recognized as wildly, wastefully diffuse. It was the political machinery Marvin Mandel rolled out to squeeze things together which rang the alarm bells. Here again the old bait-and-switch: on top, a sound principle; beneath, something nice for Dale and Irv and the rest.

Opponents caught a whiff of the game, saw the Mandel-built majority, tried to obscure by heightened voices their own shortage of votes. Senator Julian Lapides, of Baltimore City, said the bill's bonanza for Marlboro "smelled to heaven." Where Mandel followers struggled in committee to preserve the bill intact, Lapides-minded senators undertook to strip out the big dollar marks. A rough standoff ensued, threatening the bill's life.

154   *Thimbleriggers*

It was at this point that the Governor personally showed his hand. He did not show all his hand, but he showed enough, cleverly (1) to get the stalled bill moving again for the moment, but not so cleverly (2) to bring excruciating embarrassment on himself at trial three years later.

The Marlboro project, worth millions to the Mandel circle, had undergone radical surgery at the hands of the grumbling senators. Out went the fifty-eight-day bulge in racing time for Marlboro. Out, too, went Marlboro's authority to raise its daily profits by using its racing time at the larger, more lucrative tracks. Also out went obvious sops to other tracks: an exorbitant buy-out for Bowie, a fattened betting take for the others. But Marlboro emerged from senate operating rooms a disaster case.

How to recoup?

Time was running short before the legislature was required to adjourn. The senate had bloodied Marlboro . . . but only the senate. So how about retreat and reformation on the stronger political ground available in the House of Delegates? How about using the house to force again into the bill all those rich blessings for Marlboro . . . then hustle back the amended bill to the senate, this time under a fresh head of political steam . . . build up behind it, say, some other bills none dared delay . . . then presto! A majority of senators, no matter how choked with resentment, couldn't say no at the last minute, could they? Marlboro—fattened for profits, prodded by political leverage—would burst through to enactment before deadline.

One who discerned part of this planned maneuver in advance was Senator Jervis Finney, a suspicious Republican. Finney had called the original Marlboro provisions "a fantastic bonanza," then voted to knock them out, observing: "If we take all the days out, you can predict that on the very last night of the session . . . who do you think is going to be getting all its days back? Good old Marlboro, coming 'round the track." Little did Jervis Finney suspect, that April of 1972, that by 1975 he would leave the senate, be appointed United States attorney and, against Governor Mandel and his friends, sign a federal indictment for fraud. Marlboro would furnish its main thrust.

Meanwhile, still deep in maneuver, Dale Hess sensed the arrival of a critical hour and stepped forward to meet it. Marlboro must go through. As a legislative venture, the track's enlargement had mostly been left to Hess from the outset. All but unseen, he had helped write the bill that produced the fifty-eight extra racing days, then the consolidation with Pimlico and Laurel. It was a masterpiece of intrigue, of diplomatic delicacy drawing in the other tracks, finally of cool bravado in presentation to the legislature. Now all that stood threatened.

A seasoned legislative ringmaster, Hess set up Annapolis headquarters in a Hilton Hotel suite handy to legislative operations. Mandel aides moved in for the fight, leaving spare clothes in the Hess suite closets. Legislators appeared on summons, absorbed liquor and instructions, disappeared when dismissed.

Strategy evolved to resurrect the Marlboro situation to the shape it had prior to application of senate scalpels—all but the extra fifty-eight days. Hess, having originated that idea, now abandoned it as too openly grabby, too provocative. A cooperative member of the house, Delegate Paul Weisengoff, was told off as point man to see the Hess-modified package through the lower house.

Now came the critical point. The house had been hostile to the bill earlier. Were enough delegates now convertible from resentment to support?

Hess could diagnose the problem, that being his appointed role. What Hess couldn't do was solve it, that role being assigned to one enjoying political leverage denied all others in Maryland.

At Hess's invitation, Governor Mandel walked into the Hilton suite at about dinner time. It was a risk he shouldn't have taken. Hess was not yet identified as an owner of Marlboro stock; Mandel still professed ignorance of who did own it. Yet that evening the relationship between these two men surfaced all but publicly in the teeth of the Marlboro struggle. It was risky but, with disaster in sight, inevitable. So there across the table, counting votes, Hess and Mandel huddled together as a half-dozen others of mixed loyalties looked on. Two close friends, two political allies, two business partners, two men engrossed in what the two together knew best: how to navigate a shaky bill through tossing legislative seas. That meeting at that crucial juncture would double the difficulty Marvin Mandel was to have later in convincing federal jurors that, if Dale Hess owned part of Marlboro Racetrack, it was news to Marvin Mandel.

One thing Mandel and Hess unquestionably knew was how to put together a legislative package. What you did was simply cluster special interests, and nearly every legislator has at least one, sufficient to run up a winning majority. In this case, Mandel and Hess enjoyed a particular advantage: their own special interests—Hess's ownership, Mandel's pocketing of Hess checks—were carefully covered up, hence generally unknown to the legislators.

Viscerally suspicious, the legislators were. Factually informed, they were not: over and over, they had been assured, the facts were not the facts. Had it been otherwise, this massaging of Marlboro—a track picked up that same year and lovingly petted by the Governor's best friends—would have been dispelled in legislative horselaughs. Even without hard facts, the legislative mood that spring carried in it ominous thunderheads. Hess and Mandel, ordinarily not foolhardy men, might well have pulled back from a storm plainly gathering. That instead they pushed ahead suggests an overeagerness bordering on desperation. However impelled, they set the trap that eight years later would clap on them and become federal prison.

Hess, to be sure, was hardened to such risks. For years he had been bootstrapping himself upward from unlettered farm boy to swinging millionaire, exploiting inside information here, pocketing a fast real estate buck there. The law? Dale Hess had watched others in politics thumb their noses at the law and walk away untouched. Besides, with the Governor at his side, Dale Hess doubted a lawman existed who had the brass to point a finger.

For Marvin Mandel, taking this plunge was not so easy. He was a sensitive man and proud. He had not treated himself to Hess-like wheeler deals, had not acquired Hess's callousness to the law. Besides, as governor, he had farther to fall, more to lose. And yet two circumstances had begun to hem him in. One was political, the other marital. Because both involved money, of which he had little, Marvin Mandel did what he had vowed never to do. He opened the door to pressures he might have otherwise withstood.

Reelection had to be dealt with in 1974. That meant money raising in 1973, now less than a year distant. So the Kovens-Hess-Rodgers types, money raisers all, had to be placated in advance. More personal, and more urgent, was Jeanne Dorsey's gathering impatience. Their love affair, for years simmering in private, had begun with the automobile accident late in 1970 to leak into public gossip. A private Mandel dilemma was turning into a private Mandel torture.

Break formally with Bootsie, his wife of three decades and

trusty political partner? Yield at last to one of Jeanne's ever more insistent deadlines on marriage? A financial mountain—lawyers' fees, a divorce settlement, wedding expenses, Jeanne's reported dress-a-day lifestyle—intervened forbiddingly. It was a mountainous decision from which Marvin Mandel shrank. But it was a mountain that, on a Friday in April, 1972, he felt he had to climb.

Saturday morning, ascent began from the Ways and Means Committee of the House of Delegates. A handful of crucial amendments, secretly written by Hess, was clapped back into the bill consolidating Marlboro with Laurel and Pimlico. In effect, the bill was suddenly restored almost to its original luscious shape. It lacked only the extra fifty-eight days earlier agreed to by Governor Mandel and actively pushed by Chairman Newton Brewer of the Racing Commission but considered to be too gross a dose by committee members.

It wasn't as much as the new Marlboro owners had first planned on wringing from an unsuspecting legislature—they wanted perhaps twice again as much—but it was what they had to settle for. The Governor, a man financially driven, undertook to give it to them. No one but he knows with what qualms he pressed the necessary buttons.

Out of the Ways and Means Committee and through the whole house the fattened-up bill sailed. Here the Mandel allies stood thickest, here his leverage achieved a political peak. At that house victory, according to the *Sun*, "two of the Governor's lobbyists shouted with glee" and ran toward the Governor's office. Across to the grumpy senate went the bill, and here resistance stayed formidable.

Senators tend to be less subject to herding than delegates, more likely to defy orders from the gubernatorial command post "upstairs." Now pressed upon them again was much the same bill that, after tumultuous wrestling with Mandel forces, they had angrily stripped down ten days earlier. Seemingly inexorable, political heat surged from the Governor's office into the legislative wires.

What now? Was the senate, on command, to swallow its jealous pride? Its old tradition of independent action? Swallow too its mounting suspicion that somehow, somewhere in the Marlboro bill there lurked something snakily sinister?

Well, not lightly. From Julian Lapides and Jervis Finney, from Victor Crawford and Meyer Emmanuel, rebellion began to bubble.

158   *Thimbleriggers*

"Upstairs" was put loudly on notice: it had set foot, unbidden, on senate turf: the bill must not pass!

Manly words; but could the senate muster the vital muscle this time? Could it match deed to word?

Unlike three months earlier, when overriding the Governor's veto was at issue, no ambiguity now clouded the Mandel wish. That wish stood forth naked and unmistakable. The Governor wished Marlboro consolidated with Pimlico and Laurel—and with all lucrative frills attached. Off hurried the household cavalry, the "Mandelniks," to see that the wish was granted.

Down the State House stairs came Racing Chairman Brewer, trailed by legislative lobbyists and political strong-arms. Even Secretary of State Fred Wineland, normally satisfied with watching over the official Maryland seal, found himself spurred to unaccustomed action. This phalanx fell upon flinching senators with such ardor that, when protests reached crescendo, the normally gentle senate president, William James, ordered the floor swept clean of Mandel persuaders. Momentarily daunted, the Mandel drive pushed forward in another form.

Soon Senator Staten, trustiest of muldoons, a state job dangled carrotlike to keep him trusty, rose to face down the rebels—or almost. At 11:25 P.M. of April 10, it seemed, Staten had had delivered into his hand sufficient senators to bring the now-tattered Marlboro dream back to sparkling life. To the senate floor came the bill, an in-rolling political tide behind it. Desperate, sensing the wall at their backs, opponents asked for quarter: Would the senate agree to a postponement of the vote? Say, to one minute before midnight, when adjournment was required by law? Couldn't they vote then instead of now?

It was an old dodge, a killer dodge: The Mandel ranks held steady: a majority flicked red-lit refusal upon the counter board at the senate's wall. Now it was last-resort time, and Senator Lapides turned to the oldest one of all—and the most impenetrable. He was prepared, he said, to filibuster, to talk and talk and talk until midnight and the deadline for adjournment arrived. That would kill not only the Marlboro bill but also, a strategic twist, a number of other bills blocked up like railroad cars on the legislative time-track behind the Marlboro bill. It was a sobering threat. Many genuinely important bills, also many of the politically pampered sort, would be lost in a Lapides filibuster.

Consternation! The Mandel majority wobbled, eroded, gave

way. Marlboro stood postponed. The senate clock crept on toward midnight, then ten minutes past. The battle was over. Marlboro had succumbed to the filibuster, died ingloriously by the clock . . . but wait.

Senator Staten's hope hadn't died, or, if so, he couldn't bring himself to believe it. No more had hopes died among the Mandelniks, looking on wordless and tense from the senate galleries. The Governor himself awaited word upstairs: Would Staten still somehow pull it off? Defy the clock and push through against all legislative barriers the lush reward riding on the Marlboro bill?

For those around him Marvin Mandel had done all he could do. Dale Hess waited for the result. Elsewhere so did Harry and Bill Rodgers and, masquerading as Tubby Schwartz, so did Irv Kovens.

In their different ways, in the still intangible future, both Bootsie Mandel and Jeanne Dorsey may have had more at stake than anyone else in the fate of Marlboro. Drastic changes in their ways of life—one change welcome, one bitterly resented—hung indirectly on a requirement that the Marlboro changes go through. To the extent that aspects of cherchez la femme had locked in Marvin Mandel, a surge of fresh money offered the key. Marlboro's expansion was up for sale.

Roy Staten didn't know all this. What he did know was that, for him, a new job seemed to be attached to the Marlboro bill. Staten knew how these things worked. Getting a fattened Marlboro pushed past the senate meant to Staten, the chief Mandel pusher, that the Governor owed him one. Good! A disappointed Governor, maybe an angry Governor, meant hardly a generous Governor. Bad!

At 12:10 A.M., Staten made his last stand. Never mind that the legislature was supposedly ten minutes past final adjournment. Never mind because Staten seemed to have the votes to pass Marlboro. The callous old steamroller custom was clear: when you have the votes, call the roll. Call it no matter what rules you crumple in the dust. A majority, like a king, can do no wrong.

Staten took the floor, his hoped-for job maybe on the line. Scheduled adjournment be damned. Call the roll on the Marlboro bill, he said. President James stood undecided. Should he call it? Certainly, the Mandel lobbyists seemed to have lined up the Marlboro vote. Or should he not? The old clock said midnight had come and gone and, with it, the legal end of the legislative session. It was a quandary a decent man shouldn't have to face.

Lapides, still flushed with his winning filibuster tactic, watched James through slitted eyes. More bullying wasn't smart; James might turn hostile. A more perceptive insight, a gentler touch . . . yes, that was it.

The Baltimore senator rose to his feet, quietly reminded James of "the dignity of this house." The clock had passed midnight, he noted, and "this [Marlboro] bill . . . has been properly defeated." Lapides sat down. James as presiding officer could rule yes or no. James hesitated. He stared, for a moment, upward into the shadowed gallery—the one where Marvin Mandel, pipe in mouth, sometimes edged around the door for a look.

James gave a little sigh. "It is improper to carry on any business at this hour," he said, whereupon the Marlboro drive fell short. If it had the votes, and it seemed to, it didn't have the time. Here was a close-run piece of generalship by Senator Lapides and those others who detected unwelcome aromas. In the minority, they dared deflect from its iron course a probable majority because they suspected the majority was, at best, politically pressured and, at worst, criminally defrauded. What Senator Lapides could not do, however, was stamp out the Marlboro enterprise once and for all.

As noted in the previous chapter, this legislative rebuff in April of 1972 was to be outflanked the following December. Turning their backs on the legislature, Marlboro's owners simply took their thirty-six authorized days of racing time and, still under cover, handed them over to be run instead at Bowie, a larger and more profitable track. Doubled days, a doubled take per day: thus the coup engineered and put into effect by the Marlboro owners, all within the year 1972. In the fall of 1973 the Racing Commission ratified the shift, and the baffled legislature followed along.

The risk had been huge. And yet for nine years—the period between April, 1971, when Irvin Kovens first made inquiries into Marlboro's value, and April, 1980, when the Supreme Court brushed aside the last appeal against mail fraud convictions—the Mandel circle evaded punishment. As against the risk, the price tag offers some curious human insights.

To buy Marlboro the initial outlay had been $2.4 million, mostly borrowed. The selling price, after a year of political inflation, was $4.5 million. So the net profit as of December, 1972, was $2.1 million, a bit short of the original investment. A quick $2 million, hence a profit not to be sneezed away by ordinary investors. But this profit was scarcely ordinary.

Was it worth, for example, the risk of prolonged public humiliation at trial? The federal prison terms then given four of the six? The question of worth is especially pointed in that the $2 million had to be sliced six ways among men already millionaires several times over.

Mandel was no millionaire, nor was Cory. But Kovens nursed a pile perhaps $15 million high; Hess, Tidewater blessed, held as much as one-third that much. The Rodgers brothers had earlier topped a million apiece, and by 1971 were well on their way, via their sprawling Tidewater operations, toward a life higher and more velvety still. Excepting only Mandel, who had use for every penny, these men didn't need the money at all.

What's more, all were men of personal pride. None had a criminal record, not even criminal reputes. Each in his own way carried a certain position in society: Mandel as a governmental statesman, Kovens as a prominent community leader, Hess as a developer-tycoon in bud, the Rodgerses as newly bright lights in the business establishment; Cory as a likeable politico-lawyer. These men were surely not raw raiders, although Mandel, for one, tended to think himself and the others treated as outsiders. Rather they enjoyed the sort of status all the more carefully cherished because, being new, it had little resilience to shock. By a trial, by a prison term, they, their wives, and their children would be certain sufferers, their fondest hopes gone down the drain.

So why this big gamble? Why for a handful of crumbs tumbling off a chopped-up couple of million most were getting along nicely without?

Perhaps no one ever has enough money. Money begets money, meaning it begets the yearning for more, hence begets strong motive. Money newly acquired, in particular, generates its own gnawing appetites, appetites self-devouring and insatiable. One former prosecutor long seasoned in snaffling rich-man felons discerns a macho strain, a small-boy pride in financial muscle. It's not, this man says, financial security they're after, not extra comforts or even exotic luxuries. They have all that, and still they reach out for the risky extra million.

To them it is not so much money for spending as it is notches on a gun, scalps slung from a belt, medals pinned on a tunic. These things you don't spend. These you count: You count more notches, scalps, or medals than I? Then you're the bigger, better man. Same with dollars clumped up by the million, clumped unspendably high. Yet uneasily you keep clumping and counting, clumping and counting because—who knows? Around the next corner comes a man clumped higher than you. From his pinnacle, he looks down on you, as soon does all the world. For all you know is money making. It's all you are, and you've come up short of the next man. Your own damning yardstick, a crucial million missing, measures you a failure.

So run ruminations on the perils of insecure wealth. So runs Sammy—and Irv and Dale and Harry and Bill and Ernie. But not Marvin, a man found in a different context. To Marvin Mandel money was real and spendable, not some bedeviling abstraction. And of the six men convicted for mail fraud, it was Marvin Mandel who pocketed the greatest number of shadowed dollars.

One document was crucial to the jury's decision on Marvin Mandel. Looked at one way, the document was innocent, a mere device to pay the Governor some leftover legal fees owed him by Dale Hess. Looked at another way, it was guilty, a bribe in return for Mandel's help in fattening up Marlboro Racetrack.

Useful in unraveling this puzzle is the amount conveyed by the document from Hess to Mandel. If the amount was $15,000, as Mandel said, it was probably legal fees. If instead it was up to $320,000, as some calculations indicated, it was probably a bribe. So the question was, just what did this document convey? Something small? Or something large?

On its face, the document assigned to Mandel 4 percent of some part of a partnership called Security Investment Inc. That was plain. But what part? Four percent of the company's income alone? Or, a part larger by far, 4 percent of the entire partnership, its capital as well as its income? $15,000 or $320,000? Legal fees or bribe?

The agreement between Hess and Mandel was signed by each and dated December 1, 1971, a time when the Marlboro Racetrack deal was first being put together. To determine what role in the deal the Hess-to-Mandel assignment played, if any, consider first this exchange in court between Barnet Skolnik and Marvin Mandel:

Skolnik—And you had certainly, by April of 1973, when you were telling us when you got out of Security Investment Com-

pany, you had certainly by that time read the assignment that
you are holding in your lap which says that you own 4 percent of
any assets which Mr. Hess owns; isn't that correct? You had read
it, hadn't you, sir?

Mandel—I had read it, and all, as far as I was concerned,
Mr. Hess was conveying to me was four-ninths of the income that
he would get from Security Investment, and that is the monthly
income, and that's all I ever got.

Consider second the pertinent parts of the text of the assign-
ment itself:

THIS AGREEMENT is made this 1st day of December, 1971, by and
between W. DALE HESS, of Fallston, State of Maryland, first party (hereinafter called "Hess") and Marvin Mandel, of Baltimore City, State of
Maryland, second party (hereinafter called "Mandel").

EXPLANATORY STATEMENT

Hess is a General Partner in Security Investment Company, a limited
partnership, having a 9% participation therein. A copy of the partnership agreement of said Partnership is attached hereto and made a part
hereof as though fully set forth herein.

Hess has contributed capital to said Partnership in the amount of
$90.00. Hess is further obligated to advance additional sums, all as more
fully set forth in said partnership agreement. Mandel has paid to Hess
the sum of $40.00 the receipt of which Hess hereby acknowledges, for a
44.44% interest in Hess' 9% participation therein (or an interest equal to
4% of said entire Partnership).

NOW, THEREFORE, in consideration of the sum of $5.00 and of other
good and valuable considerations, the receipt of all of which is hereby
acknowledged, the parties hereto have agreed, and by these presents do
agree, as follows:

FIRST: Hess acknowledges the receipt of $40.00 from Mandel and
declares that Mandel is the owner of a 44.44% interest in Hess' 9% participation in the limited partnership referred to in the Explanatory Statement hereof, and has the right to participate in Hess' capital account,
income, profits, distribution and assets to the extent of such interest.
Hess hereby acknowledges that (subject to the provisions of Paragraph
SECOND) to the extent of said 44.44% interest in Hess' participation in
said partnership, Hess is holding same as agent for Mandel, it being the

intent hereof that (subject to Paragraph SECOND), Mandel shall be deemed the absolute owner of said 44.44% interest. It is understood that the percentage interest of 44.44% hereunder is intended to be equal to 4% of said entire capital account and partnership income, profits, distributions, and assets, and no more.

SECOND: Mandel agrees to pay to Hess within 15 days of his written demand, 44.44% of any sums which Hess may be required to pay under said partnership agreement and, further, agrees to pay to Hess 44.44% of any sums which Hess may be required to pay by virtue of Hess' signing any notes or other obligation in connection with any mortgage or deed of trust executed pursuant to the terms of said partnership or any other liability which Hess may incur by reason of his participation in said partnership.

THIRD: In the event Mandel fails to meet, in writing, his obligations hereunder, he agrees promptly to offer to sell all of his right, title and interest in Hess' participation in said partnership or under this Agreement without first offering, in writing, to sell the same to Hess at and for the fair market value of said interest. If Hess shall not accept said offer within 45 days, it shall be deemed rejected. In determining the fair market value of said interest the parties shall first attempt to agree, within 30 days of the date of said offer, as to said value and shall use their best efforts to do so. . . .

Hess agrees to give to Mandel promptly copies of all reports given to him by the partnership, and to keep Mandel fully informed as to the said partnership's activities.

Hess further agrees to pay or assign to Mandel when received, 44.44% of any monies, land or anything else of value which he may receive under the terms of said partnership. . . .

IN WITNESS WHEREOF W. Dale Hess and Marvin Mandel have signed and sealed these presents this 1st day of December, 1971.

WITNESS:

_____   _____(SEAL)
                                          W. Dale Hess

_____   _____(SEAL)
                                          Marvin Mandel

166

By April of 1973 Marvin Mandel had been warned by advisors, he said, that public disclosure of this arrangement with Hess could be embarrassing. People might suspect something untoward was afoot. To squelch any such suspicion, the Governor said, he canceled the arrangement. He did this in a curious way.

On his own he hand wrote out this statement and dated it "4/10/73":

> The within agreement is hereby declared null and void and of no force or effect and is cancelled in full.
>
> Marvin Mandel

Although Dale Hess had signed the original agreement, his signature does not appear with Mandel's signature on the cancellation. Nor does the signature of any witness.

Mandel wrote out his cancellation on the back, not of an original document, but on what appeared to be a Xerox copy of an original document. This copy did carry original signatures penned by Hess and Mandel, but a mystery remained: What became of the original document itself, as originally typed?

Despite government demands, this original agreement was never produced in court; only a copy of it made an appearance. Prosecutors speculated, more or less openly, that the original did exist, that it too was signed, that it was worth a small fortune to the Governor, that it was in hiding somewhere, and that, since it seemingly stood uncanceled, Marvin Mandel still owned his 4 percent share of Security Investment. Defendants said that wasn't so.

10.

The Snoopers
Begin to Snoop

Barney Skolnik had never before seen Frank DeFilippo when, early in February of 1974, a reporter friend of both pointed out DeFilippo across a crowded courthouse floor.

Skolnik stared. "That's DeFilippo?"

"You want to meet him?"

"I'm going to meet him . . . later. Oh, I'm going to meet him. Later, yes."

A flicker of prosecutorial steel? A vengeful hint at the future?

More likely flickering was Skolnik's own unquenchable irony, his self-parody of the macho enforcer circling his targeted quarry—Marvin Mandel was then DeFilippo's boss—more than eighteen months in advance. And yet, ironical or not, the remark was in fact made, perhaps a subliminal prophecy.

To this day, Mandel sympathizers discern sinister maneuvers. See! they say, see how early Skolnik said that! His words prove it was Mandel the feds were after all along, not Hess and Rodgers, certainly not Joseph Alton. Even getting Agnew was an accidental detour on the way to Mandel. For the Mandel investigation, they insist, drew its spark from a high-level political feud. It was Nixon Republicans out to persecute Mandel Democrats, Washington hunting down political challengers in Maryland. For flavor, hints about anti-Semitism were sprinkled in, hints hard to believe considering that two of the three men on the prosecuting team were born Jewish.

Shreds of this obsession would cling to the Mandel case for years, receding only grudgingly before the dispassionate onroll of judicial machinery. Political overtones rang out all right, if of an uncommon variety. His subsequent DeFilippo encounter had the bizarre effect of presenting Skolnik with (1) a moment, rare for him, of almost total speechlessness and (2) a fragment of testimony seemingly so thunderous he later used it on two separate occasions to keynote his case against the Mandel circle.

For DeFilippo did what no one else could do or, anyway, no one did. He injected Mandel early and deeply—for a paying job—into a highly prejudicial bed. This was the bed already abounce with the men from Tidewater Insurance, a bumptious band happily accustomed to cuddling politicians like disco club pickups. He gave strong color to the damning liaison each of six defendants denied most fiercely and which, in the end, crushed all in its scabrous embrace. What gave DeFilippo's testimony its special credibility was his militant personal loyalty, not to the prosecution, but to the defense where his own roots grew. Plainly, and regardless of the consequences, the man was telling the truth.

Truth from DeFilippo was the last thing Skolnik had expected. Maybe it was the smoldering presence at DeFilippo's shoulder of Governor Mandel, the man he served as chief of staff. Maybe it was the combative nature of DeFilippo himself, a spirited ex-newsman in the damn-your-eyes Hildy Johnson tradition. Whyever, Skolnik had led his list of Mandel associates "not to be trusted" with the name of Frank DeFilippo.

It was November of 1975 and late in the investigatory phase when Skolnik discovered his mistake squarely before the grand jury. Not that DeFilippo went soft under the Skolnik probe. To the contrary, his manner before the grand jurors openly proclaimed cold anger, his firm dislike of the man he perceived as bullying the Governor. Yet in answer after answer, even to questions he could have safely lied in answering without detection, DeFilippo's words rang to Skolnik surprisingly true.

Almost a day was consumed in this chilly duel. Skolnik thrust, DeFilippo parry. After six hours only routine cleanup questions were still to be ticked off. A little wearily Skolnik touched on the fairly remote matter of Mandel's own contingency planning. Political life is notoriously unstable: Had the Governor ever discussed his personal future with DeFilippo? If so, when?

Oh, not long after the legislature first elevated him in 1969 temporarily to succeed Spiro Agnew, gone up from governor to vice-president.

Well, what if Mandel lost at the polls in 1970? Any job offers in advance?

Uh, yeah.

Skolnik, as if absent-minded, loosed a long shot question: Any talk of Mandel going to work for Tidewater Insurance?

Skolnik had little but guesswork to sustain a question so far-fetched. Besides, of a half-dozen Mandel cronies questioned earlier, all had roundly denied any job offer by Tidewater to the newly hatched governor. Had DeFilippo too said no, as expected, Skolnik would have shrugged it off as probably true.

DeFilippo did not say no. Instead, he said yes . . . yes, there had been talk of Tidewater and a job there for Mandel.

Skolnik maintained an outward calm. Inwardly, he froze in astonishment. Had he caught DeFilippo's words correctly? Was the Governor's chief of staff, of his own free will, offering up the Governor's head on this Tidewater platter? Later, Skolnik would list the moment among the investigation's "incredible bomb-shells," but at the time he feigned an unruffled aplomb fitting for a panther surely stalking a freshly laid spoor.

Oh? Elaborate unsurprise. Next, a pretense of information already in hand too heavily documented to permit contradiction. Oh? How much of all this Tidewater matter do you recall? Your own words please.

Comfortably, free of twitches, hence quite believably, DeFilippo let his memory run. This exchange had arisen early in 1970, he said, about the risk of the upcoming elections. Marvin Mandel explained, he went on, that that awkward possibility—personal unemployment—had already been taken care of. As DeFilippo remembered it, the Governor said he had reached an understanding with Harry Rodgers, the dominant partner in Tidewater Insurance and a personal Mandel friend. The understanding was, a Tidewater job awaited Mandel when he needed it. An "option" he could pick up.

What's more, DeFilippo recalled, Mandel had said something about a letter that put this understanding with Harry Rodgers into writing. DeFilippo said he never actually saw this letter. But that would have exceeded the secretly jubilant Skolnik's giddiest dreams. A letter never did turn up and, anyway, the loss didn't really count.

What counted was this revelation of the Tidewater understanding, this potential Mandel job, and, mainly, this believability with which DeFilippo as a first-person, authoritative witness invested his own testimony. Here was stage-setting beyond price. Here, in vivid poster paint, was a cozy connection linking a needy, almost threadbare governor on one hand and, on the other, a swinging, politically prehensile corporation populated with close Mandel friends.

It was a connection that carried two impressions few could miss. One was that, at the end of his gubernatorial term, Marvin Mandel was awaited by Tidewater, its corporate arms open. A juicy salary, surely in the six-figure range, beckoned. The second impression, confirming the first, was that Tidewater thereafter held Mandel by the throat, that he must leap to Tidewater's spur as long as he was governor, or risk losing its generous goodwill.

This connection, furthermore, was no belated product of the closing Mandel years. DeFilippo dated his conversation with the Governor in the opening weeks of 1970. This meant the Mandel-Rodgers understanding could have been struck as early as 1969, weeks after Mandel took office. So, if DeFilippo was to be believed, Mandel knew throughout his time in power that Tidewater and a personal prosperity he never dared dream for himself beckoned nine years down that road. Tidewater became his rich uncle, his safety net, ultimately his Valhalla. He had but to behave.

Skolnik was sure that at trial DeFilippo's words would make a quick and lasting dent in the minds of most jurors. Consequently, he used DeFilippo—who was loyal to the Governor, who hated to wound him yet found it necessary to tell the truth—as his leadoff witness in each of the two trials. His testimony was not hard evidence, not tangible enough to nail down a conviction. What it furnished was the essential framework of atmosphere, readily grasped, in which an otherwise somewhat miscellaneous series of facts would later fall together in a pattern. An overriding sense of corruption would take hold. A sense of guilty action must emerge.

Another bearer of somewhat the same message was Nathan Cohen, who, in a parallel connection, would quote Dale Hess as saying: "We [Hess, Rodgers, and Rodgers, all Tidewater men] take care of the Governor in various ways, such as giving him a participation in business ventures we may be in." Hess too, according to Cohen, spoke of hidden business deals backed up by letters to Mandel. But Cohen, unlike DeFilippo, seemed personally vulnerable: he had been caught in questionable zoning maneuvers then still unresolved. This led to attacks on his integrity as a witness, to defense sneers at testimony by the government's "scared rabbit." Even so, Cohen's words added to the dire atmospherics of the case, or thus reasoned Barney Skolnik, a man so enchanted by on-stage flavors that he personally once volunteered as spear carrier in a Washington theatrical production he liked.

DeFilippo's candor was not the investigation's first dramatic turn. It was only one episode, and a late one at that, in a long, noisy overture to indictment. This overture was as theatrical as it was political, as vindictive as it was extralegal. If with a clatter quite uncommon, the Mandel trial got underway informally outside the courtroom long before charges were filed inside. This pretrial contest was fought out between what would become, once securely reined into the courtroom, the prosecution and the defense. Many who came to deplore all this as unseemly stayed to look on with relish.

Rules were in short supply, elbows flew on both sides. Press, radio, and television furnished the public stage. Politics, theater, and something resembling the law furnished the action. What no onlooker could miss was that the heat was on and that Marvin Mandel was fighting for his political life.

Frank DeFilippo, fastest tongue on the Severn River, furnished the Governor's first line of defense. Disparaging "information," of course, leaked freely under both doors. News reporters joyously wrung out both sides; no amount of editorial harrumphing in Baltimore and Washington settled the bubbles.

Still, beneath the surface, maneuvers were cool and deliberate, for large purposes stood directly in conflict. At each turn, cards dealt high and low to each side had to be plunked down as if winners.

With the government lay the initiative, an immeasurable advantage. It could start proceedings, stall for tactical reasons, sashay deceptively sidewise. The government knew where it was leading;

the defense could but follow willy nilly. An asset at least as telling was the government's long-seasoned team of investigators.

Barnet Skolnik, with his associates, had just brought down a vice-president of the United States, plus a half-dozen others. Skolnik was the team's acknowledged leader: quick and brilliant, a tireless tracker, as loquacious as he was ironic. A plump, dark figure on the verge of legendary legal repute. Ronald Liebman was the team philosopher and, in private, the practical joker who to long-strained evenings of investigation could restore a measure of perspective. Daniel J. Hurson was a little junior but the legal scholar: it was Hurson who haunted the law libraries, checked out statutes, found the pertinent precedent. They made a formidable team, all still in their 30s.

Masterfully they had learned to load, aim, and fire the awesome federal weapons at hand: Internal Revenue Service, FBI, grand jury subpoenas, Justice Department. For the routine defendant, as well breast a whirling buzzsaw.

Still another federal asset—however vague, however unacknowledged—was the then-dour mood of Maryland. By 1975 the state's record for political corruption was long and stained. To their own dismay, Marylanders had been forced by the Johnson-Brewster-Baggett-Rocks-Anderson-Alton-Agnew round of shames to question, in political cases, the ancient presumption of innocence. Mandel's political origins—Jack Pollack and George Hocker, Dale Hess and Irv Kovens—were scarcely reassuring. If there wasn't a presumption of guilt, there lay in the community a sad sort of presumption that something was more likely wrong than right.

Adroitly, the U.S. attorney's office left that dreary cloud to hang in the air, unexaggerated but also undisturbed. As a result the defendants never resolved a deep conflict of their own: whether to flee mortified Maryland, via change of venue, or instead to stand and fight out a trial in their home ballpark. The question was not easily answered.

For the defense had its assets too, chief among them the prestige of the strongest and probably most popular public figure in the state, Governor Marvin Mandel. He had proven an effective administrator, an artful compromiser. Twice at the polls, in 1970 and 1974, he had shown a matchless ability to seize the public confidence and hold it. He felt certain he could do that again. He felt particularly confident if in advance of trial he could detour past the law's grasp to his own political grounds, there to resolve safely the struggle he foresaw gathering on legal ground where he felt less at home, hence less secure.

So it was that the Governor undertook to shake loose betimes from the unwelcome inhibitions of a federal courtroom. George Beall and his senatorial brother, Glenn, were early targets of a barrage soon rolling out of Annapolis. George came under fire because as U.S. attorney he had launched the investigation of Hess and Rodgers; Glenn, because his senatorial campaign in the 1970 elections had imbibed, incautiously, a $200,000 draft poured out anonymously by Richard Nixon's Washington money raisers. This was the "townhouse" operation, made to sound evilly like a Watergate subsidiary.

Why, the Mandel quarter accusingly asked, hadn't brother investigated brother? Brotherhood alone? Or was it because both were Republicans, not Democrats like Hess, Rodgers, and their patron, the Governor? Touché! or more accurately, only semi-touché: it had been George Beall, earlier, who had hauled fellow Republican Agnew from the vice-presidency.

When Beall gave way as U.S. attorney to Jervis Finney, another Republican, Annapolis raised fresh complaints. Finney, who signed the papers indicting Mandel, had been in his days as state senator an open Mandel enemy, hadn't he? Carrying on an old personal feud, wasn't he?

Finally, when it turned out Skolnik was the true sparkplug of the investigation, there came a telephoned voice to a newspaper editor. Skolnik? said the voice. Look up the sorry details of Skolnik's divorce action in New York, then print it. The gritty voice was that of Irvin Kovens, the Governor's oldest and best friend. As if by paradox, the divorced Skolnik had sympathized personally with Mandel's own agonized divorce. Also, voted for him in 1970, but not in 1974.

Higher still as the investigation grew more menacing shot the arrows from Marvin Mandel's bow. Now it wasn't just Nixon's underlings stabbing unfairly at the Governor: it was Nixon himself, a president quoted (third-hand) in 1972 as counting Mandel among the five ablest Democrats across the nation, men he feared would soon turn up to challenge him from the floor of the United States Senate. So pick off Mandel in advance was the supposed Nixon instruction to the Justice Department. If you don't believe that version, Marvin Mandel said, go ask Nixon's attorney gen-

eral. John Mitchell himself, Mandel said, had told him personally. He added that the Justice Department still housed the telltale
records. To date, he has not produced them.

What Marvin Mandel did do, at about the time Skolnik was
wrapping up his legal investigation, was wrap up his own pretrial, rear-guard maneuvers. This took the form of a detailed letter
of protest, including many of the above items, to the Justice
Department: it was a Mandel cry of persecuted innocence, of
unfair tactics, of history misunderstood. A bugged telephone,
intimidated witnesses, prejudiced prosecutors, other public officials who did worse: such was the infuriated tone of the Mandel
letter. Get these devils, it said in effect, off my back. This extraordinary document was dated November 7, 1975—less than three
weeks before Mandel and five others were indicted. When on
December 3 the Mandel letter began appearing in the daily
papers, it seemed as though it had been leaked unofficially, from
Annapolis.

The following day, at arraignment proceedings, Skolnik ver-
bally brushed off all these allegations as "totally devoid of truth"
and "simply fatuous nonsense." He tossed in as analysis the old
legal saw: "If the facts are against you, pound the law; if the law
is against you, pound the facts; if both the law and the facts are
against you, pound the prosecutors."

Indeed the letter, largely a product of Frank DeFilippo's flash-
ing pen, had little to do with the law but a lot to do with political
perceptions. It amounted to Mandel's final desperate stab at a
political life preserver, at a last-minute rescue from the legal
waters he saw rising ominously about him. He had lost the investigatory phase of the struggle. The next phase meant abandoning
the Governor's own field of political expertise for Skolnik's courtroom, a source of relief for the essentially apolitical prosecutor.
Now, formally laid out before a jury, the main event could begin.

This breakthrough had been slow, even uncertain in coming. A
year earlier investigators picked up supposed footprints almost by
accident and, baffled in the pursuit, all but gave up the trail in
September, 1974. These footprints, anyway, had not been identified as left by Marvin Mandel. Instead they were those of Dale
Hess and Harry Rodgers, a twosome thought to be contemporary
practitioners of an ancient and hard-bitten art. This was peddling
political influence, with payoffs cleverly piped through corpo-

rate, hence unsuspected, channels. The influence Hess and Rodgers were thought to have for sale, to be sure, emanated from the governor's office inhabited by Marvin Mandel. Even so, at this stage, no finger pointed at Mandel even indirectly. No credible accuser called his name.

What had alerted investigators was word from witnesses— themselves frankly guilty, hence deeply frightened—left over from federal cases against the immediately preceding set of Maryland misbehavers. After the fall of Anderson and Alton and Agnew, witnesses against them said, corruption declared no holiday in Maryland. Instead, the old tradition was called alive and well—indeed, it seemed to have resurrected refinements at the hands of Hess and Rodgers.

One refinement rested on performance bonds, a financial commodity pressed down upon contractors by a politically muscular bond agency. The second bore national overtones. It was an exercise in trading off funds raised for a presidential election in return for the award, postelection, of juicy federal leases. Each was potentially criminal, neither easy to prove. Both involved tentacles of the Tidewater Insurance octopus, a phenomenal corporate creature half-seen and half-unseen. Tidewater was known at the investigation's outset to inhabit the political deep. At the end, its key men were found awash on a rocky beach.

The investigation stalled inconclusively as 1974 unfolded. One reason was preoccupation in the U.S. attorney's office with other, seemingly more important, derelictions. The Anderson case developed hang-ups; Agnew's retreat left titillating mysteries. Only a half-hearted push went into digging up Hess-Rodgers answers. Still, bits later proved provocative were unearthed, first about their performance bond operations.

Here is a familiar arm twister, long established and lovingly played by locals out to make politics pay. Its fulcrum is a state law, as in Maryland, which for excellent reason requires that a contractor undertaking, say, a difficult bridge construction furnish a financial guarantee, or bond. This is reassurance to the public that he will actually perform the job he contracts to perform. So far, clearly, so legitimate. Thereafter political leverage moves in.

What bonding house, for example, is to furnish the contractor his performance bond? Many companies, many agencies, elbow for position; all hustle after this high-profit, low-risk business.

Seasoned contractors know this and know, too, that a bond source that enjoys political relations with the state government awarding contracts is a bond source with an extra dimension. Red tape can be cut from contracts, hard specifications softened, approvals and overruns hustled through.

A piquant delicacy in all this is that no real connection, no inside track to the contracting authority, is really necessary. The name is as good as the game—no, actually is the game—and Tidewater in those days had played upon its own ambivalent position with skill and authority.

A crafty Georgia insurance man once confirmed for the *Washington Post* that this relationship may be partly factual, partly fanciful, but fully operative either way. As he told it to the *Post*, Paul F. Morrison had a Georgia client seeking a contract with the Maryland government, which was beyond Morrison's reach. But Morrison counseled his client: go to Tidewater for your bond; in Maryland, it's the "politically right, anointed" firm, one of which is found in every state.

Why "anointed"? Because of Tidewater's Mandel connection or, anyway, its repute for linkage on high. Earlier, under Agnew, this same Morrison had steered hopeful Georgia contractors to a different Maryland insurance agency, one rated friendly to Agnew. Upon the switch of governors in 1969, Morrison deftly switched inquiring clients over to Tidewater. It was no more than a businesslike recognition of a shift in political realities.

To that extent, it was also an exercise safely within the law. No Maryland statute forbids giving business to political friends over political enemies, provided all else is equal. What federal agents began to pick up, however, were reports that all else was not necessarily equal.

Was it possible, as some witnesses said, that Hess and Rodgers were twisting contractors' arms? Was a Tidewater-provided bond the only ticket to a contract in Maryland? Conversely, did sudden, unwelcome obstacles arise to plague contractors so brazen as to secure bonding elsewhere than with the anointed Tidewater? Did letters exist which could be called threatening?

That possibility threw a different, harsher light on Hess and Rodgers and the Mandel connection. Political leverage was obvious, maybe ominous. Was there a hint of extortion here? A refrain suggested itself: get bonded by Tidewater, Mr. Contractor, or go build birdcages and not bridges. Beyond that, what of the Governor himself? Was Mandel too somehow cut in on the happy bonanza?

For bonanza it had become. An inquiry by the *Baltimore Sun* uncovered in mid-1974, more than five years after Marvin Mandel took office, Tidewater's extraordinary good fortune. The first five Mandel years brought its partners $185 million in performance bonds for state roads alone, a leap from less than 5 percent to 25 percent of the total. In one particularly flush year, Tidewater handled almost half the performance bond total in the state. Federal investigators thought that near-monopoly curious, considering that the road contracts emerged from state machinery dominated by Marvin Mandel, close friend of Dale Hess and Harry Rodgers.

A second enterprise the federals found provocative was the sudden leap across party lines performed, in 1972, by the same pair of Mandel friends. Rodgers and Hess, lifelong Democrats, abruptly turned up as active leaders in the Maryland presidential campaign for Richard M. Nixon, the Republican incumbent. Leaping Nixon-ward with them was a still-closer Mandel friend, another once-sturdy Democrat, Irvin Kovens. Mandel's own trio of political money raisers began, simultaneously, to raise political money for the Republican president. Mandel himself kept to lukewarm loyalty for the Democratic nominee, Senator George McGovern.

It was true that Maryland Democrats had long been a contrary breed given to party inconstancy in presidential season. Still, this Rodgers-Hess-Kovens trio had scarcely been known for ideological impulse. These were deliberate men, political brokers at home in the wheel and the deal, in the big-dollar dinner, then in the exertion of leverage for purposes other than principle. So why the $17,000 and more they personally gave to keep Nixon in office? Why did Rodgers take on the chairmanship of a Democratic group that raised up to $150,000 in Nixon money? What did Nixon matter to Harry Rodgers?

The Justice Department hadn't far to look for an answer. A little inquiry uncovered $5 million in federal leases, one batch on buildings at Baltimore-Washington International Airport, another at the Social Security complex in Woodlawn. The $5 million was collected annually by owner-partners in the buildings, including Hess and Rodgers; escalators for inflation were included. Rich as this arrangement was, it had stumbled into an awkward tangle in party affiliations.

At birth, the arrangement was soundly Democratic. Its origin lay in the later years of the Lyndon B. Johnson administration. To cement that liaison, the Woodlawn lease included among its partners Clifton C. Carter, a Johnson White House assistant. Suddenly, in came Nixon and the Republicans: Would the leases survive a party changeover? To keep the $5 million rolling and perhaps to better it, Maryland Democrats for Nixon emerged, with Harry Rodgers, understandably, as its chairman.

Spicy particles emerged from this federal poking about in the affairs of Hess and Rodgers and of their many-oared vessel, Tidewater. And yet, concrete evidence was insufficient to justify a trip to the grand jury, at least not along the influence-peddling line under inquiry, and not in 1974. There were fragments and indications, probabilities and must-have-beens; there was not a prosecutable case. By November, investigators had all but abandoned Hess and Rodgers as game lying exposed to the gun. Later, fresh trails would appear. And fresh quarry, larger by far.

What 1974's investigation did begin to open up was the labyrinthine growth of Tidewater and its potential, at least, for exploiting government in Maryland. Tidewater turned out under scrutiny to be more than a single company, more than the simple insurance business as which it first set out. It had metastasized into a series of companies and partnerships, sometimes separate, sometimes interlinked. From their insurance base, Tidewater men had reached out to touch real estate and development, contracting and construction, leasing and maintenance. A stab at banking in western Maryland brought upon Hess and Rodgers the embarrassment of a formal legislative investigation into whether they were peddling influence, whether Governor Mandel's son Gary helped them. After the Governor personally, furiously, intervened, the investigation grudgingly shut down.

The net of it was this: unobtrusively, with startling speed, Tidewater was becoming one of Maryland's most dynamic conglomerates. It was a conglomerate that seemed to have drifted on stage from nowhere in Maryland's identifiable business world. It was a bootstrap product, instead, of the state's political world, opportunists skilled at making the most of inside connections to break into what had long been thought an almost unbreakable business establishment. It would identify Marvin Mandel as a sort of political interloper himself and, with loving hunger, would swallow him too.

For all their upstart parallels, Mandel did not invent Tidewater or it him. George Hocker, a jumped-up beer lobbyist, shoved each along at a critical moment, little dreaming that his own tumbrel was attached. All Hocker had in mind, when he planted the Tidewater seed in 1959, was to cultivate some campaign financing for his own patron, J. Millard Tawes, just inaugurated governor. Though Tawes was a gamesman long adept at political patronage, and though no form of patronage existed more fruitful, financially, than a tame insurance agency, there was a hitch. As an Eastern Shoreman and non-Baltimorean, Tawes enjoyed no trusty insurance connection of his own in the city's financial establishment. Would Hocker manufacture one?

Hocker would, and did, whereupon the new firm was huffily denounced by old-line insurance agencies, themselves long at the political feedbag. Tidewater was political, they said self-righteously, as if they had never known the taste. It jostled them at this feedbag; it was outrageous. Tough Hocker stood unperturbed. Dispenser of jobs, raiser of money, backstage wielder of influence for the gentle Tawes, he shaped Tidewater with a sure touch. With Philip Tawes, the governor's son, as a partner, bond-buying contractors could not easily miss the political banner raised aloft. Another partner was Harry Rodgers, a genuinely keen insurance professional: he would run the business. Finally, Hocker took a third partnership for himself: he would keep Tidewater responsive to Tawes administration needs.

Prosperity, so baited, could not hold back. By the time Millard Tawes went out of office in 1967—and assumed, symbolically, the company chairmanship for himself for a time—Tidewater ranked among the top three insurance agencies in Maryland. Hocker, laboring both for his governor and for himself, had created in the state a new political fact, an enduring one. Within three years after Tawes, Tidewater would skillfully reposition itself under Marvin Mandel, there to proliferate exuberantly. Ultimately, it would feel the lightnings in federal court.

The advent of Tidewater carried a significance broader than its part in the Mandel collapse. It marked the conjunction of two trends already visible, maybe inevitable, in Maryland's political unfolding. One was the ever-nagging, increasingly urgent need for a new source of political money: television alone, already recognized as the make-or-break medium at election time, proved a ravenous consumer of dollars. Next, contrarily, the old techniques and the old machinery for raising money were eroding rapidly. Neighborhood political clubs faded, party discipline went soft; job holders bared defiant teeth at election-time shake-downs. Too often for complacence, the legendary "Mr. Wiseinski" limped back to party headquarters with his "little black bag" only skimpily filled. Something had to be done.

What George Hocker began to do was convert the Democratic party, once a political organization, into a money-raising vehicle. Tidewater, fueled by performance bonds, hummed away largely out of sight, hidden under the party hood. To this input Hocker added a newly sharpened version of the once-genial old testimonial dinner: at $100 for a $20 plate, a neat profit was turned, and businessmen who somehow had avoided Tidewater's clutch were pointedly advised to buy tables of ten. One eager understudy of the Hocker fund-raising elegancies, Irvin Kovens, developed a dossier of vulnerable names to whom he could consign dinner tickets wholesale. The understanding was that the recipient of tickets faced a stern choice—either retail the tickets elsewhere or eat ten testimonial dinners himself.

Tawes election campaigns, thanks to Hocker, seldom suffered a money shortage. Later, enjoying enhancements by Rodgers and Kovens and Hess, money raising for Mandel's campaigns would be converted from a political art almost to a military science. So aggressively was money extracted, so complete was the coverage, that one would-be challenger to Mandel surrendered in advance in 1974. Financially, Sargent Shriver found he faced scorched earth, Rodgers-Kovens-Hess having smoked out Maryland fat cats weeks earlier. Shriver turned elsewhere.

All this made an unlovely scene. Reformers winced, editorial writers viewed with alarm, political cartoonists drew belching hippopotamuses. But the law stood helplessly still, trapped by the United States Constitution. True enough, in the common view, that this money-raising machine depended on someone holding public office, that trading political influence for money was illegal—or should be. Overriding that stood the First Amendment with its guarantee of free speech, which by extension had been held to include the gift of money to political candidates. Giving money was one way an American was called free to express himself, to back his opinion in the public forum. George Hocker's profitable invention was better than fool-proof. It was cop-proof too, at least in its original version.

As those who live by the sword also tend to die by it, George

Hocker failed to survive for long the end in 1967 of J. Millard Tawes's years in office. Spiro Agnew's post-Tawes two years as governor provided only a brief interregnum; wanly, Tidewater trod Republican water. In 1969, that suddenly changed. Up went Agnew to vice-president; to replace him as governor, in came Marvin Mandel. A Democrat was back on top in Maryland, but for George Hocker not the right Democrat, not Millard Tawes. Never mind that Hocker had engineered Mandel's earlier elevation to Speaker of the House of Delegates, never mind that without that political springboard Mandel's chance for governor was highly doubtful. Never mind, because the Hocker-Mandel relationship was cool to hostile. Philip Tawes stood no nearer this new well-spring of political power.

Besides, Harry Rodgers was impatient to try on the larger political visions long vetoed by the cautious Hocker. As the only genuine insurance man of the three, it was plain to Rodgers by 1971 that Tidewater's assets other than his own expertise were worn perilously thin. He shucked off this Hocker-laid political pipeline to the governor's office as casually as he would have turned in a balding tire.

Amid a scuffle half-hidden beneath Tidewater's covers, out went Hocker and Philip Tawes. They had turned politically obsolete. Beckoned in to replace them was Dale Hess, a man who brought Rodgers not just one enticing new asset but two. Hess carried with him, first, his matchless personal tie as Mandel's friend and protégé, his one-time legislative roommate and law client. Second, Hess had demonstrated on his own an almost eerie insight into the mysteries of political real estate, a sophisticated field into which Rodgers had recently been steering Tidewater.

That Hess personally seemed the hayseed of rudimentary education was immaterial. That he had sent the city slicks at the legislature into paroxysms when he deplored "beating this dead horse to death" was irrelevant. The point was, Hess held the politico-financial combinations. Of six toll exits cut through from the new Kennedy expressway, four happened to stand at least in part on land owned by Hess's family. By 1967, according to tax records, Hess had gathered in a net worth in excess of $1 million. He would make his second million from Tidewater, for in recruiting Hess as partner Rodgers set in motion a train of events soon proved fateful.

Marvin Mandel passed up *few* opportunities, both as governor and after, to berate
privately what he regarded as The Estab-
lishment in Baltimore. He thought it was unwholesomely peo-
pled by a handful of the richest bankers, by big-firm lawyers and
contractors, by stockbrokers and insurance fat cats, by newspaper publishers and similar pompous asses. It was ingrown, self-
serving, inefficient, arrogant and, he was pretty sure, anti-
Semitic. Where these dismal people customarily met, he
believed, was in a gray stone building on North Charles Street
called the Maryland Club. Just here, Marvin Mandel would say,
The Establishment laid its plans to scuttle him and his newly
arrived, hence non-Establishment, friends.

The facts carry an ironical twist. It is true that the largest deal
for the sale of Marlboro Racetrack in 1971 was negotiated at the
Maryland Club. It's true too that this Marlboro deal was the one
which, six years later in court, would sink the Mandel group on
charges of mail fraud and racketeering. To this extent, the Governor's suspicion of the club as the scene of the beginning of his
downfall could be called accurate.

Where irony arises is in the negotiator of the fateful Marlboro
deal. It was not one of the pink-shirted Establishmentarians of
whom Marvin Mandel stood wary. Instead, it was Ernest Cory, a
small-firm, non-Baltimore lawyer working in the interests of
Harry Rodgers, Dale Hess, and, Cory half-suspected, Irvin
Kovens. This was the Mandel group itself, his closest personal

and political friends. In 1977, Cory would be convicted along with the rest.

At the moment the deal closed, however, Cory was rather pleased with his success. He had brought off a difficult negotiation between the old Marlboro stockholders and the new. When a news reporter asked him about it, he said yes, he had worked things out over breakfast at the Maryland Club.

Gaines McMillan, then president of the club, read the story in the newspaper. McMillan was angry. He telephoned Cory.

"Gaines gave me hell," Cory reported later.

Cory's offense, apparently, lay not in the company he was keeping or in his clients. No, he broke the rule against doing business in the club and, worse, letting that fact get into the newspaper.

The Establishment had spoken—if, in truth, there was any Establishment at all.

11.

"Fatal Mistakes in the Movies"

W hen Alice Riley updated her typing style, it went from rural schoolroom sprawl to urban office slick. She might as easily have updated her hairdo or her nail polish, and maybe she did those too. What mattered was her typing style, upping of which—followed, tellingly, by a make-believe downing—placed in the delighted hands of federal prosecutors, in the fall of 1975, a crucial key. It was a key to unlock the darkest puzzle of Marvin Mandel. Later, in court, Alice Riley's pursuit of this perkier style did more than any other single bit of evidence to flummox the Mandel defense, to proclaim deception, to establish bribery. It went far to convict six men of using the United States mails fraudulently.

Alice Riley's own motive was disarmingly simple. All she wanted was to please her boss, Dale Hess. For that she decided the letters she typed for him needed a more contemporary look, a fresh stenographic chic. After all, their workplace, hers and Dale's, had taken on a dramatic new sheen, hadn't it? No more frumpy little real estate office out in the sticks feeding on a suburban land boom. No, this new place was more sophisticated. Commandingly it perched at the edge of the vast spread of Baltimore-Washington International Airport and, as if echoing the great throaty jets, it surged with a deep financial thrust Alice Riley had not experienced before. She wanted Dale's letters to match this rich new rhythm exuded by Tidewater Insurance.

185

Draperies there hung like velvet, carpeting massaged the instep, furniture stood elegantly understated. It was an insurance office expensively designed to lure expensive people. Mom and Pop, hopefully in search of comprehensive coverage for their dream cottage, need not apply. Tidewater was a corporate octopus, many tentacled. It reached out over the heads of Mom and Pop innocents, grappling instead for the biggest fish in the sea.

Clearly, Tidewater's menacing splendor demanded something classier than Alice Riley's bush-league approach to the typewriter. She must pull up her secretarial socks. She must clasp her rambling paragraphs into modish bunches, shift the salutation and the yours sincerely to a smart flush left. She must inject a crisp dash into old friend Dale's letters, now that he had joined Tidewater as an executive and hustler. So she did and then, one day in 1974, Dale told her a certain letter was sort of special.

What made the letter special, he explained, was a little chronological adjustment. Dale Hess told her she should date it not May, 1974, which it was, but March 22, 1968, which it wasn't. Also this: Why not go back to the county, to the old office there, Dale said, and type this special letter on the old typewriter she used to use in 1968 but didn't use anymore? A final tiny touch: down in the lower left-hand corner of the letter, in the place where the typist's initials appear, Alice was to be sure she typed in ''ahm'' for Alice H. Morrow, which, in 1968, had indeed been her name. What she was not to type in was ''amr'' for Alice M. Riley, which, by 1974, after divorce and remarriage, she had become. This letter should begin ''Dear Marvin.'' He would sign it ''Dale.''

All of which is just what Alice Riley dutifully did.

And slipped. She forgot the style change. She forgot that between 1968, when the letter was supposed to have been written, and 1974, when it was actually written, her new letter-writing style had evolved. Specifically, she forgot to put aside her fashionably bunched new style and to use instead, for this one letter, the old sprawly style she had used in 1968. She typed in the new style, whereupon for the investigators the houselights shot on unexpectedly. They revealed the theater curtain half-open on a stage in disastrous disarray. Invented date, resurrected typewriter, undivorced initials—all dissembled in vain. One flash of truth, the forgotten new typing style, betrayed the game. On such trivia large events can turn.

In this case, the "Dear Marvin" letter emerged revealingly skewed. Its ostensibly old date and its manifestly new typing style contradicted each other. Something was wrong: old date and new style locked in between them a huge aberration. It showed the letter itself to be intrinsically, deliberately false, to carry at its heart an unsoundness hard to reconcile with the open, honest transaction between two men it purported to be. Plainly Dale Hess had something in mind more complex than a simple note to his friend and lawyer, Marvin Mandel, a man who in the spring of 1968 had scarcely dreamed of being governor. In 1974, he had been governor five years.

On its face the letter does look simple. In it Hess acknowledges a routine debt to Mandel for legal fees, long overdue, amounting to $17,000. He says he cannot afford to pay all that just now. He can pay $2,000 now, by giving Mandel a share in a hotel venture. The remaining $15,000 is to be paid in installments. He hopes Mandel approves. "Sincerely . . ."

Up to this point lawyers for both sides might stand in substantial agreement. The Hess letter—admittedly manufactured, absent-mindedly flawed in the typing—could make or break a court case. Each side recognized a strategic turning point. But turning which way, the defense way or the prosecution way?

Was the letter a turn to innocence, as Hess insisted? Was it a mere rectification of business data in order to present his personal records more accurately to inquiring agents of the Internal Revenue Service? Not improbably, Hess said he expected an IRS audit.

Or was the letter instead a glittering clue to bribery, the government's belief? Did it suggest, despite its bland businesslike surface, a hasty raking over of ashes to conceal the criminal flame beneath? Such questions were central.

Yet Alice Riley's typing was not enough, by itself, to sink the Mandel group. Much else not quite so central but still raising pointed questions would arise as evidence unfolded. Came a stream of expensive clothes and jewelry, a separate stream of lush vacations: all went to the Governor or his family, all came from these uncommonly generous friends. A quiet land speculation on the Eastern Shore of Maryland, accidentally opened up by the press, linked friends and Governor directly. The Mandel divorce and remarriage were cruelly costly: one friend ponied up bonds in six figures, and the Roman Catholic Pallottine Fathers—in maybe the most bizarre turn of all—allowed themselves to help out with alimony costs. Overall, the take on the Governor's side neared $500,000.

On the friends' side, the return was more substantial. It arose mostly from sleight-of-hand maneuvers surrounding the purchase and disposal of a dusty little country racetrack called Marlboro, a profitable turnover to which the Mandel touch was vital. Four friends stood to gain at least $2 million from their investment.

In bare essentials, as the government saw it, so stood the foundations of conspiracy. To the grand jury, this was painted as a scheme to pay off the Governor in various ways; in return, Mandel's part was to arrange for the fattening up and profitable disposal of Marlboro Racetrack. Thus, bribery was the aroma detected, bribery of the Governor—but bribery studiously concealed, as in the Dale Hess letter.

If the defense accepted many of the government's facts, it did not accept the intent the government said lay behind the facts. Defense counsel disputed every step, substituting for each question raised an innocent version of the government's guilty answer. The Hess-Mandel letter was routine business, said the defense. So with all the other exchanges within the group of six. Good friends these were, innocently exchanging presents—innocent because the Governor did not know where his good friends' business interests lay, so did not know how his actions helped them. No, said the defense. This is not criminal. It's how good friends help one another: honestly. If there was concealment, it arose from legitimate political prudence.

That much of the case rested fairly openly on the question of intent, on whether or not a plot to deceive was deliberately manufactured. A more ticklish point, and the one on which the defense scored heaviest, emerged from conflicting interpretations of the law. This point was the seeming need for the government to establish linkage between benefits flowing to the Governor on one hand and, on the other, benefits flowing in return to his friends.

Quid pro quo? Maybe, but was there a demonstrable pro, as the late Louis Azrael asked in his *Baltimore News American* column, connecting the quid and the quo? Or were the two sets of benefits separate and independent of each other, hence not bribery and not criminal? Here the lawyers split violently.

Whether bribery was satisfactorily proved or instead only strongly suggested would remain a lingering puzzle. Three times this puzzle beset federal appellate judges; it continues to beset lawyers and informed laymen throughout Maryland. Six years later, it was the most unsatisfying residue of the Mandel case. Aspects are discussed later in this book. Also, Ray Earnest, a neutral analyst and note editor of the *Maryland Law Review*, dealt with the matter in 1981; a portion of her opinion appears in the Appendix.

Such intricacies did not trouble investigators for the United States attorney's office when, late in 1975, they first unraveled Alice Riley's unwittingly perfidious typing. This was an investigator's coup, also a fair sample of the dogged paper chase that set apart this investigation from earlier trials and the plea-bargaining techniques used to unhorse defendants. "Insider" witnesses, squeezed to incriminate higher-ups, added little if any to the Mandel prosecution. Documents did it, and Eugene Twardowicz put his finger on the soft spot in Dale Hess's letter to Marvin Mandel.

"Pete, the Polish Prince" to his federal colleagues, Twardowicz was an investigative bulldog then on loan from the Internal Revenue Service. He had sensed in the letter a put-on: Why had Hess gone out of his way, Twardowicz wondered, to set out in writing years earlier the fact that he was then paying money to Mandel? True, other investigators in January of 1975 had stumbled on the fact that Hess, with Harry Rodgers, had secretly bought control of Marlboro Racetrack. Also that the track, shortly afterward, had undergone odd handling at the legislature, a body commonly subservient to the Governor. Still, where was the Mandel connection? The Hess letter looked innocent. It was dated six years before Mandel became governor and, besides, it spoke only of past legal fees.

Twardowicz had stared at the letter for months. Only when he spread ten other Hess-dictated letters across his desk, letters ranging over a decade, did the truth pop out at him. A dividing line separated Alice Riley's old typing style from her new; the line occurred early in the 1970s. That meant one thing. The letter's typing style stamped it unmistakably a product of the 1970s whereas its date, "March 22, 1968," cried out deception. Hess was paying money to Mandel—not back in 1968, before Mandel was governor, when it didn't much matter—but in the 1970s, when he was the Governor. What's more, they were trying to hide it. That mattered very much. Mandel entered the suspect circle, along with Hess and Rodgers. Could the Governor be on the take?

No, it's Twardowicz's "outlandish theory," said one assistant U.S. attorney. "Yes," said another, "Twardowicz has done it again," and this one was right. Pieces hitherto strewn bafflingly loose began to draw together.

To the investigators, here was the clincher for the entire Mandel case. Here was the bribe-bearing document that bound giver and taker together, that on its admittedly spurious face proclaimed a damning attempt at concealment. Here was not just one more random, misty clue. Here was documentary evidence admissible in court, evidence factual enough to satisfy a testy judge and dramatically revealing enough to grab a jury in its guts.

To Barnet Skolnik, chief of the investigating team suddenly handed this prosecutor's prize, what it told was "devastating . . . like a fatal mistake in the movies." Beside this pivotal letter all other morsels of evidence, while necessary and supporting, shrank to secondary roles. Instantly Skolnik knew the Hess letter gave him a criminal case against the Mandel circle. He believed the case to be winnable.

Not that the back-dated letter that Alice Riley created at Hess's instruction was direct evidence of fraud. It was only a letter conveying an apparently routine business message from Hess to Mandel. In it Hess did not say Marvin, let's you and I defraud the citizens of Maryland of their right to honest government. It did not say, let's make a deal: you trick the legislature on this racetrack bill of mine and lie to reporters about it. Then, I'll pay you off and hide the payments. The letter, on its face, made no such incriminating statement. Direct evidence played little part in the Mandel trial.

Yet it was in things the letter did not say, in the unwritten words hidden between the letter's lines, that investigators discerned what they would call mail fraud. As an example of indirect, circumstantial evidence, Alice Riley had accidentally produced a masterpiece.

The investigation at that point paused on Hess's intent in writing the letter, not on the words he wrote. What made the letter so electrifying a find was that it seemed to breathe deception— deception in its date, in its physical form. Also in the excuse Hess gave for having it written: he told prosecutors of possible Internal

Revenue auditors. In fact, it turned out, he had dictated it within days after being officially notified, not by IRS of an impending audit, but by the U.S. attorney's office that he was under investigation for mail fraud. The letter's intent, investigators decided, was not to reveal but to cover up.

Nor did the deceptive letter stand alone and unsupported by other deceptions. It was only the final, most telling link that hooked Hess and Mandel together in a chain of many links, artfully contrived. Finally, the defense of innocent coincidence became hard to sustain. An overriding intent to deceive argued strongly the other way.

As noted, most evidence in this case was circumstantial rather than direct. That factor changed its whole complexion from that of the Agnew case, in which no fewer than four witnesses pointed fingers squarely at Agnew as accepting cash bribes. In the Mandel case, documents such as the Alice Riley letter furnished the government its strongest platform for prosecution. A glance at the process leading up to Pete Twardowicz's discovery of this letter–this "fatal mistake in the movies"—tells more of how federal investigators earn their keep.

Four slash nine: 4/9. A date, of course. The customary shorthand for April 9. Don Bell had deduced that easily enough, poking about in Dale Hess's personal financial papers. April 9, April 9, repeated over and over and over. Yes, yes, yes. April 9. But so what, dammit? So what? So what?

Abruptly, after weeks of befogged noodling, two pieces came together inside Don Bell's head.

Wasn't this April 9 the very day prior to that historic day, April 10, 1972? And what made April 10 historic? It was the date, wasn't it, on which the Marlboro Racetrack balloon, until then grossly swelling at Annapolis, had been pricked by outraged Maryland senators? Of course!

Don Bell knew he was close to something important. What he saw, or thought he saw, had jumped out from Dale Hess's check spreads. These were two lists, extricated by grand jury subpoena, which recorded all the checks Hess had written in 1972 and 1973. It was to unravel just such documentary puzzles that Bell, an IRS agent like Pete Twardowicz, had also been tapped temporarily by the Hess-Rodgers investigators. The paper trail, it was believed, would lead them all to the Hess misdeeds the feds were pretty sure by now existed.

So April 9 seemed a tantalizing clue. It was Bell's own catch, perhaps the long-sought loose end in the otherwise seamless web Hess seemed to have draped cunningly about his own operations, about Tidewater's political leverage, about God knew what other unsavory revelations. But wait now: Was it really a clue?

It wasn't. The trouble was, as things turned out, April 9 was no clue at all. It was an illusion, not a trail; or maybe a false trail literally too good to be true. Bell tried it on as a date this way, then turned it around that way. Nothing led anywhere. Four slash nine wasn't even a date, the weary Bell finally concluded. The two deceptive pieces in his head slid apart again, whereupon two quite different pieces slid together. This time, the pieces clicked into place.

Of such agonized reshufflings is an investigator's trade constructed. A date? No, not a date. Four slash nine, achingly reconsidered, must instead be a fraction: four-ninths. All right, but a fraction of what? Well, what was Dale Hess dividing? With whom? And why? Starting with such pointed questions, the trail Bell was following went from cold to hot.

It would lead straight to a second chunk of evidence comparable in importance only to the Alice Riley letter, and directly linked to it. On this fraction the government would later rivet down its central assertion: Marvin Mandel was given a bribe and accepted it. Here was no casual gift, no token of friendly warmth. Immediately, this transaction was worth at least $300,000 to Mandel. Built-in escalators suggested that value would swell to more than $500,000. For what the Governor had been given was a juicy share in the federal lease, privately held, on a huge building in the Social Security complex standing just at Baltimore's edge.

Federal authorities called this gift a bribe. They said it was a secret payoff for services that, as Governor, he improperly rendered his friends. Elaborate efforts to hide this Mandel holding—to deny, even, that it was his holding—were hardly convincing. For prosecutors were able to call up damning documents bearing dates, signatures, dollar marks, to cement their indictment in place.

As noted, some pretty exotic government weaponry was trained on Mandel and his friends. But it was the Social Security item that furnished the courtroom blockbuster. From that numbing blast the defense could find no credible hiding place.

What's more, sheer chance at time of trial furnished the Social Security building, as evidence, a psychological wallop of its own. Because of two bits of jury tampering, a mistrial had been called; because of the mistrial jurors in a second trial were held in sequestration. Where they were sequestered night after night during the twelve weeks of the trial was in a Ramada Inn gazing east upon Baltimore. Just there the Social Security cluster arose, gray and faceless, stack on stack of architectural egg crates.

The result was, as they were bused to and from the downtown courtroom, each morning and evening, these jurors had spread before them the stacked-up egg crates that, the prosecutors told them, were really stacked-up bribery, fraud, and racketeering. Twice daily, though coincidentally, the government's strongest evidence passed physically before their eyes. The jurors might as well have criss-crossed the pertinent cemetery en route to and from a murder trial.

Once again it was Dale Hess's Alice Riley—loyal, trusting Alice, slightly absent-minded Alice—who unintentionally gave the government its critical break. Probably the investigators, with their vacuum-cleaner thoroughness, eventually would have sucked up the facts regardless of Alice Riley. Probably her oversight did no more than shorten the government's search. Still, a document that by mischance she bundled up in the wrong place gave away the biggest game of all. For investigators, this document would rip the mask off a transaction displaying Dale Hess on the giving end and Marvin Mandel as receiver. Here at its best was the documentary approach to evidence which placed on the Mandel trial a distinguishing mark.

The uncovering of Marvin Mandel was not altogether unexpected by the federals. Only an investigator both blind and numb to political reality could fail to sense that, upon inquiry into the business affairs of Dale Hess and Harry Rodgers, the road beyond might lead to high government levels where policy is created, to fund raisers Hess's and Rodgers's personal friend, Marvin Mandel. Closer to the bone: Wasn't there a flourish of political name-dropping in the way the twosome snaffled new insurance business away from the older, more settled insurance companies? The name they dropped was the Governor's. Investigators blind and numb seldom last long as investigators.

And yet, across the outset in early 1974 of the government's Hess-Rodgers inquiry, Marvin Mandel personally seems to have cast only a distant shadow, dimly seen. The Governor, despite his own suspicions to the contrary, all the federals insist was not the opening target. Hess was certainly a target; so was Rodgers. It was Hess's personal papers, winnowed from a documentary haystack raked up by government subpoenas, which broadened the investigative focus. Alice Riley, by accident, had handed over one paper too many.

When the federals put their hands on this documentary treasure trove, it was neatly stacked in the office of Hess's accountant, Alfred Sachs. Long before the government came around, Sachs had reason for puzzlement in the spring of 1974. He stumbled over an oddity in some figures Hess had furnished him, financial figures on which he was to compute the Hess income tax return for the previous year, 1973.

Here stood a listing of Hess-signed checks, Sachs noted, which included four monthly payments made out to Marvin Mandel for about $520 apiece. Strangely, to Sachs, each of these entries carried the notation "legal fees."

"Legal fees"?

What made that puzzling was that, in the similar Hess check spread for the year earlier, 1972, a string of eight monthly payments to Mandel began in May in about the same amounts: they had not been called "legal fees" at all. They were marked, instead, "Sec Inv." And what was "Sec Inv"?

Well that, Hess had earlier told the inquiring Sachs, represented the earnings of Mandel's share of Security Investment, the company that owned the Social Security buildings. Hess himself held 9 percent of the company, he said. Of that share four-ninths, or 4 percent of the company, Hess said he was holding in his own name for Mandel. He explained to Sachs that when his own monthly checks came through, he simply sent on four-ninths of each to Mandel. That was the arrangement. Understand?

Sachs understood at once too little and too much. Hess's version be damned. What his own eyes told him was that a running stream of checks which had been plainly labeled "Sec Inv" in 1972 had suddenly, when resumed in 1973, become labeled "legal fees"–and without explanation for the change. Why was

"Sec Inv," Sachs wondered, abruptly obliterated? Worse, Hess now wanted Sachs to deduct these payments to Mandel—suddenly called "fees," totaling $7,249.04—from his income tax return as legal expenses in 1973. Warily, Sachs demurred.

The odor was queer, his own professional repute stood on the line. Suppose Internal Revenue asked the same suspicious questions Sachs asked? How would he explain this strange financial zig that Hess insisted, inexplicably, was really a zag?

Perhaps Hess could help Sachs out. Maybe furnish some illuminating paper, some document to establish these payments to Mandel as indeed the "legal fees" claimed and not—Sachs couldn't help wondering privately—as something different, something a little shadowy suggested by the "Sec Inv" checks from the previous year. Would Hess help?

Sure. So was born in April of 1974, but falsely dated "March 22, 1968," the Alice Riley–typed letter set forth at the beginning of the chapter. The letter's self-betrayals—its 1968 pretensions, its 1974 typing style—would explode in court. That was later. Just then, to still Alfred Sachs's tax-season qualms, the letter worked perfectly. In it Hess wrote Mandel with disarming casualness about the $17,000 legal fees owed, how he was short of money just now, that he would pay as he could. All right with Marvin?

No objection was recorded, none from Mandel, none from Internal Revenue. Alfred Sachs breathed a little easier, for about a year.

In fact, federal investigators of a different sort were already on the Hess trail, and Hess knew it. It was April 5, 1974, when both Hess and Rodgers were sent what the Justice Department calls "target letters." They were under investigation for possible violations of federal law. Subpoenas followed shortly, reaching out for myriad documents pertaining to their business affairs. The message was clear: Hess and Rodgers had better get their act together. They were standing close to the federal flame.

It was apparently the target letter to him which singed Hess, then worried him into his covering-up maneuvers. The back-dated letter was only the second part of that. Almost as revealing was the first part, in which he had Alice Riley try, at least, to scrub out beyond trace the tattletale lines linking Security Investment and Marvin Mandel. He told her, for example, to recopy the entire list, or spread, of checks he wrote during 1972. She was to make one change and only one: she was to eliminate "Sec Inv" as an identifying label on each check drawn to Marvin Mandel. In its place she was to substitute "legal fees," and leave all the rest the same, thus making the 1972 check spread seem to match the 1973 check spread questioned by Alfred Sachs. Both would say "legal fees"; neither would say "Sec Inv." The cover-up was under way.

This change was no small job. Checks by the dozen had been recorded in detail—source, payee, check number, date, purpose—and ran to more than eight closely written pages. It took several days to redo it all.

What struck investigators later was that Dale Hess, if making no more than the honest bookkeeper's correction he said he was making, could have had it done in twenty minutes. Alice Riley could simply have drawn a line through the "Sec Inv" entries, and then written in "legal fees" instead. This was not, after all, an official document. It was simply an informational record, mainly for accounting use by Alfred Sachs. Instead, every single item—with that outstanding exception, "Sec Inv"—had to be rewritten just as in the original version. A smooth record unblemished by question-raising cross-outs was what Hess wanted.

Here was the response of a man who had learned officially a week or so earlier, April 5, that every scrap of paper he owned was soon to be subject to government scrutiny. Obviously, he couldn't hide the payments to Mandel. His checks, after all, were recorded in half a hundred other places beyond his control, hence beyond revision. Even his own original check stubs, dutifully labeled "Sec Inv," could not be completely rewritten. Some clumsy erasures were attempted with doubtful success. What Hess could do was try to use the altered check spread as his basic record, which it wasn't, and on it camouflage the purpose of the check payments to Mandel. Change "Sec Inv" to "legal fees"; that is, make guilt look innocent.

The game began to fall apart at the outset, even before the government came nosing around. Alfred Sachs did get a copy of the back-dated letter. What he did not get, apparently, was the new, falsified version of the 1972 check spread, the one Alice Riley had painstakingly recopied to obliterate the giveaway "Sec Inv." Sachs received only the original, unexpurgated version—and either Alice Riley or Dale Hess forgot to call it back from him. One more "fatal mistake," it lay there in Sachs's Dale Hess folder when the investigators picked it up.

They already had from Hess the second, or doctored, version.

The Sachs file gave them the first version and the makings of the truth. Side by side, the two versions were laid down: out jumped the "Sec Inv" alteration, plus the excessively time-consuming method by which Hess had tried to conceal the fact that it was an alteration. He was covering up the cover-up, investigators reasoned, whereupon suspicions darkened and broadened. Financial records deliberately altered amount, for federal agents, to a tack upturned in a chair seat. They produce an abruptly energizing effect.

How, investigators began to wonder, did all this look on the receiving end, the Mandel end? If with a gulp—this was, after all, a powerful and increasingly angry governor they were now directly confronting—they reached out with their subpoenas for Marvin Mandel's own papers. It was June, 1975. More than five months would elapse before indictment, but the federal focus was coming clear and sharp. It fell on the Governor himself.

What the subpoenas now turned up was no less tortured than on the giving, or Hess, side. First, there were Mandel's declarations of his income tax for 1972 and 1973; they told an embarrassing story. In the spring of 1973, figuring his 1972 income, the Governor found his series of checks from Dale Hess added up to $6,065.47. What to do? He could scarcely report them as what they honestly were, income from his hidden share in Security Investment. Nor could he, at that stage, safely identify Hess as the source: the back-dated Alice Riley letter had not yet been created to sustain that myth. Still, he dared not deny the Security Investment income altogether.

Cornered, Marvin Mandel happened early in 1973 upon a different covering device. He duly reported the checks as income and duly paid the tax on it: but he reported it as income not from Hess, not from Security Investment. Instead, there was $7,265 in "dividends" received, he said, from a firm, G&E Realty, owned by Barbara Mandel's family. The hitch was, Mandel's actual dividend from G&E for 1972 wasn't $7,265; it was only $1,200, the G&E treasurer, Mayme Oberfeld, testified later. Here was a $6,000 gap between truth and cover-up. Investigators found the difference eloquent.

Tax season in 1974, by which time the gubernatorial quarry was alerted, produced a quite different version of the Security Investment checks piped for the second year through Hess. This time they were called "fees": Alice Riley's back-dated letter was now in existence, plus its newly manufactured scenario about legal fees owed by Hess. So $7,249.04 Hess paid Mandel in 1973 went into Mandel's Form 1040 as "fees"—but even that brought a couple of betraying bobbles. Earlier, Mandel had told the *Washington Post* that this money was his share in an investment program run by his old law firm; it wasn't. Next his accountant, ignorant of the "fees" game afoot, had typed in "lecture fees"; again, it wasn't. Mandel caught that one when the declaration, filled in, was returned for his signature. He erased the word "lecture," so "fees" unspecified was the way the transaction was played out. It squared with Hess's freshly revised check spreads. It fit the back-dated letter. The cover slid into place, or almost.

Still another document, however, arose to protrude awkwardly through the package otherwise smoothly wrapped in innocence. This was the formal agreement in which Hess gave Mandel outright a substantial share (the four-ninths of his own 9 percent share) in Security Investment, of which Hess had just been made a general partner.

Mandel was supposed to pay Hess $40 for this share, but evidence never appeared that he paid anything at all. Indeed, the cost to Hess for his own share had been specified as only $90, and he apparently never paid that. So far as investigators could determine, both men were simply handed gifts cost-free. Each gift had substantial value.

As to what value we have Dale Hess and Harry Rodgers as authority. His own share of Security Investment, the 9 percent, Hess said in his personal net worth statement early in 1973, would bring $725,000 if the building were sold. Rodgers opined about the same: his net worth statement put his own 8 1/2 percent share at $718,000. In light of these two estimates—probably conservative since Security Investment enjoyed a cash flow of $3 million annually from U.S. leases—the dollar value of Marvin Mandel's 4 percent share begins to take shape and weight.

His four-ninths of the Hess share was carefully specified. It was not simply sharing in the cash flow, as Mandel maintained. Instead, the document that both signed as of December 1, 1971, plainly refers to Mandel as "absolute owner." So read, his share would stand well above $300,000. Escalator clauses written into the Security Investment leases suggest that, by their termination twenty years later, values would have at least doubled.

Clearly, this was far from the couple of free suits and paid-up trips to Florida said by some disparagers of the government case to be the lone underpinning of the bribery charge against Marvin Mandel. Security Investment was no such frivolity. This was heavy money, a small fortune shrewdly invested to expand rapidly over the years and to ensure that the Mandel life, presently and in the future, was a comfortable one. It was also a pointed token: there's more to be had, the 4 percent cut seemed to say, where this came from. By itself, once fully unveiled, Mandel's Security Investment holding might well have secured his conviction. The suggestion of bribery was powerful.

Both givers and takers seemed to think so, judging by their maneuvers to cover up Mandel's holding. Consider the role of Hess, the man central to the action throughout. Outwardly, it had been Hess who was picked up first by the Tidewater partners, then enfolded by much the same people in Security Investment. They converted him from rustic speculator, nickel-and-dimeing his way up to middle-class swagger, to a senior entrepreneur with the sky his limit. But why pick up Hess, a man clumsy and crude by their keener, more sophisticated standards?

Unspoken, or anyway carefully unwritten, but plainly understood all around, was the inner reason. Hess held the ear and the confidence and the friendship of Governor Mandel, a man uniquely situated to enlarge the financial interests for which this group eagerly reached out. For their purposes, Hess was Mandel; it was Mandel they needed and wanted. So when it came to cutting Hess into the Security Investment deal, Mandel had to be cut in too—but cut in, as always, under the covering shadow of Hess.

The Hess 9 percent share in Security Investment was a gift, virtually free. But the private understanding that went with that, as the investigators saw it, was the telling part. It was that four-ninths of this, or 4 percent, was to belong secretly to Mandel. On the face of it, Hess was to "hold as agent"—meaning hide—Mandel's share for him (why "hold," Hess could never be brought openly to say). He would pay Mandel interest in regular installments disguised as the aforementioned "legal fees." Both would deny under questioning that Mandel actually owned any part of Security Investment. Each was to say no, the income to Mandel is payment on some leftover bills Hess owed him. As scenarios go, it wasn't too bad in concept.

It started to break down in two places, however, one in the

contradictory facts turned up, the other in circumstances that the scenario sadly failed to fit. A sample fact: when Hess wrote Mandel "in 1974" that he could not just then pay him the $17,000 he had supposedly owed him for years, Hess by his own declaration was worth well over $1 million in principal, with an annual income in six figures. Another fact, larger still: the formal legal agreement in which Hess simply transfers to Mandel 4 percent of Security Investment. This is not an allotment of income, complete with time limit, to settle an old debt. What this agreement deals with is a solid chunk of principal. "Absolute owner," it calls Mandel. Nothing suggesting a temporary flow of cash, nothing to blur clear ownership.

And yet, under oath, cash flow is what both Hess and Mandel said the agreement was limited to. Out came the old-debt legendry again: Hess owed Mandel legal fees and, short of cash, used this way to pay him. Never mind, we are told, that the language of their signed agreement says nothing about fees or any other debt. Ignore its plain references, instead, to a capital transaction. Mandel, once a practicing lawyer himself, would stoutly maintain on the witness stand that this legal agreement did not mean what it plainly said it meant. Jurors were asked to disregard what their own intelligence told them was true, a vastly damaging truth at that. Mandel, thus pinned down to his own words, signed and dated, tried to retreat once more into his too-familiar corner. Instantly the impact of the agreement as evidence was multiplied. More still was to come.

Just the existence of this Hess-Mandel agreement, stark and explicit, furnished a hard core to the government case. Less flinty, but no less revealing as evidence, were the circumstances in which the agreement was born and, less than two years later, oddly obliterated.

Hess had it drawn up in the spring of 1972, then back-dated it to December 1, 1971. This placed the largest gift of all to Mandel in a period peculiarly suggestive: it was the period when the Marlboro Racetrack bills entered their devious course through a legislature heavily dominated by the Governor. He was thus paid, on a regular basis, from the outset of the Marlboro operation. December, 1971, was indeed the very month in which the Hess-Rodgers group launched the Marlboro operation by buying the track. Linkage of the two actions, to be sure, was achieved only by the phenomenal closeness of their timing. No document, no witness, said yes, here is where it all began.

Predictably, the defense dismissed those dates as coincidental, hence irrelevant. No such easy dismissal was offered for the agreement's abrupt demise. The Governor himself stated the obvious truth: he canceled it to avoid public revelation of this secret financial tie to Hess. A new law had just taken effect. Mounting irritation in the legislature with under-the-table dealings had led to this law, effective in 1973, which required state officials to lay bare publicly all assets and income. That April, to dodge the embarrassment of disclosure, Mandel in his own handwriting canceled his agreement with Hess. Or said he did.

Was the original agreement, some wondered, still uncanceled and still in effect? Similarly undisclosed was the source and dimensions of the income that kept the Mandel family in comfortable circumstances during and after the Governor's nineteen months in prison.

F or a while in the spring of 1977 too many pressures converged on Marvin Mandel. Huge bills accumulated, he was desperate for money to pay them, his usual financial avenue to "the boys" was shut off by the trial. And the trial itself was going badly: every day the media flung up some new embarrassment revealed in court the day before. The walls seemed to close in and Marvin Mandel—a sensitive man, hence an embittered man—momentarily fell apart. He was admitted to a hospital in Prince Georges County. A brace of respected Johns Hopkins doctors diagnosed some kind of stroke. It was important, the doctors said, that stress be lifted. That included the stress of governing Maryland, the duties to which Marvin Mandel had clung despite the trial.

But the state machinery could not stop in its tracks. It must maintain momentum, so who would do the steering?

Brightly, protectively or possessively, maybe a little jealously, Jeanne Mandel volunteered her services. She would, Jeanne announced publicly, serve as Marvin's "eyes and ears" until he was better. She would carry messages between him and his State House assistants. She would ease the now-prohibited stress but, at the same time, keep Marvin's hand on the gubernatorial wheel. She did not have to mention that she would keep others' hands off. In effect, Jeanne seemed to some to be saying, she would govern Maryland herself.

And why not? Mrs. Woodrow Wilson had personally taken up

the slack when her presidential husband collapsed. Evita Peron proved a more than adequate substitute for her husband, Juan. In Maryland, not everyone agreed.

One large obstacle was the state constitution, freshly amended at Marvin's own instigation to cover just this situation. It provided a lieutenant governor as official substitute for his fallen leader. What's more, that job housed an inhabitant long trained to state authority, personally selected by Governor Mandel, eager to take charge. Blair Lee III, ever the graceful Princetonian, bit his tongue quietly at word of Jeanne's presumptions. He had already put up with enough condescension from that quarter. Being elbowed out of his clear duties, constitution be damned, was too much.

Lieutenant Governor Lee paid a formal call on Governor Mandel in the hospital. Either he would govern in Marvin Mandel's place, Blair Lee said, or else he would resign as lieutenant governor—and tell why. The threat worked. Jeanne backed off, Blair Lee took over the Governor's duties until as a brief gesture near the end Marvin resumed them temporarily.

What didn't work was Lee's own follow-up. In 1978, by now on-the-job governor, he undertook to win election in his own right. Of those in the field, he was by far the best qualified—with one overriding exception. He was perceived, rightly or wrongly, as the political heir to Marvin Mandel, hence to the aromatic tangle of corruption, of fraud and bribery, still fresh in the nostrils of Maryland Democrats. Blair Lee had rid himself of Jeanne, only to succumb in the Democratic primary to the lingering redolence of Marvin.

Harry Hughes had been among the first to point publicly to corruption in the Mandel administration. In protest against a state contract he believed to be tainted, he had resigned his position as state director of transportation. His reformist credentials were established. Thereafter, as Marvin Mandel glumly but instantly perceived, a reform path to the governorship lay open to Harry Hughes. Hughes took it.

12.

Friendship?
or Fraud?

A popular fallacy holds that the Mandel circle was upended by a few free suits and a couple of trips to Florida, these in exchange for doing something about Marlboro Racetrack which was a little shady but scarcely unprecedented. It is a fallacy that both distorts and diminishes the hard evidence presented.

The fact is, formidable bulwarks upheld at each of its two ends the charge that bribery occurred. One bulwark was the $300,000 worth of Security Investment handed over to Mandel, the bribe itself. The other was the $2-million legislative boost the Governor's response to the bribe furnished in return to the secret owners of Marlboro. On these two episodes—detailed, documented, cemented together in a fraudulent context—the crux of the case stood clinched. The case was not clinched, however, by these two alone.

Suits and Florida trips, a land deal and borrowed alimony did indeed flow Mandel-ward. And if they happened to blur the popular grasp of the crux of the case, they also furnished a secondary layer of confirmatory incidents. These were less darkly damning and, in some important ways, more illuminating. Tiny, telling perceptions are often caught only in the corner of the eye.

Consider the central assertion of the defendants about their warm personal relationship. Each insisted that exchanges called criminal were, in fact, no more than the wholesome give-and-take common among close friends. Adding force to this argument, the Governor and his friends genuinely did enjoy their mutual com-

204

pany. Each trusted the rest, none betrayed another—certainly not in the way Spiro Agnew's "friends" had cravenly betrayed him two years earlier. And yet just here the defense edged itself backward onto a precipice of logic. From it the only exit was a leap, outright jury boggling, into logical thin air.

The trouble was that a second defense contention undermined the first. This held that, at the time the Marlboro legislation was afoot in 1972, these close friends of Governor Mandel did not tell him they had quietly bought the track. Their silence, they said, was designed to head off a political uproar that would embarrass the Governor and imperil Marlboro's fate. Still, it was they who stood to make a quick $2 million on the legislature's approval. And it was the Governor who, in supposed ignorance, used his considerable political muscle trying to squeeze approval through.

Hence the logical collision: Would such close and loyal friends of the Governor deliberately mislead him into disaster? Would they, behind his back, loose a train of events plainly loaded with the threat of carrying him and them together into court, conviction, prison?

Logically, that was too thick to swallow, and the jury couldn't choke it down. No, the jury answered in effect. No, good friends like these do not behave in this way. No, his friends did not trick the Governor, did not misuse him, did not maneuver him into an unwitting fraud on the citizens of Maryland. No, because the Governor knew from the outset what his close friends were up to.

Fraud was committed all right, in the jury's view, but there was nothing unwitting about it. The Governor knew who owned the track. He knew it when he put his own political push to doubling, in one flash of the electric vote counter on the senate wall, the investment he knew they had made. Not a juryman, not a jurywoman, flinched when, after the verdict was spoken, defense counsel had them polled individually. Guilty, each said. Guilty.

How so? What combination of circumstances, what fatal aperture in the legal battlements the defense threw up with royal expertise gave these jurors the discernment, uniformly held, that fraud was on display?

Reading the collective mind of a jury is a rash undertaking, and yet an objective look is possible at the melange of attitudes jurors watched defendants unfold. Here, a taste of the political spoilsman; there, a tangled supposition of historical justification. Now, a cavalier sense of being above the law; then, a simple impairment of judgment as to the difference between right and wrong. Contrarily, there turned up too a sometime consciousness of impropriety, a consciousness that led to endless evasions, unlikely explanations, palpable lies. Time after time, their behavior fell into patterns that argued against unwelcome truth.

Particularly so the Governor himself. His testimony in court, like his comments earlier at news conferences, exuded an air laden with a reasoning too disjointed for easy belief. As a result, even the best of the defense case—and counsel offered many strong points, shrewdly argued—emerged tainted. Of the myriad facets of self-betrayal, a handful is illustrative.

Ray's Point Farm, a real estate venture, had been brought on first as a newspaper exposé. To the still tolerant public eye of 1972, it seemed to be little more than another shabby political joke. B'hoys, it was thought, would be b'hoys. Baltimore politicians joining together in secret to buy themselves a farm? On Maryland's determinedly rustic Eastern Shore? It seemed inexplicable, hence provocative, finally uncomfortably amusing.

Such was the journalistic guffawing that the Governor was at last stung into an explanation. It was outright startling in its shy demureness. Marvin Mandel was not, he implied, the hard-bitten, city-seasoned pol he was commonly taken to be. Inside, he suggested, there lurked a wistful strain of Tom Sawyer, Holden Caulfield, maybe Henry Thoreau.

This came about after a reporter asked at a news conference, "Don't you think your participation in a land deal in Talbot County is putting you in a situation of some conflict of interest?"

Marvin Mandel answered with customary asperity, also with the clouded plausibility soon recognized as a Mandel trademark. He said: "I don't know how. No, I don't consider it any conflict at all. I think buying a farm, well let me put it this way: I think every boy who grows up in the city always has a desire to own a farm sometime in his lifetime. . . . Frankly, I feel the same way and I have grown up and I have a 15 percent interest in a farm and I don't see any conflict."

Political cartoonists, a sardonic crew, found this farm-boy motif irresistible. The Mandel circle began to turn up on editorial pages in their pointy-toed city shoes hunched over a split-rail fence, munching thoughtfully on a wheat stalk, eyes straw-hat shaded. Startled cartoon cows were milked, a cartoon pig slopped. For perceived veracity, the Governor might as well have put the Brooklyn Bridge back on the market.

The U.S. attorney's office was not amused. In 1974, nearly two years after it surfaced in the papers, Ray's Point began to show a glint more specifically sinister. What had turned up was . . .

That the Governor had been cut in at the token price of $150 on a $350,000 land deal worth at least $35,000 to him, and

That his name had first been written casually on the record of the land corporation as an owner, then hastily expunged, and

That, unlike his partners, his personal guarantee did not go on the purchase mortgage, and

That the mocking publicity drove Ray's Point owners to pretend to sell out to others but

That the "others" they sold to were in secret mostly themselves, namely, the boys from Tidewater. The sale was a blind.

Whether Mandel personally abandoned his share of Ray's Point, as he said he did, or instead maintained his financial holding underground, as the others did, remains a question.

As evidence Mandel was bribed, his share of Ray's Point did not carry the crushing weight of his share in Security Investment. Charges could scarcely have been brought, much less sustained, on the strength of Ray's Point alone. But it was not alone: as part of a pattern, as a further demonstration of Mandel interacting financially with the Tidewater group, as characteristic of its surreptitious modus operandi, Ray's Point carried advance echoes of Security Investment and Marlboro. What's more, the Ray's Point purchase and the sharing out to Mandel was bracketed closely in time with the Security Investment and Marlboro deals. Spring, 1972, was a season filled with questionable exchanges. Ray's Point was included as a formal count under the headings of bribery and mail fraud.

In court, defense attorney Arnold Weiner dismissed Ray's Point as largely a government trump-up. Weiner drew the jury's attention sharply to the "personal liability" matter. As Weiner stated, Mandel had volunteered to share liability for the loan—"go on the hook"—but was brushed aside by the others. The fact was, Weiner went on, citing a somewhat parallel arrangement for Judge Thomas Hunter Lowe, Mandel had actually earned his share as a finder's fee for helping locate Ray's Point.

Weiner added: "And if that's all there was to it, as every credible witness tells you, there is no way in the world to suggest that Ray's Point was a bribe. . . . A man who is being given a bribe, . . .

a free ride, isn't going to agree to go on the hook for anything. They [the prosecution] never mentioned that to you because it is a . . . startling piece of circumstantial evidence that works completely and thoroughly against their theory."

For the government, Ronald Liebman sounded the contrary refrain that ran throughout the prosecution side of the Mandel case.

"Common sense, folks," Liebman said. "Take that common sense into the jury room with you. Think about this transaction, think about the value involved, think about the way it was handled.

"What was in the minds of the boys at Tidewater when they let Marvin Mandel in? What was in Marvin Mandel's mind when he took 15 percent interest for $150 with no personal liability? . . . Friendship or was it something else?

"Remember, this is a case about fraud . . ."

The episode casting the Pallottine Missionary Fathers as abettors of (1) bribery of the Governor and (2) a set of divorce arrangements was, once sorted out, as extraordinary as any the trial produced. So complex was the cover-up attempted, so naked the fear of exposure, so unwashable the Governor's explanation, so blunt the government's open court charge of "lie," that the facts as they unrolled came to seem more Byzantine than Pallottine. Here emerged a marvel of panicky invention, a roll of hollow laughter.

Marvin Mandel sat flat broke when, in early September of 1974, his first alimony bill came due. He owed the first Mrs. Mandel, freshly divorced, the sum of $42,000. He had no money, no collateral. He could not borrow money from any bank and—worse—faced an imminent Democratic primary for renomination. Had he tried to fob off his ex-wife with a bouncing check, he had been stiffly warned, he would have been whisked into court the next day—with election day two days later. For a political candidate, a dilemma indeed. What to do?

What was done was something like this.

By phone, Mandel put it up to Dale Hess, who, as usual, had the money all right but, as unusual, had a qualm. He had just learned officially that he was under federal investigation: Business use of political influence was the ticklish subject under inquiry. Dare Hess, with federal eyes trained menacingly upon his every move, be seen openly handing over $42,000 to Governor Mandel? No, he dare not.

Similarly braced by federal "target" letter, and so similarly unmanned, was Harry Rodgers when Hess put the Mandel problem to him. No, Rodgers didn't dare touch it either. Still, neither Hess nor Rodgers could afford to let this Governor of theirs, this golden business asset proven not quite beyond price, go down some dismal divorce-dug drain. They needed Mandel, needed him in office. Only money was called for to protect their investment, only $42,000 at that.

If Hess and Rodgers daren't, what about the Pallottine Fathers? They always had plenty of money, were always alert to a shrewd investment. Best of all, not even the inquisitive feds would lightly poke about behind this money-raising arm, however hairy, of the Roman Catholic Church.

The Very Reverend Guido John Carcich, S.A.C., the order's fiscal genius, at first demurred, possibly out of sensitivity to his church's deep-set repugnance for divorce. He too didn't quite dare. Still, there were other ways, weren't there? One other way was Donald Webster and his nephew Dennis, each a past political chore doer for the Mandel circle, each enjoying a business association with the Pallottines. Enter Donald Webster as the obvious go-between. Willing to help when Hess called him, yes, but wasn't he personally a bit too obvious as the hander-over of $42,000 to the Governor? The Websters were traceable to Hess by marriage, so Donald Webster produced a newer name still: William May, a man Webster had used before.

William May as cover was almost too perfect. He was unknown to Mandel, unknown to the Pallottines. He was an obscure salesman of motorcycles, remote from politics in a varooming world of his own. A front man, just as for Kovens Tubby Schwartz was a front, as Hess fronted for Tidewater. No one would think to look behind a motorcycle salesman, see? Courage seeped back into the others, if circuitously.

Hess would put up $15,000. Donald Webster would put up $10,000 and Dennis Webster $17,000. Lumped together, this $42,000 would funnel in to William May, whose own check would then be made out to Mandel. After a short interval, maybe a few weeks, Father Carcich would then lift everyone gently off the hook. He would refinance May's $42,000 loan to Mandel, using Pallottine funds.

No one on the inside would be hurt. No one outside would know where the money really came from. At a Sunday party at the Webster house, all the principals including Father Carcich gathered. Either Father Carcich or Donald Webster, but not William May, handed Mandel May's check for $42,000. The Governor and the motorcycle salesman had never laid eyes on each other before. The perfect cover?

Perhaps not quite. Marvin Mandel himself was now to draw it closer, the government said. A disturbing glimmer of light shone through the name, Marvin Mandel, which William May had written on the face of his check. In spite of all the multiple wrapping, would investigators be able to spot the May check as puzzling when they looked into the Mandel checking account? Layer by layer, couldn't they then leaf it back to its Dale Hess origins?

Marvin Mandel did not deposit the May check in his checking account. Instead, he gave it to his son Gary Mandel and, in return, deposited Gary's check for $42,000 to his own account. Both checks were dated and deposited the same day, September 9, a Monday. That way, the only check to emerge from this long transaction and to show up deposited to the father's account was a check from the son, not even from the motorcycle salesman. Prosecutors called the check laundered.

At any rate, the circle of insulation came complete. Gary Mandel insulated William May, William May insulated the Websters, the Websters helped insulate Dale Hess and, presumably, Harry Rodgers. Shortly, Father Carcich would come along and insulate them all by picking up the debt, in effect would make the Governor's alimony payment to his former wife using Catholic funds supposedly reserved for the needy. Father Carcich did not stop here. Not long after, he furnished the Mandel family $12,000 more, this time payable to the second Mrs. Mandel. She had trouble, it appeared, raising from her ex-husband money due for child support. The Pallottines, nudged by the Mandel circle, obliged both Mandel wives and, by extension, their mutual Governor.

Word of the Pallottine loan had leaked to the newspapers, so a reporter asked the Governor about that.

"I never borrowed any money for my divorce from that organization, which is the Pallottines, period," said the Governor. Then he added: "I'm not going to comment any further. They had absolutely nothing to do with my divorce."

The Governor seemed to take the position that his divorce was one thing, his alimony payments something quite different and unconnected. So discerned, the Pallottine connection was supposedly unobjectionable. Months later, in June of 1976, this delicate bit of reasoning left many onlookers unconvinced, judging by the Governor's own comment that the Catholic Church still "was being unfairly criticized in the newspapers." He undertook to do something about it.

He did not hurry to give the Pallottines the money back. He did not call a news conference to explain, in detail and in public, the many hands that secretly shuffled checks behind the Pallottine loan. What he did, instead, was pay a private call on Archbishop William Borders, overall head of Catholics in the Baltimore area. His object: to explain to the archbishop how "totally unfair" public criticism of the church had been.

In court, under questioning by Barnet Skolnik, Marvin Mandel recalled his message: "I told the Archbishop Borders exactly what I know about it, and how I knew it, and what I know about it. . . . And I told him that it [the loan] was not involved in any divorce."

Skolnik pressed harder: "Did you tell Archbishop Borders that the Pallottines had provided $42,000 to refinance a loan that had been made to you for your alimony payments in connection with your divorce?"

"No, sir . . ." Then later: ". . . I told him that they had in no way been involved in my obtaining my divorce."

This was too much for Skolnik. He burst out: "Governor, isn't it a fact that you were not telling the truth when you told the public in December of '75 that the Pallottines had nothing to do with your divorce, that you did not tell the truth to Archbishop Borders in repeating that in June of '76, and that you are today telling the same falsehood because you are locked in by having lied about it twice in the past?"

The Governor said that was "not true, and you know it." Sputtering on both sides ended the exchange, which then turned to other things.

Here again, as with Ray's Point, the proverbial smoking pistol never appeared. One rather long reach by government investigators tried to establish that the $42,000 wasn't a loan at all and was, in fact, an accumulation of income owed Mandel on his 4 percent share of Security Investment—which, contrary to his testimony, he never renounced at all. True or untrue, this assertion depended almost exclusively on a mathematical computation too abstruse for ready comprehension. So that Mandel was being bribed was not at this point concretely demonstrated.

Instead, bribery was deducible only from a combination of circumstances. Came the Governor's private call upon people he had exchanged favors with, then the quick response of the Tidewater boys. Their sudden display of arm's-length caution suggested fear of the law. So did the bewildering flutter of checks backstage, the improbable front presented by the motorcycle salesman, the curious coincidence of a same-day check exchange for $42,000 between father and son, Marvin Mandel's own strained distinction between divorce and alimony.

Perhaps the Pallottine loan boils down to atmospherics, to a laying out of suspicious circumstances instead of facts locked up. It was not formally included as an item in the grand jury indictment. Still, contrarily, it scarcely strengthened the high posture of innocent, open friendship where the defendants insisted their relationship began and ended. It carried the aura of guilty knowledge, even if of knowledge discernible only in circumstantial outline.

In still another way, the Mandel divorce settlement drew substantial help from the Governor's fellow defendants. Irvin Kovens, specifically, furnished $155,000 in bonds. This money was the central and most concrete part of the 1973 agreement by which Barbara Mandel was induced, after five months embattled in the Governor's mansion, to pack up at last and leave. An irony is that Kovens had tried to dissuade Mandel from divorcing Barbara but, when he failed in this, came up with the bonds that made divorce possible. This sum, not uncovered until late in the investigation, was the first big chunk of money the government found going from Kovens to Mandel. Until then, Koven's indictment had seemed questionable. Not afterward.

Clothes, jewelry, vacations. Some free, some discounted, all oddly explained. These comprised the chicken feed the government said his bribers tossed the ever-receptive Mandel. In magnitude none of these gifts approached the great weight of the Security Investment transaction, none its elaborate camouflage. For audacity, none touched Ray's Point. The Pallottine loan stood by itself in paranoid insulation from prying eyes. But hand-out clothes and the rest served their own purpose as evidence.

In their smaller way, they provided glimpses of the startling generosity of the Mandel circle and, by their characteristically devious earmarks, suggested that at least someone therein was conscious that something wrong was being done. The effect was cumulative. It amounted not to the portrait, full-face, of fraud in action. Here was more the sketching in of background scenery, of men half-seen as they veered off habitually in directions other than straightforward.

Neither Bootsie's bracelet nor Gary's engagement ring figured in the indictment. But each shared with Security Investment and Ray's Point, the two bribes charged, a now-familiar circumstantial resemblance.

Neither cost Marvin Mandel real money. Both were paid for by cash, hence were untraceable except by exhaustive documentary research. Tidewater Insurance, or at least the boys there, handled both transactions. Bracelet as well as ring carried cover stories not altogether impervious. The old refrain, in short, rang out again—this time in a key too minor for indictment.

The diamond bracelet for Bootsie (by check, $5,000, by cash $4,500—cash generated at Tidewater) bore three conflicting explanations. Dale Hess called it the payoff on a bet he lost to Bootsie on the 1970 elections for governor. No, said Harry Rodgers, the bracelet was to reward Bootsie for the hard work she had put in on the election. Prosecutors offered a third version, quite different: the bracelet, they believed, was to pacify a Bootsie hurt and humiliated by Marvin's growing romance with Jeanne Dorsey. Handily, Tidewater then carried not one but two special funds. These were comfortably stretchable to embrace everything from bad bets to backstairs love and tended to be disbursed as cash.

Gary Mandel's engagement ring, while comparatively uncomplicated in purpose, did display quirks of its own. It too was paid for in cash, though whether in Tidewater cash or Gary's own cash was left unclear. The curiosity here was the means chosen for transporting the cash from Baltimore buyer to New York seller. A Tidewater courier was singled out for the job. Hess handed this courier cash totaling $2,600 (if by check, $3,300 had been demanded) in a brown paper bag or envelope and instructed him, first, to wear a green suit, then, second, to fly to Kennedy Airport in New York and, still at the airport, await a public page. This page came, finally, from a man named Fischer, the diamond cutter who liked to pick up his payments, as Tidewater put them out, in trackless cash. No track of either transaction turned up in Maryland until Fischer, the brother-in-law of a Tidewater associate, was brought protesting from New York to Baltimore, records in hand.

A bracelet and a ring did not draw down bribery charges upon the Mandel circle. No more so did a handful of vacations to Florida, each a gift. Nor several thousand dollars worth of custom-made clothes, likewise on the cuff. Questions arose of propriety and judgment, yes. Why did Governor Mandel think he was being so warmly massaged by men with keen interest in state contracts?

Close personal friendship was the explanation, happily wholesome, that most of them offered. Christmas trees were mentioned, jolly hunting trips, family dinners, poolside chats in the Florida sunshine. The friendship seems to have been largely authentic too; these people really liked and trusted one another—men not dissimilar in gravelly background, in a common drive to heights new and unfamiliar, in a shared relish of a lifestyle richly material. Overemphasis on friendly trust between defendants was to boomerang, however, later in court. It would present defense counsel with one of its most excruciating dilemmas.

Kovens, closest to Marvin Mandel, could tell him what the others couldn't. If he was going to be governor, Kovens said, he ought to dress like a governor—and in green sharkskin he didn't. Kovens was a man of lush haberdashery himself. He seems to have fastened on clothing the Governor as his personal contribution to uplifting Maryland; Johns Hopkins, Enoch Pratt, and Henry Walters, Kovens believed, would have understood.

As early as 1969, shortly after Mandel became governor, a funny thing happened to his clothes. New, fancier suits—laid-back cuffs, some with embroidery—began to appear. The bills for these, however, began to disappear, indeed to fade away like smoke. The Governor ordered several custom-made suits, sent to have them picked up, was told they had already been paid for. By whom? Well, they had been billed to Charlestown Racetrack as "guards' uniforms." Kovens owned the track.

Later came another set of suits, and Charlestown stood up again. In 1972, during a trip to Florida, bills for nearly $1,000 to dress up the Governor were paid by the boys from Tidewater, needled by Kovens. These were called birthday presents. Prior to a formal trip to Israel, the Governor was again outfitted at Kovens's expense by one of the most expensive tailors in the Baltimore area. Kovens, personally snappy in styled hair and white-on-white shirts, had undertaken to smooth out his governor's wrinkles and bulges. At least the ones that showed.

"Marvin Mandel . . . discarded the old green sharkskin," the

Evening Sun noted sadly, "and, with it, large chunks of the prudence which had safely bolstered him most of his life. Big treats here, big treats there. How he was expected to treat back he could guess easily enough, then push right out of his head. . . . It's dangerously humiliating for a man, as Spiro Agnew could have warned Marvin Mandel but probably didn't, to be the only one poor in a small circle of rich."

Millionaire Kovens and millionaire Hess enfolded him, so did the millionaire brothers Rodgers. First a sparkle of new clothes, then a sparkle of Florida sunshine, no less unaccustomed. The first of several journeys southward (this one on Kovens) took place in the spring of 1972: tensions were extraordinary. Marvin's affair with Jeanne Dorsey had become more and more public, Bootsie correspondingly irate. Hess and Kovens had tried to talk Marvin out of his fling with Jeanne; when he demurred, they thought a Florida vacation might at least patch up things with Bootsie. It didn't.

Another difficulty was an insurance bill, resisted by Harry Rodgers and others in the industry, which Mandel had just pushed through the 1972 legislature. On that, Florida's soft breezes did work a reconciliation.

But another, quite different, bill had failed at the very end of the same legislative session, the Marlboro bill in which all of those in the Florida party were vitally interested. And who was the acknowledged master of legislative action? Who had mercilessly pushed the Marlboro bill until, in a midnight blowup, the senate rebelled in a mad flurry of accusations and epithets? Why, it was one of their own circle, old and trusted friend Marvin Mandel—the man they had raised more than $500,000 to put in office and would raise $1 million more, had lavishly cultivated while he was there, had promised lucrative employment at his term's end.

So what did these friends whose central defense was their close relationship have to say, during their Florida vacation together, about the Marlboro outburst of a few days past? Were there recriminations? Surrender of hope? Or, instead, bright plans laid for the future?

None of the above, so the Mandel circle insisted. Marlboro, they said, was never mentioned—certainly never when the Governor was present. Why not? Well, because the Governor still didn't know their big secret from him, namely, that it was his best friends and biggest benefactors who owned Marlboro. Again, why not?

Because he might leak the truth to the news media, whereupon an outcry would arise from the Racing Commission, the legislature, the public. That's why the Governor wasn't told, why even a week later in the intimacy of Boca Raton, Florida, the Marlboro bill was never discussed in his presence.

So argued the defense, helplessly laying open the cruelest gap of all in their common credibility. They were helpless because they could not admit the Governor knew the secret as well as they did, specifically, that he knew it when in the spring of 1972 he was pushing the Marlboro bill toward enactment. For if he knew it at that time, then he was knowingly benefiting his friends, the friends who had so richly—and so recently—benefited him.

Favor for favor, a criminal bribery of Marvin Mandel would become obvious, a concealing fraud by all established. No, the Governor must not be seen to know, let alone to admit it. Logically, it was a position distorted beyond repair. It carried at its heart a betraying flaw that no amount of persuasion by the eloquent legal battery expensively marshaled by the Mandel circle could dispel. They never did, and the jury spoke accordingly.

B enjamin Sapperstein, an accountant thought to be the holder of many secrets, proved crustily determined to hold tight to them. Federal investigators were infuriated. They complained loudly of Sapperstein's delays in producing documents they had subpoenaed. To their questions he gave oral testimony that was partial, misleading, and at least once, according to Barnet Skolnik, outright false. But because they needed Sapperstein's information, investigators pressed him so mercilessly that they furnished Governor Mandel one large item, justified or not, in his letter of complaint to the Justice Department.

In fact, Sapperstein was frightened for himself and asserted Fifth Amendment rights. He needn't have. Prosecutors didn't want Sapperstein's skin; they wanted his documents, documents that would pin down charges of fraud and racketeering soon to be laid against the Governor and his friends. Sapperstein had kept the books for Harry Rodgers, for Dale Hess, and for the Tidewater Insurance Co. He was thought to be the possessor of evidence beyond price. Samples of their verbal exchanges before the grand jury show the prosecutors' determination, the witness's resistance, the mood they created between them:

Sapperstein— . . . I can't remember everything. I am only human. If there is a possibility that you know that I spoke to someone what in the name of God is there to . . . for you not to tell me so that I can intelligently discuss it with you? . . .

Skolnik—Mr. Sapperstein, it is not our job to be helpful to you.

A. — I am beginning to see that.

Q. —It is your attorney's job to be helpful to you. It is our job to investigate crime including, but by no means limited, to the crime of perjury committed in this room.

Q. —We asked you [Mr. Sapperstein] what did Mr. Sidle tell you and your answer is that you don't recall. If you are consciously aware as you gave that answer that it is false you are committing a crime.

A. —I understand.

Q. —And your subsequently discussing it with Mr. Sidle tomorrow or the next day or the next day is not going to change the fact that you committed a crime, is that clear?

Q. —. . . It's my understanding, Mr. Sapperstein . . .

A. —That I am physically . . .

Q. —That you are tired.

A. —Tired and worn out and I have a little diarrhea and it's just that maybe some of the answers have not been as lucid because I am physically tired. . . . I think that with a good night's sleep . . .

Q. —All right . . . you may leave.

Q. —. . . There is very substantial evidence to indicate that your client, as well as some of the individuals with whom he has been associated, lied to you and misled you and deceived you and in many ways caused you, deliberately and willfully caused you, to do things that should not have been done . . .

A. —Excuse me. If it ever comes out in a subsequent trial, any of these individuals, that I failed to do, elected to do certain things. I would not like the different bar associations or accounting associations to know that. . . . Maybe that's one of the things that made me feel a little ill yesterday, primarily when you said several times, Mr. Sapperstein, I don't believe you. That is worse to me than if you would pick up a knife and stick it in my finger or on my shoulder.

Q. —I'm sorry for that but I think it the better course for me to be candid with a witness than for me to con him. Very often, if I just don't plain believe a witness, I'm going to tell him rather than smiling at him and pretending that everything is fine, when inside my head bells are going off that I don't believe the witness . . .

13.

Winning/Losing, Three to Three: A Deeper Look

Because Francis D. Murnaghan, Jr., was the new boy on the Court of Appeals for the Fourth Circuit—so new he hadn't even read the file of the Mandel case—a degree of circumspection might have been expected. But no. Judge Murnaghan is not a circumspect type. He is red haired, blue eyed, given to snappy comebacks and occasional comeforwards. Irish irreverence is his trademark. The posture of the Mandel case as it neared its end in November, 1979, struck him as a court-wrought outrage.

It struck many others the same, if for varying reasons. Judges disliked what they called "federal intrusion" into Maryland affairs. Lawyers were disturbed by liberal admission of hearsay evidence, also by court meddling with political decisions traditionally made at the polls. The *Maryland Law Review* carried a thirty-nine page outburst of disapproval (see the Appendix). Laymen wondered, regardless of legal niceties, if Marvin Mandel and his friends had been convicted for doing little worse than others before them, than statesmen still piously enshrined in marble.

Not even the prosecutor's office found its satisfaction total. Russell T. Baker, Jr., U.S. attorney during the appellate stage, estimated later that up to 25 percent of Marylanders were dissatisfied with the result, a percentage he called unhelpful to building public confidence in the court system. My own count of grumblers was higher.

219

Judge Murnaghan's complaint was simple and direct. He didn't question the evidence or the prosecutor's theory of the case or the lower court's handling. What upset him was the blotched, confusing record his own appellate court had run up just before he joined it. Briefly, the record stood like this.

Following the jury's guilty verdict in district court, a three-man panel was told off from the Court of Appeals to hear the defendants' manifold objections. By two to one, Judge John D. Butzner, Jr., dissenting, the appellate panel reversed the lower court. Thereupon, the prosecutors asked for a full court rehearing. They got, this time, a six-man bench. Upon review the six split three to three, on whether to sustain the panel's earlier finding. By precedent, this even split had the effect of (1) overriding the two-to-one panel and (2) restoring the lower court result. So back to square one, guilty on multiple charges of mail fraud and racketeering.

That three-to-three split was what first drew Judge Murnaghan's ire. Stiffly, he tipped his hat to the "dedication, skill, compassion, and concern" of his fellow judges. Then he told them what he really thought: "Those considerations have not deterred me only because of a strange certainty, transcending the ordinary confidence one has in one's own convictions, that the court's failure to decide this case constitutes an important injustice."

As a remedy, Judge Murnaghan called for still further rehearing by the Court of Appeals. He hoped that the addition of new judges, or, better, one new judge, could produce a result clearer than this ambiguously even split. Above all, he demanded a clear tilt one way or the other, a genuine decision perceptible to all as decisive. Such was not to be, and the Murnaghan call rang unheeded in the judicial wilderness. It was a sorry turn to what Judge Murnaghan said was "no ordinary case . . . its consequences on the entire political system of the State of Maryland are enormous. It cries out for a proper resolution."

Which it did not get. Presented with a formal petition for a fresh rehearing, the court again split helplessly, this time four to four.

Frank Murnaghan had put his finger, at that stage, on what seemed this case's weakest link. Whoever heard of a ballgame lost three to three? An election won four to four? Worse, who could relish the spectacle of men sent off to prison when half the judges sitting on their case seemed to say serious mistakes had been made at trial?

The net of it was, the Court of Appeals added fresh vitality to a legend already born and already unwelcome. It was the legend that somehow, through a blur of technical twisters, sly feints, maybe a few solid blows below the belt, the Mandel group had been railroaded. The Governor was responsible for prearranging the legend. In the weeks immediately prior to indictment he had publicly stormed at the grand jury investigation as politically inspired, as vengeful, as traceable to Richard Nixon's paranoia. So here, to cap all that, comes the Court of Appeals with its supposedly solemn rulings, its nondecisive decisions, which had the bizarre effect of hustling him and his friends behind federal bars. Mandel legendry fattened accordingly: The man was robbed, wasn't he? In the confusion left by the appellate findings, few could convincingly say no.

And yet the Court of Appeals turned in a better, clearer job than it was generally seen to do. Masking its central position were the evenly split decisions, often taken as signs of the court's inability to separate innocence from guilt. Commonly overlooked was the court's effective message. This was a series of other decisions where clear majorities did emerge. These ran almost universally the government's way, one by one rejecting complaints raised by the defense. If prosecutors stood wounded at the moment of final triumph, the wounds were but skin deep. The defense lay largely flattened, appellate splits and all. If few got around to listening, the court's words were pretty plain.

A score-keeping exercise helps decipher what the court finally wrote. To start, both the first and last appellate decisions may be temporarily laid aside. The first, two-to-one, panel decision to reverse the district court was itself reversed, hence obliterated. The final, four-to-four, decision was purely procedural—to re-re-hear or not to re-re-hear?—and quite divorced anyway from the actual machinery of the case. So the substance of the court's position resided in its cluster of six-judge decisions, of which the three-to-three decision was only one. The rest of the decisions, several central, threw the other defense arguments to earth.

Mostly the court spoke in opinions as decisive as four to two at least. At some critical turnings even the two judicial doubters joined the majority ruling against the defense. Here the count stood six to zero, a stern rejection seldom acknowledged by adherents of the Mandel-was-robbed school of sympathizers. Anyway, guilt or nonguilt wasn't the court's focus, certainly not directly.

As usual at this midlevel court, questions presented for judgment bore on how the case was managed in trial court: whether statutes and precedents had been fitted correctly, defendants' rights observed, constitutional principles adhered to, and so on. Not the trial jury's verdict itself but how the verdict was reached is the business of appellate courts, and so it was here. How competently, for example, did district Judge Taylor handle his duties? Was the mail fraud statute properly applied? What of the presentation of evidence? Fair to the Mandel defendants or unfair?

To the barrage of questions flying at them, the appellate judges held ample power of response. They could affirm the verdict in the lower court or reverse it for judicial error. They could affirm in part, deny in part, or send back for a new trial. The court in Richmond, Virginia, flexed at one phase or another all of these judicial muscles, adding to the confusion Judge Murnaghan understandably complained of.

Confusion need not and should not remain impenetrable. At the outset, the underpinning of the case was quickly clarified and confirmed. The defense had undertaken as its main thrust to strike at both the mail fraud and the racketeering statutes on which the indictment had been based in Baltimore. Complaints arose against federal meddling in a state's historic right to police itself, also against court intrusion into procedures essentially political. This strategy carried a high constitutional ring: it got nowhere. Even the two judges of the three-judge panel who for other reasons wanted to reverse held that, in the essential framework of its indictment, the government had built soundly. The six-man court agreed.

Also dismissed was a defense complaint against Judge Taylor's use in trial court of the modified Allen, or "dynamite," charge. This he set off in order to jostle along to a decision the twelve jurors who, after several days of cogitation, thought they were unable to agree. Here too the six appellate judges apparently gave unanimous support.

Thereafter unanimity eroded, to be followed by splits on a pattern of four to two. The two holdouts were Judges H. Emory

Widener, Jr., and Donald S. Russell, the same pair who had comprised the majority for reversal on the original three-judge panel. Generally, these two defended their earlier rulings. They met, however, a new and contrary group of four judges who coalesced when the six-judge bench agreed to take over.

On this pattern two defense complaints that echoed outside the courtroom were brushed aside. They concerned prosecution use of, first, evidence that was plainly hearsay evidence and, second, a state code of ethics which did not apply to Mandel. Both were called unfair weapons. No, said the appellate judges. No, not unfair. The majority reasoning, so far as could be determined, was based on the generality that in fraud cases the intent of the accused is of paramount importance, hence that extraordinary flexibility is permitted in trying to answer that always tricky question: What was going on in the accused's mind when he did this or that? The general rule against hearsay evidence carries in it an exception. The court ruled that the exception fit this case. As to the code of ethics, while not applicable to Mandel, it amounted to little more than a bland statement of clean-government generalities, a presumed expression of current community belief about political right and wrong. The court majority said it had no objection, since it helped illuminate Mandel's intent. On both complaints, it ruled four to two against the defense.

What remained to bedevil the six judges, and to produce their lamented three-to-three split, was one issue. This was the proof required for mail fraud itself. The sticky part was the still relatively new concept of fraud, not just in the familiar marketplace sense, but fraud by public officials. Federal courts have taken many different positions, often mutually contradictory.

Essentially, the question as it arose in the Mandel case took this form: Was the language of the statute forbidding mail fraud to be taken literally, word for word? If so, and the prosecution argued so, the jury was to determine for itself from the evidence presented by both sides whether fraud had been committed. If not, and here the defense came closest to an upset, the trial judge wrongly had failed to define bribery as in this case the legal task vital to pinning down the mail fraud counts.

Was it sufficient that bribery-type activities were self-evident? And that Judge Taylor did meticulously instruct the jurors on bribery in the same charge but in a different place as it bore on a separate count, racketeering? Or should the bribery instruction have been given twice instead of only once? The question was somewhat more than technical and procedural. It touched on the clarity of the jurors' understanding of what was required of them.

Plainly, subtleties were abundant. Plainly, too, both prosecution and defense found ample room for maneuvering between two competing concepts: the prosecution for a broad, enveloping mail fraud concept, the defense for a concept more precisely pinned down to bribery underlying the fraud. The first left open doors through which to introduce more evidence of different sorts. The government, not unnaturally, leaned that way. The second, tighter, concept put a heavier burden on the prosecution, especially the requirement to spell out an interlocking quid pro quo exchange between the briber and the bribed. Here, unsurprisingly, stood the defense.

It was this second concept that, as it turned out, furnished the defense its cutting edge inside the appellate court. It fetched Judge Widener and Judge Russell, led them to vote to reverse the conviction found in trial court. And, at the en banc hearing by six judges, a third judge never publicly named joined the Widener-Russell view on the one point—disapproval of part of the trial judge's instruction to the jury—but on none of the rest of the defense objections.

Hence the three-to-three split and its effects. One, by established custom, was to wipe out the earlier, two-to-one, reversal by the panel and to restore the trial court findings: guilty. A second was failure to establish a precedent for future use—instruct for bribery, or not?—in a mail fraud case where bribery is central to several other wrongdoings charged. Only when a clear majority emerges is a precedent established. The upshot was this: the Fourth Circuit's nondecisive decision left formally unanswered the most ticklish question raised by the Mandel defense. Other cases to come would have to struggle along without binding guidance from this one.

On all other points, notably the most substantial ones, the outcome was different. The court majority spoke either explicitly or implicitly in favor of the prosecution and against the defense. Most important, for onlooking laymen blinded by legalistic flash and counterflash, was the flow of actual evidence of wrongdoing. Here the court found the evidence sufficient to warrant conviction. The finding was implicit, to be sure, but without a finding of sufficient evidence a retrial would have been obligatory and would have been ordered. It wasn't ordered and so, as a practical matter, the trial court's verdict of guilty was reestablished.

There lingered the vexing question: Why? On what grounds?

Perhaps unfortunately, the opinion came down terse and without explanation. Only Judge Widener, this time in dissent, undertook to set out his reflections (joined as usual by Judge Russell). Of the others who stood alike on most points, none undertook to lace these points together in judicial symmetry, much less in philosophical contour. Apparently, they simply read the rival briefs—the statutes, the precedents, the evidence, the procedure—and found the district court right in the first place. They did not say why, thus bringing the case to its ragged close.

Judge Murnaghan's stab at clarification was novel, even quixotic. When the defendants asked for still a further rehearing following the three-to-three ruling, the court membership had been increased from seven to nine. Yet as in the earlier, "full bench," hearing, the bench wasn't quite full. One judge—Harrison Winter, of Baltimore—excused himself because of previous, peripheral, contacts with some of the defendants. It was the Winter withdrawal that had shrunk the seven-man court to six. Now, exercised again, it would shrink the nine-man court to eight.

Instantly another even split loomed, this time four to four. Judge Murnaghan contrived, in theory, a rescue from the same pitfall. He tried it on in advance. How, he said, about this? He and Judge James M. Sprouse were the two new members of the eight-judge court, hence the two without known position on the Mandel case. Why shouldn't one or the other of them simply withdraw, thus creating a court uneven at seven members? Thus the stage would be set for the decisive, authoritative court ruling up to now so sorely lacking. Let Judge Sprouse, Judge Murnaghan went on, decide first whether to step aside. If he did, the seven-man court would become a reality. If he did not, Judge Murnaghan volunteered to withdraw. Either way, a clear decision was guaranteed because the court would be left odd-numbered.

Why was he able to take this in-or-out posture? Because, the judge said, of professional reasons so "tenuous and speculative" for excusing himself that he felt justified in either picking up the reasons or putting them down. He felt free to take either course, stay in or get out, which would produce the objective he considered overriding, an authoritative decision.

Judge Murnaghan's was a visionary proposal, creative and daring. Successfully carried off, it might well have sealed up one way or another the persistent drip-drip leakage of discontent which was destined to stain indefinitely the public impression of the finale of the Mandel case. That it didn't was traceable to the sudden intrusion of a killing flaw, a Catch 22 or, in this case, Catch 8. Judge Murnaghan couldn't get there from where he was: he couldn't win from the eight-man court the relatively minor but still vital first step. He couldn't persuade the court to reduce itself to seven, then to vote on whether to rehear the case.

Four judges stood fast by the old rule. Four voted to try the new Murnaghan way. So it was four to four, back still again to guilty as convicted, no further rehearing. An added irony: It was Judge Murnaghan's own vote that made the fourth in favor of rehearing, thus precipitating the very four-to-four split he eloquently deplored.

Even the Supreme Court, when asked later by the defendants for review, said no. At least six justices of the nine discerned nothing worth their serious attention emerging from the courts below. Four justices or more must agree to Supreme Court review.

No wonder Russell Baker, sampling as U.S. attorney the public response to this convoluted progress through the courts, sensed a confusion greater than ordinary. No wonder, even, that the courts themselves in one case broke evenly and several times angrily on important issues. What both citizens and judges faced in the Mandel trial was not a clear-cut violation of a statute—murder, robbery, tax evasion, bigamy—long familiar from many trips around the judicial track. Mail fraud, as used here, seemed a newfangled notion hardly convincing to the average onlooker. Racketeering, the other charge, sounded outright bizarre.

Both deserve closer inspection, especially the concept of mail fraud by public official. This holds to the proposition, startling to many, that a public official owes his constituents—really, his employers—an honest administration of their government business. Honest, that is, in being undistorted by bribery or other betrayal of the trust publicly established in his official position. The law, in short, insists on honest government. It tries actively to enforce it.

Maybe technically the law always stood for this sort of honesty, but the actuality was different. Dating from the Revolution at least, Americans have been skeptical of nearly any government at all, especially of the officials who run it. Outright cynicism suffused the common view of government figures: the only way to look at a politician, the sour old saying went, is down. So demeaned, politicians responded accordingly. As both writers and enforcers of the law, government figures managed to elude the clutch of their own legal fingers with ease. They heard little outcry from a public that habitually drew perverse satisfaction from watching its worst expectations of corruption come predictably to bloom.

New, sterner views long preceded the righteous outpouring that followed the shock of Watergate. A series of road-building scandals in Louisiana had precipitated a fresh look in the 1940s at the relationship between public servant, or politician, and public employer, or citizen. Before that development occurred, fraud, like rats, was long a familiar byproduct of the commercial marketplace: it was cheating, pretending a product was good instead of bad. It was flimflam, a deception aimed at unfair deprivation of something of value. Fraud, coupled with use of the U.S. mail, was made a federal offense as early as 1872. So well understood was this ordinary, marketplace fraud that a federal judge commented: "The law does not define fraud; it needs no definition; it is as old as falsehood and as versatile as human ingenuity."

When federal courts in Louisiana began to switch something ordinary and old to something else extraordinary and new it was the birth of a notion, at least a notion sharply refined. A citizen, it was held, has a vested right to honest government as fair return on the taxes he pays. When deprived of this right, he loses something of value, something that need not be measurable in money. When lied to about his loss, he is defrauded. Finally, when a letter is mailed to further this act, the federal statute forbidding mail fraud is violated.

All of which amounted to a bubbling up, at last, of long-smothered popular resentment against flagrant corruption in public office. Mail fraud, as a federal crime, became recognizable in government just as it long had been in the marketplace.

By the 1970s the new idea gravitated to the fountainhead of political corruption, Chicago. There the most prominent to fall was the tallest public figure in town: former governor of Illinois, at that time federal judge, potential presidential material, Otto Kerner. The Kerner case showed striking parallels with the

Mandel case. It involved the secret sale of racetrack stock at a fraction of its true value. Kerner, as governor, pushed racetrack legislation to help his benefactor. Kerner's interests were hidden behind nominees. When he sold his interests, he profited by $140,000, money piped to him via convoluted channels. Kerner misrepresented the money's source on his income tax return. Documents created in 1966 were back-dated to 1962. And so on. Set forth was an Illinois preview of the closely similar transactions soon to unfold in Maryland. Marvin Mandel and his friends might well have studied technique at the feet of Otto Kerner: his troubles occurred two years too late for the Marylanders to be aware that Kerner would be indicted, tried, convicted, and sentenced for mail fraud in 1974. Most of the would-be Mandel exchange took place, undeterred by the Kerner lesson, in 1972.

One who was more than a little interested by the similarities of the two cases was the same Judge Taylor, who formed probably the closest linkage between them. It was Judge Taylor who was called from his Tennessee court to Chicago to preside in the Kerner case. Afterward in Baltimore—when first Judge Herbert F. Murray had been edged aside quite innocently because a former law partner had some early association with the case, and when following that Judge John Pratt had stepped out after calling a mistrial for attempted jury tampering—Judge Taylor picked up where they left off. It was the Taylor personality, firm but twinkling, as astute as worldly, which gave the Mandel courtroom a good-natured relaxation. It was the Taylor judicial philosophy— open the jurors to as much evidence on both sides as possible, then give them ample opportunity to exercise their own judgment—which fixed the character of the trial. Mainly, it was Judge Taylor's earlier seasoning in Chicago with the vagaries of mail fraud and bribery which gave his Baltimore rulings sharp authority. His final charge to the jury, on only one point of which the defendants were able to secure a three-to-three appellate split, had been carefully modeled on his earlier charge to the Kerner jury. That too had survived appellate scrutiny.

For the U.S. attorneys in Baltimore, the Kerner trial validated the mail fraud statute as a framework in which to test the still-uncertain concept of corruption in a public official. The bribery aspect of the Mandel case made a neat fit; both briber and bribed could be ensnared without reference to the Maryland bribery statute, which some called tricky. As to criminal intent, always the element vital in establishing a mail fraud case, no turncoat witness showed up. What did come flooding to hand was a cascade of documents: documents altered, documents back-dated, documents falsified. Here was a situation where the documents, although circumstantial evidence, promised to be more probative than some direct evidence of a witness eagerly trading for his own immunity. Still, a faint uneasiness troubled the prosecutors.

In Maryland, unlike Louisiana and Illinois, federal mail fraud had seldom been pinned to public officials. Would the federal bench there feel comfortable with the idea of a citizen's right to honest government? Would the judges discern that right to be as substantial, if not as tangible, as his right to own private property? Could a judge newly come to this delicate notion come so far as to acknowledge the further proposition that a private citizen's right, so held, must not be damaged or diminished by a public official? That an official corrupted by, say, a bribe was damaging that citizen's right? Finally, that by concealment of his act the official was not just damaging the citizen's right but damaging it fraudulently, which is to say, criminally?

Here ran a line of judicial reasoning increasingly accepted elsewhere as sound. Ask Otto Kerner, a federal judge himself, languishing in federal prison for mail fraud. And yet would Marylanders accept it? If not, if a federal judge in Baltimore quarreled with the U.S. attorney's application of the federal mail fraud statute, the Mandel case with all the months of investigation which went into it might be pitched out of court on the trial's first day. The U.S. attorney's office wanted to avoid such a risk.

Prudently, prosecutors looked around for a backup, a supporting line of attack. Prudent, yes, but here prudence didn't pay. It cost them heavily instead, nearly sinking the whole case they thought they were buoying up. Infuriatingly, as things turned out, they hadn't needed the treacherous buoyancy after all.

All that became apparent only in hindsight. What drew Barnet Skolnik and his team to the mail fraud statute in the first place was its breadth and flexibility. It covered bribery, the essence of their case, but covered more besides. It also covered deception of government agencies, and the evidence at hand seemed to point unmistakably to doubletalk and half-truth, to willful distortion and downright lie. Further, the statute recognized in fraud an element of conspiracy, an offense that may encircle not just the principals, bribers and bribed, but also people only partially involved. The government was out to bag the lot, six men of varying shades and sorts of guilt. It needed mail fraud's net, not bribery's stiletto. Mail fraud held out the weapon of choice, but was it a weapon wieldable in the Maryland jurisdiction?

Perhaps not, whereupon the prosecution took its fateful turn to another and quite different fallback weapon, racketeering. Here again was a relatively new law, one dating back only a decade to congressional impatience with organized criminals who muscle in on legitimate business. If a circle not noted for social daintiness, Marvin Mandel and company were scarcely Mafia dons. That didn't matter. The language of the antiracketeering statute fit nicely about the government's evidence against them. What's more, the statute carried in it leverage to extract from the defendants, by means of forced forfeiture, any illegal gains their wrongdoings had won them. Mail fraud alone did not.

Almost as a last-minute addition, Dan Hurson's suggestion was taken up. Write in a couple of racketeering counts, he advised, as a strategic safeguard. Install a spare legal option to rescue the case in the event, unlikely but remotely possible, the main mail fraud counts strike the trial court judge as too newfangled and unrefined by earlier trials to suit this one. Should mail fraud thus be thrown out in the opening moments, then the racketeering provision would open up like a legal parachute to spare the prosecution a fatal fall to earth. Skolnik liked Hurson's idea too as a way to wheel in a formidable piece of prosecutorial machinery for use in other trials to appear later in the Fourth Judicial Circuit

Then loomed the trouble, months in the shaping. Wrapping up mail fraud counts and racketeering counts with the same indictment, and making them partly interdependent, was to prove an operation almost too delicate to carry off with legal finesse. The slippery item was bribery. In the Mandel context, bribery seemed only implicit to mail fraud; to racketeering, however, bribery had to be explicit or the case wasn't proved. Because the same evidence was brought to bear on all counts, mail fraud as well as racketeering, the question of establishing bribery turned into a tormenting puzzle.

Must bribery be pinned down in the precise, quid pro quo way? The Maryland bribery statute, after all, had been brought in as part of the racketeering counts. Or was proof of the more generalized sort sufficient, the sort often used in previous mail fraud cases? Here arose the sort of professional wrangle in which lawyers delight, jurors despair, and judges decide.

The government's formula was to give the overriding indictment a flexible either-or posture. Bribery was alleged, but, if mail fraud was held by the jury to be established by the evidence, then that would establish racketeering as well. Precise proof of bribery, in that event, became unnecessary altogether. A mail fraud conviction would cover both sorts of count. So argued the prosecution, despite an early and continuing series of objections by the defense. At trial, Judge Taylor ruled consistently the prosecution way.

Still, all this made for some pretty intricate mating of two legal species not altogether compatible. Arnold Weiner sensed from the outset of the trial that in the contrasting approaches to bribery—close-hauled vs. winging—lay his best bet to eviscerate the government's case. What he had to do first was belittle the mail fraud concept as no more than an ill-defined accusation of noncriminal concealment. That disposed of, he could turn squarely upon bribery and demand from the prosecution a close demonstration of guilt it might have trouble producing. After all, Weiner could say, bribery flavors ran all through the indictment: implicit in mail fraud, explicit and indeed charged under racketeering. So let the government prove bribery. Let it hew to the line of tight precedents long familiar, long in place.

What Weiner strongly suspected was that if the government had been truly confident of its bribery evidence it would have made bribery and not mail fraud its main case. It did not. Consequently, as a sound tactician, Weiner played his own strongest card. He pushed for the form of a bribery trial, a trial the government hadn't brought and didn't want. The success he won was fleeting and limited; indeed, it may have come as a private surprise to even its perceptive author. Weiner's stroke which turned out to be damaging was not even the first one in a rolling barrage of complaints he laid down in the main brief for appellants. It was listed third in line, behind legal-political conflicts and behind federal intrusion. Only then did he complain of the lack of bribery instruction. Even so, in retrospect this seemed the most skillful defensive footwork the Mandel side produced.

On his side Barney Skolnik kicked himself once the framework of the case began to fall into place. First, his fears about getting mail fraud established as the question at the center of proceedings proved groundless. Three trial court judges in a row showed themselves comfortable with the new Illinois cases. They accepted Skolnik's presentation. So far, so good: but then came the racketeering counts, including the specific charge of bribery.

Here Skolnik had to watch Weiner pounce, hammering on bribery as the indispensable ingredient not just to racketeering but to mail fraud too. Bribery was bribery, Weiner kept saying, no matter what shape the formal count took. Skillfully he converted the racketeering-bribery counts from the saving parachute Skolnik thought he was designing to an anchor tied, maddeningly, to the prosecution's tail. The trial judge resisted Weiner. He was convinced that a mail fraud trial was one thing and a bribery trial quite something else. After thirteen days, if with a hesitant gulp, the trial jury went along. But Weiner from the outset had aimed over trial court heads. Baltimore be damned. His target was Richmond and a winning appeal.

A legal rule of thumb is that district courts are more sensitive to the pressure of evidence, to the documents and witnesses with which the Mandel case bristled. Still another rule holds that jurors are largely uninfluenced by the trial judge's—Judge Taylor's, for example—long, droning instructions and rely instead on their own visceral sense of innocence or guilt.

Not appellate courts, not appellate judges. They look to procedure, and it was on a point more elegantly procedural than grittily substantial that Weiner scored at last upon his long-range appellate target. It was on a point of Judge Taylor's instruction, or lack of it, about bribery that two Weiner-prompted members of the three-judge panel found "error." They reversed the jury's vote to convict Marvin Mandel and his five associates. They ordered a new trial.

This reversible "error," if that is what it was, was not altogether procedural. What Judge Taylor had failed to do, despite Weiner's request, was instruct the jury that to convict for mail fraud it was required to find explicit bribery; something of value had to be exchanged for something else, quid pro quo. A lesser failure, in appellate eyes, was his lack of instruction that to be found guilty Mandel must be recognized as being aware, which he denied, that his friends owned Marlboro.

Two other appellate objections—to admitting hearsay evidence, to admitting a state code of ethics inapplicable to

Mandel—would be brushed aside later by the six-man court. This was a matter of establishing intent. Though troublesome to many onlookers, nearly any evidence from either side, provided it threw genuine light on what the defendants were actually up to, was tolerated by the appellate court. Intent is commonly the make-or-break issue in mail fraud cases.

What remained to stick in the appellate ear had been thoughtfully inserted there by Weiner. This was the puzzle about the precision with which bribery must be proven. Here lay the crux of the all-important three-to-three split, the appellate court's final judgment.

Judge Widener was the spokesman for close definition of bribery. His sharpest point was framed in the question: Where runs the line between small, innocent gift and large, guilty bribe? Many private companies, the judge correctly observed, by custom hand public officials small tokens of goodwill: dinner or ballgame tickets, cases of liquor, weekend use of a hunting lodge. These are not necessarily bribes, not in the sense that the public official's judgment is corruptly twisted to return the private giver something of value, something he does not deserve. They are instead simple insurance that a phone call will be returned, a letter answered, a name remembered at cocktail parties. What may be the origin of the word *tip* is not inappropriate: to insure promptness.

Some jurors, in Judge Widener's opinion, might not recognize this category of private-public gifts as nonbribes, hence noncriminal. What was needed here and not given, he said, was precise instruction by the trial judge as to what a bribe is and what it isn't. What's more, he went on, it was needed at the point where the instruction on fraud was given. Short of that, Judge Widener noted, a juror might feel genuine confusion about the guilt he should attach to the gifts, large and small, given to Marvin Mandel. And a vote for criminal guilt must be a vote beyond reasonable doubt.

At first some doubt had indeed beset the jurors. Three days of deliberations brought from the jury foreman the admission: "We are unable to come to a unanimous decision as to the existence of a scheme to defraud." Originally four jurors had held out for Mandel's innocence, for the belief that the others—especially Hess, Kovens, Harry Rodgers—had duped him into a criminal deal he naively misunderstood: so they told newsmen later. Nine more days of deliberations changed that. Mandel's own testimony, several jurors said later, was his undoing. They decided they couldn't believe what he said, let alone what the other defendants said about him. They told newsmen they thought he took bribes and lied to cover them up. The verdict of guilt, if long coming, was unanimous.

There eventually followed, as noted, the decision, that in effect, affirmed the trial court's verdict of guilt. Two other appellate judges followed the Widener reasoning, or parts of it. That nevertheless left the six-judge court one short of the four votes needed to sustain a reversal, whereupon the defense achieved its high watermark and fell back. It never regained momentum.

The other, prevailing, three members of the appeals court said little to clarify their opinion. Why did they back away from the two-to-one reversal first produced? What analysis of the contending sides, prosecution and defense, did they accept as correct? On this they stood virtually silent, as reviewing courts often do, stating only that "a majority" of the court—unnamed, uncounted—"would affirm the judgments of conviction" against all of the contentions of the defense. To this the lone exception was the "claim of [Judge Taylor's] error in the charge to the jury." On that, the court said, there was "equal division," meaning three judges found error and three did not. For future courts, let alone for historians, the Fourth Circuit's terse, two sentence ruling left unsure guidelines. It read:

> The judgments of conviction are affirmed by an equally divided court.
>
> A majority of the members of the en banc court would affirm the judgments of conviction against all of the contentions of the appellants except the claim of error in the charge to the jury which was the point upon which there was equal division.

It's a treacherous undertaking to paw about in the haze left by a court that, for reasons unstated, deliberately shunned clarity. Here lurk the wishful "probablys," the doubtful "must have beens," the uncertified "reasonable assumptions." How the pitfalls yawn on a road to truth for which the judicial map stands virtually blank. Helpfully, if not transcendingly, one set of articulated clues to the heart of the opinion does turn up.

These appear, ironically, in the dissent offered by Judge John Butzner to the earlier panel ruling. This judge thought the trial court finding of guilt should stand just as, in the end, it did. What's more, the judge said why and said it emphatically. So the Butzner dissent offers the most revealing peek behind the dark curtain the appellate ruling drew about itself. One man, one insider, had spoken. The rationale here is that when the en banc ruling found the panel majority wrong, the result was that the panel dissenter—Judge Butzner—was right.

What flaws this rationale somewhat is that two wrongs, especially when perceived through rhetoric so billowing, don't necessarily make a right. Also that judges may well tend, while disagreeing on subordinate matters, to consolidate on a central or controlling opinion. The short of it is, no outsider knows what part of the whole court thought of which part of Judge Butzner's dissent. Still, shaky clue though it is, it is the best clue. The Butzner opinion came out on the same side as, for practical purposes, the final court ruling, namely, affirmation of conviction. Subject to obvious reservations, Judge Butzner's written words throw the best light available on why the six-man court found as it did. It helps explain where Marvin Mandel failed in court and why he went to prison.

The Butzner dissent is vigorous, blunt, and clear. It embraces all the objections cited by the panel majority in its reversal—jury instruction, hearsay evidence, misuse of code of ethics—and calls them wrongly raised. Finally, Judge Butzner goes beyond the majority opinion and considers, in addition, the sufficiency of evidence brought by the prosecution. This evidence, he wrote, "amply" established guilt. He said conviction should be affirmed.

Affirmed it was to be, but later, and by a six-judge court, not by a three-judge court. To the extent that this Butzner dissent at first forecasts and then reflects from within the otherwise almost silent position of the prevailing trio of which Judge Butzner was a member, it calls for inspection not ordinarily given dissenting opinions. Here is what courts call the best evidence available on a court performance left otherwise murky. Serious questions were raised by the appellants; many of these questions still stand open in the public mind. The Butzner dissent makes plain one set of answers, at least, to where and why the Mandel appeal fell apart.

As noted earlier, the majority of the appellate court stood at least four to two against the appellants on all points but one. Not surprisingly, Judge Butzner had earlier turned his most searching attention to the lone issue on which the court would split three to three. This was the issue of jury instruction, of whether Judge Taylor had dealt adequately in his charge with the somewhat floating question of bribery. Had bribery as a crime been sufficiently brought down, in a mail fraud context, to judicial earth? Was the jury told beyond question what it must find to convict of mail fraud? Of racketeering? Or did Judge Taylor fuzz up his instructions so sadly that jurors were left adrift in a bewildering fog?

Judge Butzner found no fog at all. Turning directly to the text of Judge Taylor's instructions, he quoted from them eight plump paragraphs dissecting the pivotal point: What is bribery and what isn't? What is the required quid pro quo relationship, the something of value corruptly given in exchange for something else?

To Judge Butzner this instruction fit precisely the instruction on bribery which in a recent case, designated *Arthur*, this very Fourth Circuit had approved. Still, not even Judge Widener, in writing his panel majority opinion, had objected to this bribery instruction as set forth at that point in the charge. What had troubled him was that it was set forth only under the racketeering counts, that it was not set forth a second time under the mail fraud counts, even though bribery furnished the central hinge of the fraudulent wrongdoings. Wouldn't that omission, Judge Widener asked pointedly, fatally confuse a conscientious juror?

Not at all, said Judge Butzner, not at all. On the contrary, he said, for a trial judge to go plodding twice through the same meticulous instruction on bribery would really confuse a juror. Precedent held no requirement for such double instruction. Besides, why give the same instruction twice when the same evidence was being used to support both allegations, mail fraud and racketeering? No, said Judge Butzner, Judge Taylor did not fail. He did his judicial job well.

Judge Butzner said:

> The trial of this lengthy case required the able experienced district judge to whom it was especially assigned to make many rulings involving the admission and exclusion of evidence and to explain to the jury in clear and concise

terms the principles of law on which both the prosecution and the numerous defendants relied. To do justice to both sides, he had to exercise in full measure the discretion entrusted to a trial judge . . . but . . . he must necessarily exercise judgment in applying the stark letter of the law to the facts that are the subject of controversy.

My study of the record convinces me that the trial judge responsibly discharged his duty.

To what extent these earlier words of Judge Butzner's, written in dissent, carried in them the later judgment of colleagues who then joined him is not known. Only this is indisputable: the central point is that conviction of the Mandel circle was affirmed. The rest fades to nuance and detail which, however provocative of lawyerish debate, did not change the practical outcome of a long and closely fought case.

The Mandel appeal had sprung to life, momentarily, in a ruling by a divided three-judge panel. Thereafter a six-judge court, sitting together, could not support the panel. Also divided, it upset the panel and restored the original findings of guilty as made in trial court in Baltimore.

So ended the facts. Speculation began, speculation invited by the virtual silence surrounding the final court ruling. Contrasting analyses of the court's position are available from two anonymous sources, each closely familiar with these judges' habitual method of operation. One analysis tends to rationalize the court's seemingly erratic course, to discern an underlying purpose. The second analysis does not: it discerns little but internal chaos and only an arithmetical, almost accidental decision to affirm the Mandel conviction.

The more philosophical of the two analysts perceives the significant division not as three to three, but as four to two, the majority by which all but the question of bribery was decided. Within that dominant four-judge bloc, he read this mood of judicial practicality: These four judges would have been happier if Judge Taylor had included mail fraud within his bribery instruction, given only for racketeering, in his charge to the jury. Instructing twice would have been unnecessary. A simple way would have been to give the strict quid pro quo once, then say it applied to both the mail fraud and the racketeering counts. Still, if failure to do this was judicial error, it was harmless error and not serious enough to warrant reversal. What compelled the judges whose opinion prevailed was the record as a whole, the totality of the case.

Looked at that way, the central pieces fitted together. The bribery instruction was fairly given under the racketeering counts. Since the jury convicted on racketeering, the implication of a bribery finding was strong. That implication carried over to the mail fraud counts, even though the bribery instruction was not given precisely there. So in the total context, if a little willy nilly, a mail fraud conviction was justified by a finding of bribery under racketeering. That clinched the crime, the heart of the case.

The second analyst holds to the view that three to three, not four to two, was the telling count of the judges. He goes on to say that no unspoken agreement to affirm existed, that no collegial arrangement prevailed on the court. On the contrary, it was each judge for himself, leading to a sharp general dispute on the bribery instruction. The final agreement to affirm reflected no more than the arithmetic of the way the judicial votes fell point by point. Thus the court had no overall message framed up; it sent none. Here was, in this view, a grave abdication of judicial responsibility—even though this analyst, like the first, believed the defendants to be guilty. He called the appellate process a judicial fumble.

Maybe the debate is academic. Maybe the four-judge majority that held on most of the issues was persuaded on fundamentals. If so, it was unwilling to dismantle and send back for retrial a case already mistried once, tried a second time for three months, with jurors thirteen days in deliberation. It was a case fairly tried on all key points, a case by now impoverishing some defendants, and, on the government side, severely draining time and manpower. Besides, sufficient wrongdoing had been demonstrated, whatever the technical label pinned on it. The Governor's friends had rewarded him too richly, too often for innocent explanations. The proposition that he did not know of their Marlboro connections, hence that the help he gave Marlboro was unwitting, strained credulity to the breaking point.

The quid pro quo exchange, the nugget of the case, was obvious. It was obviously corrupt. Conviction was the just response.

F or prosecutors, to bring a criminal case to verdict is no less delicate than for a pregnant woman to bring her child to birth. One hazard is standard defense tactics: counsel often feels duty bound, contrarily, to try to abort.

This is especially so where the evidence piles high and damning, as in the Mandel trial. Mistrial! cry the defendants, looking for every aperture to make a backdoor exit. Defense tables tend to pour out a stream of complaints against alleged misconduct by the prosecution, alleged regional prejudice. All these characterized the Mandel trial. Even collapses by defendants are commonly alleged: Marvin Mandel was said to have suffered a midtrial stroke, Irvin Kovens a bad heart, Ernest Cory financial ruin and a nervous breakdown. Those judges who are blessed with inward security commonly sit unjostled. They commonly brush aside transparent maneuvers toward the cheap, unearned victory held out by a mistrial. In December of 1976, however, someone caught the Mandel court off-guard and vulnerable. Someone went too far.

The someone, Barney Skolnik was sure, was "a shark" he couldn't quite identify but who frightened him all the same. "We are frankly concerned, is the mildest word we can find about the situation," he said, relating in a secret conference in the judge's chambers what seemed to him to be happening. "It's like we are swimmers and there is a shark out there that keeps nipping at us." They had been nipped as many as four times, he said.

Twice, the shark drew blood. Twice, attempts were made to fix the Mandel jury, and the trial was indeed aborted, by a mistrial declared thirteen weeks along. Twice men were caught and jailed. The whole prosecution case was left open on the record, while the defense was still clearing its throat. Many thought proceedings could never be resurrected and that the six defendants had, on a fluke, gone free. Others suspected it was no fluke at all but a desperate plan drawn in cold blood. But drawn by whom?

Hardly by government prosecutors, not after nervously gathering and cuddling their evidence for nearly two years.

In open court, Judge John H. Pratt showed where most suspicions lay: "It goes without saying that publicity concerning a charge of attempted bribery . . . is perhaps the most prejudicial type of publicity since any juror, including a conscientious juror, would draw the inference of involvement on the part of some defendant."

A jury suspicious that "some defendant" was trying, by bribery, to fix his own case was obviously not an impartial jury. So Judge Pratt reluctantly granted a defense motion for a mistrial.

Prosecutors were heartbroken. Defendants pronounced themselves heartbroken too, a position not everyone took altogether seriously. Certainly not those of the defense staff who filled three jolly tables in the restaurant of the Baltimore Hilton a half-hour after the mistrial was declared. Thomas C. Green, attorney for Harry W. Rodgers, III, closed one eye, according to the Baltimore Sun, and "twisted his mouth into a toothy grin and entertained the group with his imitation of a shark."

One last toast followed: "To the shark!"

So who?

Several tried to point a finger at Irvin Kovens—a sometime Kovens confidant and tough guy, the late Jimmy Hoffa of Teamsters fame, had been jailed for jury tampering—but nobody came up with any hard evidence against Kovens. Nobody knew then who the shark was and, at the time of this writing, still nobody knew.

The facts of the two documented passes made at the jury, and the consequent mistrial, are briefly recounted. Five seconds of a television news bulletin was overheard by at least six jurors in the Mandel case early in December, 1976. "Baltimore area man held on charges of jury tampering in Mandel trial, and now reports of still another attempt." That sent up the balloon. As noted, Judge Pratt thought jurors would suspect the defendants, rightly or wrongly, and hence be unable to give them an unprejudiced hearing on the main event, the trial on mail fraud charges. Regretfully—at the urging of defense counsel, resisted by prosecutors—he called a mistrial.

Up to the moment of the infectious telecast, all sides—prosecution, defense, Judge Pratt—had struggled in their respective ways to keep two dirty secrets from poisoning jurors' minds. First, there had been Charles E. Neiswender, apparently a clumsy schemer. For $20,000, Neiswender told Arnold Weiner, Mandel's lawyer, in a telephone call made shortly after the trial began, I can get at least one, maybe two, jurors to vote for acquittal. The jury would be hung, the case dismissed, the defendants free.

Would Weiner cooperate?

Weiner, shocked, pretended he would. Instead, he turned Neiswender over to federal authorities, who secretly arrested him. What was Neiswender up to? Two versions exist.

Neiswender's own version is that he had counted on Weiner, an honest man, to do what he did: tell it to the cops, loosing a blast of obviously prejudicial publicity, then a mistrial. Neiswender said he had been put up to this—and paid—by someone unidentified, someone "in the Baltimore area." In short, some shark.

Another version is that Neiswender was, instead, a confidence man himself who in fact had no juror for sale, who simply hoped to winkle a dishonest dollar out of the Mandel circle via his approach to Weiner. No shark here, more a dolphin with a sweet tooth. Neiswender served nearly twenty-one months in federal prison.

The second dirty secret was Walter Weikers, a West Baltimore furniture salesman who, two months after Neiswender, brought a stranger case. Weikers directly approached his own relative by marriage, Oscar Sislen, a Washington-area limousine chauffeur who was serving as juror in the Mandel trial. If Sislen would hang the jury with a vote for acquittal, Weikers told him, he would pay him $10,000. Sislen, after dithering, turned Weikers in, and at trial Weikers said it was Sislen who invited a bribe. Taped conversations firmly undercut Weikers, who, upon conviction, served seventeen months for obstruction of justice.

To keep all this away from the eyes and ears of the jurors, thereby preserving their objectivity, panicky efforts at insulation were made. They were too little; they were too late. Word did leak through to the news media—in one case, astonishingly, from Judge Pratt himself—and all but instantly hit Baltimore television screens. At this point, jurors had been sequestered belatedly in the downtown Lord Baltimore Hotel, supposedly fenced off by United States marshals.

The marshals fumbled. At least six jurors were left watching a hotel television set when Jerry Turner, WJZ anchorman, came on with the flash report about jury tampering. Not just the marshals were to blame. So was Judge Pratt who, despite warnings obvious in the Neiswender attempt, waited weeks to sequester the jurors and to sequester them properly.

"If I goofed," the judge said, "I goofed."

At least in the case of the authorities, the goof had arisen from good intentions. No such muddle softens the verdict on Skolnik's "shark." Neither Neiswender nor Weikers had any clearly visible motive of his own for laying hands on the jurors. Both referred to a hidden instigator—someone "in the Baltimore area," "my contact"—as having put them up to it.

The mistrial, according to Barney Skolnik, gave "the shark just what he wants."

George Beall, a former U.S. attorney, agreed: "The bad guys won."

In the second trial, when it got underway more than four months later, the lesson had at last been learned. Jurors were sequestered from the outset. They spent twelve weeks stoppered, in effect, inside a test tube.

14.

Quid pro Quo
v. Democracy

I n December, 1981, a celebrity arrived at Baltimore-Washington International Airport. Onlookers cheered and wept. Cameras snapped hungrily. At the center of it all, triumphant in the embrace of his beloved, stood the hero of the hour—a man freshly released after nineteen months of confinement in federal prison camp at Eglin Air Force Base, Florida.

Michael Olesker, columnist for the *Baltimore Sun*, heard the huzzahs in astonishment. "Was this," Olesker wrote the next day, "Marvin Mandel coming home to Maryland, or Scarlett O'Hara arriving back at Tara?"

The airport flutter would come and go, Marvin Mandel fade into a restless obscurity to which he had not been accustomed for at least a dozen years. Some saw him a poignant figure. He was a man all but destroyed, broke and debt-ridden, an outcast by disbarment from the legal profession. His lofty political past now hung about him as humiliating shadows, his future was a gloomy mystery.

He did have Jeanne, golden curls agleam, and some sort of job, never clearly defined. He also developed a helpful if curious sort of amnesia. It blocked out for him any sense of guilt, of any crime committed. He continued to insist, just as if jurors and judges had never spoken, that no Marylanders had been wronged. It was he, not they, who had been wronged. There was no flicker of remorse.

Indeed, he managed to invest his postprison reflections with an almost convincing sanctimony. Rehabilitation of convicts, he told reporters, was supposed to take place in prison, but in fact "nothing is being done" to straighten out most prisoners. Maybe he would do something for them personally. He might "lend" himself to help correct the rehabilitation system he had seen firsthand at Eglin, had seen failing. This carried a responsible, constructive sound.

It also carried a question: What guidance was he offering to "lend," this man as stonily unrepentant as the day he entered Eglin, a living monument to rehabilitation's failure? Or had remorselessness become the guiding star to rehabilitation?

Maybe the real truth is that Marvin Mandel never understood the government machinery that first raised him up, its apparent darling, then in fickleness cut him down. Maybe his tragic error was to weave about him a political cocoon, tight against light as against air, and inside it to imagine himself safely walled off in the 1950s against the new reality evolving over the years outside.

What the foregoing chapters relate is one aspect of a state government in adolescence, of the approach to maturity in Maryland's political ethics. The process has been neither smooth nor easily grasped. Others than Marvin Mandel found themselves baffled by a public as ambivalent to corruption as to reformers' protests. Consequently, movement forward has been slow and erratic. The stop-and-go signs stand unevenly spaced, a path runs maddeningly elusive.

Nor is perfect purity yet at hand or likely to be soon. As recently as 1982, a promising president of the Baltimore City Council, a man symbolizing political enlightenment, confessed to illegal pocketings growing out of, yes, a contract to haul the city's sludge.

The point remains intact. A century of hesitant advances linking the end of the Civil War to the beginning of Marvin Mandel's tenure as governor amounts, when set in historical perspective, to a cultural revolution. It has been a revolution in the popular view of what's right and what's wrong in the way public officials personally conduct themselves at the controls of the great governmental powers entrusted to them.

Arguments are heard that Marvin Mandel was a victim of changing rules, that he was more to be pitied than censured. Also his midlife romance, plus his otherwise sound record as an executive, are often bundled in as sympathetic makeweights that somehow balance off convictions for mail fraud and bribery. If there's a little something to this, there's not enough. It comforts mainly those who tend to edit out ill-fitting wiggles when they draw their cool, clear judgments.

What are the enduring facts? What are the illuminating historical themes that draw together in the fall of Marvin Mandel?

When Mayor Frank Hague of Jersey City said "I am the law," he did not mean what was in the statute books. He meant the power that pulsed, unofficially, often illegally, in the political machinery he commanded there in the 1930s, a naked form of the power that by the 1970s had eroded in Maryland as in New Jersey. But Marvin Mandel grew up and fed politically on the old fashioned machinery lingering as late as the 1950s. The Hague-like attitudes it prompted, if prudently diluted, were part of his political heritage. He—as well as Irvin Kovens, Dale Hess, the Rodgers brothers, and Ernest Cory—were leftovers from the old political spoils system.

Consequently, they never outgrew altogether the notion that political victory confers on the victors a lofty perch denied to all others. They were convinced, anachronistically, that they stood as far above the law as Frank Hague in his day boasted he did. The trouble was, by the 1970s the machines of Gorman and Rasin, of Mahon and Pollack, no longer extended the old protections.

That's the first enduring fact. The second is that Marvin Mandel, for all his celebrated political antennae, failed to pick up the popular call, long sounded, for a new and higher political ethic. The George Mahoney phenomenon, jangled with opportunism as it was, plainly rang the warning bells and rang them in plenty of time: people want honest government. Because he didn't hear, or didn't believe what he heard, Marvin Mandel was in effect ethically obsolete the day in 1969 when he took office as Maryland's governor. He had simply missed the message of his own time.

A third fact, also enduring, grows out of the first two. The once-proud state right's posture of Albert Ritchie's era—the right of a state, presumably, to police its own turf—had been elbowed almost out of sight. Instead a new notion was ushered in by Franklin Roosevelt, then brought to sharp focus by John Kennedy and his brother Robert. This was the belief that the federal government, not the state, had to be the top cop on the block. Against that hardening reality lawyers for the Mandel group battered and picked, sliced and undermined. Their struggle was skillful but in vain. Federal enforcement had come to Maryland to stay.

The final fact pertinent here is still unresolved, still reaching out for its own retaining wall. It is the pervasive power of private money to debase, via the pipeline of politics, the men and women who preside over the government system by which all Americans hope to live together. One small step forward has been achieved. The $25,000 salary by which Maryland grievously underpaid Marvin Mandel, leaving him vulnerable to exploitation by his friends, has been lifted to $45,000. That's still not enough, but it's better.

The larger hazard of money lies rooted, paradoxically, inside that venerable guardian of the people, the United States Constitution. The First Amendment guarantees freedom of speech; that guarantee has been interpreted as covering financial contributions to an election campaign. Election gifts may be loosely regulated but not, under the Constitution, blocked. The practical effect is, money flys uninhibited and in staggering amounts at election time. The financial contributor has yet to turn up who gives against his own best interest. To the contrary, political self-seeking is as normal to business as to labor, to individuals as to organized pressure groups. You give a buck to get two bucks back or, anyway, two bucks worth of something the government, so seduced, can return.

Political action committees proliferate in every quarter, their function being to furnish leverage by which a private money bag can bend public policy its own way. It's quid pro quo unabashed, it's sanitized bribery, and, on all this, the First Amendment smiles protectively. Free speech is the cornerstone of the republic, and which of the media dares quarrel with that?

So here runs a theme of the Mandel story which is both overriding and, unlike the others, dismayingly beyond the reach of existing governmental expertise. Hess, Kovens et al. weren't jailed for pumping millions of highly questionable dollars into the Mandel election campaigns. And yet they did, in 1969, in 1970, and in 1974, and it was legal. Thus it was they first crept into Mandel's political bed. There they made themselves indispensable to him financially. There the foundation was laid for further enterprises—but these not similarly enjoying constitutional protection.

What came next were the Marlboro escapade and the Security Investment payoff, and why not? If millions could be legally used to prop up Marvin Mandel at election time, why not a helpful few hundred thousand between elections? What's the real difference? And look at quid pro quo relationships appearing at the highest, most respectable levels elsewhere. Look how the Lockheed Aircraft Company, ornament of the U.S. defense establishment, took care of Prince Bernhard of the Netherlands and Prime Minister Tanaka of Japan. For services rendered, both turned up on the Lockheed payroll. If the boys at Lockheed aircraft could get away with that, why not the boys at Tidewater Insurance? In politics, hot dollars laugh at legal niceties. Quid pro quo, it seemed, provided the lubricant of democracy almost everywhere.

Almost but not quite. The British, long among the wisest of democratic peoples, have found ways to bottle up some of their own election-time temptations. Today election winds blow in Britain with full-throated vigor, but they blow free of the aroma of money dangling and of the decay money inflicts on a political system. British politics smells of many things, but politicians bought and paid for are not among them.

One reason is that Britain has no written constitution, hence no well-meant First Amendment to stray off into interpretations never dreamed of by the Founders. The British constitution, unwritten, means what the British want, not what they don't want. It was the British writer Lewis Carroll, who, via Humpty Dumpty, put these matters best. "When I use a word," Humpty Dumpty said, "It means just what I choose it to mean—neither more nor less."

Almost surely, however, serious, purposeful men like Marvin Mandel and his friends—let alone serious, purposeful congressmen—who might patch the leaks in the First Amendment have little time for frivolous and ill-starred advisors like Humpty Dumpty. Anyway, who says they really want the leaks patched? Among most American politicians and many businessmen, talk of giving and taking political money remains a subject altogether too ticklish for comfort.

Appendix

Note from the *Maryland Law Review*

UNITED STATES v. MANDEL:
THE MAIL FRAUD AND EN BANC PROCEDURAL ISSUES

INTRODUCTION

When Governor Marvin Mandel and his five codefendants were convicted of mail fraud and racketeering, Maryland politics seemed hope-
lessly corrupt. In a space of five years Marylanders had seen one of their
United States senators, their former governor, and then their sitting governor haled into federal court on criminal charges. Yet *United States v.
Mandel* is disturbing, not merely because it suggests that Marylanders
again were victimized by one of their top officials, but also because it
raises doubts whether the defendants received a fair trial and whether
they were properly sent to jail after half the Fourth Circuit, sitting en
banc, voted to reverse their convictions.

Doubt concerning the fairness of the *Mandel* trial arises in connection
with two of three theories on which the mail fraud charges were submitted to the jury. Because the case was presented to the jury on alternative
theories, it is impossible to know which, or what combination of these
theories, the jurors adopted. Consequently, the guilty verdicts may
reflect the jurors' finding that Mandel was bribed by his codefendants,
that he and his codefendants withheld material information from government officials, or that the defendants made false representations in order
to obtain benefits from governmental bodies. If the verdicts rested on
either the first or second of these theories, the defendants may have been
unjustly convicted. The bribery theory was inadequately explained to
the jury, and the theory that the defendants defrauded the public of

SOURCE: Excerpts from Note by Ray L. Earnest, *Maryland Law Review* 40, no. 4
(1981). Reprinted by permission. All footnote numbers have been removed.

material information was rife with conceptual problems. Nonetheless, the Fourth Circuit eventually ratified all three theories as well as the ways in which they were presented to the jury.

Of the issues raised on appeal, the question whether the jury instructions adequately explained the bribery theory was the most troublesome for the court. Initially a three judge panel of the Court of Appeals for the Fourth Circuit reversed the convictions, holding that the bribery instruction was inadequate. Upon rehearing by the court en banc, the Fourth Circuit was evenly divided on this issue; accordingly, the convictions were affirmed by the equally divided court.

The question remains whether the defendants were properly convicted under the mail fraud statute. First, the body of mail fraud case law and the Fourth Circuit's decision in *United States v. Arthur* suggest that the defendants were entitled to a bribery instruction as requested in connection with the mail fraud counts. Second, the Fourth Circuit's analysis of the mail fraud statute as it applies to schemes to conceal material information from government officials was surprisingly superficial. The court failed to deal with the question whether the allegedly concealed information was "material" and the question whether Mandel's co-defendants, as private citizens, had any obligation to disclose the information, even if it was material.

The Court of Appeals' en banc procedure also demands scrutiny. Even though the court could not reach a majority decision, it reinstated the district court judgment. This is what federal courts of appeal usually do when they find themselves evenly divided in an en banc rehearing. Arguably, this procedure is inherently unfair to a criminal defendant, for it means that he will be sentenced in accordance with a guilty verdict that one half of the en banc judges consider fatally defective. Furthermore, the decision of an equally divided en banc court is always unsatisfactory because such a decision has no precedential value. It leaves the law of the circuit unsettled, and uncertainty in the criminal law is particularly disturbing.

In light of the problems that attend the practice of affirming criminal convictions by equal divisions, it is hard to imagine that any appellate court would let an equal division stand if it had a legitimate means of breaking the deadlock. Yet the Fourth Circuit rejected the defendants' petition for a second en banc rehearing of *Mandel*, although the court was assured of reaching a majority decision in a second rehearing. It is difficult to understand the court's refusal to decide the issues presented by this case.

Although neither the en banc decision nor the panel decision has precedential value, it is nevertheless worthwhile to explore the Fourth Circuit's treatment of the mail fraud issues in *Mandel* in order to evaluate whether these defendants were treated fairly. Moreover, because at least five of the six en banc judges apparently agreed that the mail fraud counts could properly have been submitted to the jury on three theories, the court's reasoning in connection with those theories, deserves attention. If it prejudiced the *Mandel* defendants, it may prejudice future defendants.

. . . .

Conclusion

The Fourth Circuit's treatment of the *Mandel* case was disappointing for a number of reasons, including:

(1) the court's failure to deal adequately with the mail fraud issues:

(2) the court's failure to clarify the meaning of *Arthur*; and

(3) the court's failure to grant a second rehearing and decide *Mandel*, a properly presented case.

The most glaring problem with the Fourth Circuit's treatment of the mail fraud counts was associated with the theory that the defendants defrauded the public of its right to information material to governmental decisions. The panel majority's analysis of the theory that the public has a right to material information ignored the difficulties in applying that theory to the circumstances in *Mandel*. It failed to deal with two questions: first, whether the information withheld was material to a governmental decision, and second, whether the public has a right to all material information from private citizens. Half the en banc judges overlooked these problems, just as the panel majority did. This is disturbing, because under the panel majority's analysis, a private citizen can be exposed to criminal liability for withholding information from government officials whenever the officials testify that the information might have affected their decision on a particular matter. If the Fourth Circuit ever reviews another case prosecuted on this theory, the court should re-examine this analysis and either repudiate it or deal with the questions it presents.

Finally, *Mandel* exemplified the problem inherent in the present practice of affirming by an equal division. When a court affirms a criminal conviction by an equal division, there is a strong possibility that an individual defendant does not receive protection that will later be accorded to similarly situated defendants. A new Federal Rule of Appellate Procedure should be adopted to eliminate this possibility for injustice. Justice would be better served if the federal courts were to reverse whenever they are equally divided on an issue in the appeal of a criminal conviction.

Notes on the Sources

arious inhabitants of the United States attorney's office in Baltimore—George Beall, Jervis Finney, Timmy Baker, Fred Motz—were lavish with their time. Barney Skolnik, who as assistant U.S. attorney more than anyone else designed and then prosecuted the case against the Mandel circle, opened for me a new world in the art of applying justice to criminals. Pete Twardowicz, that office's fabled "Polish Prince," breached a reservoir of facts, documents, shrewd observations. Susan Nellor, of the national executive office for U.S. attorneys, helped me flex the Freedom of Information machinery in Washington to squeeze extra drops from a reluctant Reagan administration.

In the Maryland attorney general's office, Charley Monk kept me abreast of the state's struggle to reclaim gubernatorial furniture, dog food, and toothpaste. Attorney General Steve Sachs and Bill Burch, a former attorney general, imparted their philosophy about politics and the law.

As noted elsewhere, Marvin and Jeanne Mandel felt unable, after three exploratory talks, to pursue the subject further. So did three other defendants, on advice of counsel. Irvin Kovens and Ernest Cory talked freely and fully. Arnold Weiner, Marvin Mandel's adroit and thoughtful counsellor, put the whole defense case into legal perspective. His secretary, Pat O'Meara, was long enduring and productive. Norman Ramsey, Kovens's lawyer, also helped.

Special thanks go to Barbara Mandel who, before talking, thought long and hard about where her loyalties lay, then graciously answered questions.

No less special is the acknowledgment to Judge Robert Taylor, who

253

presided with insight and disarming humanity over the second Mandel trial, and who, afterward in Knoxville, Tennessee, made complicated things seem simple. Other federal judges, prudently anonymous, clarified further legal puzzles.

Representatives Steny Hoyer and Clarence Long furnished valuable guidance. So did State Senator Jack Lapides and former Speaker of the House John Hanson Briscoe. Judge Sol Liss, long a loyal Mandel friend, sketched in background. Judge Marshall Levin, a Mandel schoolmate, added more.

William Marbury was a triple contributor—to historical accuracy, to legal analysis, to literary appraisal. The late Vernon Eney added legal philosophy. Hall Hammond, former chief judge of the Court of Appeals, former state attorney general, refracted public life through his own prism. Samuel Hopkins told of good men and bad, also of the historical flavors of Maryland Republicans. Arthur Machen explained one of his specialties, moral turpitude. Ray Earnest, of the *Maryland Law Review*, provided valuable research materials.

Wistfully, Blair Lee reminisced about his days—some of them happy—as acting governor during the Mandel trial. Bravely, George Hocker, a repository of political secrets, told some things he knew about some politicians, not all.

Newsmen high and low devoured the Mandel case, and it is to what they wrote then and said later that this book owes much. Bob Erlandson and Steve Luxenberg, of the *Baltimore Sun*'s trial team, were invaluable contributors. Jeff Price and Peter Jay, of the same paper, had special insights. So had David Lightman and Nick Yengich, both of the *Evening Sun*. Jack Lemmon, the evening managing editor, and Jim Day made available their paper's store of trial testimony recorded day by day. Phil Heisler, his predecessor, made clear why one potential title for this book was less than appropriate. Clem Vitek and Fred Rasmussen, of the *Sunpapers* library, turned out a cascade of news clippings, photographs, microfilm.

The late Lou Azrael, the *News American*'s oracular columnist, was a goldmine of facts and reflections. Frank DeFilippo, also of the *News American* and once Mandel's chief of staff, told some surprising things. Bill Stump, that paper's editorial page editor, dug up photographs of striking dramatic content. Dave Goeller, of the Associated Press, recalled details that escaped everyone else. Lee Trautner, an Annapolis photographer, functioned as an observant fly on several walls.

Three certified historians—Bill Manchester, Walter Lord, and Stanley Blumberg—held my uncertified hand through some long, dark passages. Gil Sandler, another historian, unearthed not only some forgotten facts but also his brother Irv, a Mandel schoolmate. The late Dave Woods and Ed Farrell, a former part-owner of Marlboro Racetrack, talked about the gaudier days of Maryland horseracing. At Chic 'n' Ruth's delly in Annapolis, where a special red table was set aside for Governor Mandel, Chic gave his own views of governors and the like. Mike Kaplow, a state police watcher-out over several Maryland governors, offered the fruits of his long observations.

My sources for the relatively recent parts of the narrative were mainly the interviews acknowledged above. In addition, there were nearly two thousand pages of official testimony and statements recorded at the second Mandel trial and the three appeals that followed it. Use of the Freedom of Information Act produced still further documents, some of them off-the-record interoffice communications in the possession of the several arms of government which were drawn into the trial. Chapters covering events prior to, say, 1965 are built partly on sources already named and partly on historical documentation.

The manuscripts that I consulted are listed below.

Maryland Historical Society

> Bradford Journals and Papers
> Thomas Swann Papers
> Gorman Papers

Collection of Carroll Rasin

> Isaac Freeman Rasin Papers

Semans, Truman T. "Maryland's Albert Ritchie." Senior thesis, Princeton University, 1949.

Reference works consulted include the following:

Albright, Joseph. *What Makes Spiro Run?* New York: Dodd, Mead, 1972.
Baker, Jean H. *The Politics of Continuity: Maryland Political Parties from 1858 to 1870.* Baltimore: Johns Hopkins University Press, 1973.
———. *Ambivalent Americans: The Know-Nothing Party in Maryland.* Baltimore: Johns Hopkins University Press, 1977.
Baltzell, E. Digby. *The Protestant Establishment: Aristocracy and Caste in America.* New York: Random House, 1964.
Brown, Dorothy M. "Maryland between the Wars," In *Maryland: A History, 1632–1974*, edited by Richard Walsh and William Lloyd Fox.
Buchholz, Heinrich Ewald. *Governors of Maryland: From the Revolution to the Year 1908.* Baltimore: Williams & Wilkens, 1908.
Burdette, Franklin L. "Modern Maryland Politics and Social Change." In *Maryland: A History, 1632–1974*, edited by Richard Walsh and William Lloyd Fox.
Burns, James Macgregor. *Leadership.* New York: Harper & Row, 1978.

Crooks, James B. "Maryland Progressivism." In *Maryland: A History, 1632–1974*, edited by Richard Walsh and William Lloyd Fox.

Dawidowicz, Lucy S. *The Golden Tradition: Jewish Life and Thought in Eastern Europe*. Boston: Beacon Press, 1967.

Essary, J. Frederick. *Maryland in National Politics: From Charles Carroll to Albert C. Ritchie*. Baltimore: John Murphy, 1932.

Johnson, Gerald W., Frank R. Kent, H.L. Mencken, and Hamilton Owens. *The Sunpapers of Baltimore*. New York: Alfred A. Knopf, 1937.

Kent, Frank R. *The Story of Maryland Politics*. Baltimore: Thomas & Evans, 1911.

Kirwin, Henry W. *The Inevitable Success: Herbert R. O'Conor*. Westminster, Md.: Newman Press, 1962.

Lambert, John R. *Arthur Pue Gorman*. Baton Rouge: Louisiana State University Press, 1953.

Lippman, Theo. Jr. *Spiro Agnew's America*. New York: W. W. Norton, 1972.

Miller, Nathan. *The Founding Finaglers*. New York: David McKay, 1976.

Phillips, David Graham. *The Treason of the Senate*. Chicago: Quadrangle, 1964.

Radoff, Morris L. *The Old Line State*. Annapolis: Hall of Records Commission, 1971.

Wagandt, Charles L. *The Mighty Revolution: Negro Emancipation in Maryland, 1862–1864*. Baltimore: Johns Hopkins Press, 1964.

Walsh, Richard, and William Lloyd Fox, editors. *Maryland: A History, 1632–1974*. Baltimore: Maryland Historical Society, 1974.

White, Frank F., Jr. *The Governors of Maryland, 1777–1970*. Annapolis: Hall of Records Commission, 1971.

Index

257

Cleveland, Grover, 24, 25
Code of ethics, Maryland, 30, 223, 232, 235
Cohen, Nathan, 171–72
Confiscation, federal, of defendants' property, 46–49
Consolidation bill, 152, 154
Conspiracy. See Bribery; Cover-up; Fraud; Mail fraud; Racketeering
Convictions, of defendants, 1, 4, 20, 37, 38, 73, 83, 151, 164, 184; for mail fraud, xxvii, 2, 7, 47–48, 74, 147, 161, 163, 183, 185, 205, 216, 220, 238, 245; for racketeering, xxvii, 2, 47–48, 183, 216, 220, 238. See also Federal jury; Re-reversal; Reversal; Trial
Corruption, xxi, 51, 66, 99, 203, 227, 228, 244–45; and the First Amendment, 41–42, 181, 246, 247; by Gorman, 20, 23–28, 71, 127; by Maryland governors, 38, 41–44, 61, 71–73, 101, 126–27, 138, 176, 191, 203; in Maryland politics, 21, 26, 69–71, 100–102, 123–28, 151, 173, 176; in Maryland savings and loan market, 61, 103–4. See also Bribery; Fraud; Mail fraud; Racketeering; Reform
Cory, Ernest N., Jr., xxii–xxiii, xxvii, 7, 111, 117, 129, 132, 139, 245; and Marlboro ownership, xxv, 48, 65, 141–42, 145–46, 147, 183–84; personal finances of, 162–63, 239. See also Bribery, by codefendants, of Mandel
Court of Appeals, xx, xxi, 140, 152, 188–89, 219–38; refusal of, to rehear, xxvii, 151, 220–21, 225–26; re-reversal by, xxviii, 37, 151, 220–21, 223, 224, 232–34, 237; reversal by, xxvii, 2–8, 11, 220–21, 223, 224, 232, 234, 237
Cover-up, by defendants, xxi, 114–18, 134–47, 185, 188, 189, 190–91, 198, 229. See also Bribery; Fraud; Mail fraud; Racketeering
Crothers, Austin L., 34, 71, 101
Curran, William, 40, 41, 57, 58

D'Alesandro, Thomas, Jr., 39, 40, 57, 61, 69
Deception. See Cover-up
Defense: complaints by, xx, 222–24, 231, 232, 235, 245–46; effect on, of Mandel's testimony, xxi, 30, 206, 234; stance of, regarding bribery charges, 185–88, 193, 201, 207–8,

224, 231–34; trial strategy of, 222–24, 231–33, 240
Defense: friendship between defendants as, 137, 144, 188, 191, 204–5, 212, 214–15; Mandel's ignorance of Marlboro transaction as, xxvii, 63–65, 134–39, 142, 144, 150, 205, 216, 232, 238; Mandel's gubernatorial record as, xx, 173–74; tradition of corruption in Maryland politics as, xx, 21, 27, 37, 69–70, 99–100, 102, 125, 219, 243. See also Trial; Weiner, Arnold
DeFilippo, Frank, 168–72, 175
Democratic party, 32–33, 181; machines of, 23–28, 33, 39–41, 58, 69, 245; in Maryland, 56–60, 68–69, 71, 102, 103, 123, 181, 203; in Maryland, and Mahoney, 50–52, 54–58
Divorce, B. Mandel and Mandel's, xxi, xxvi, 80, 83, 90; alimony payments following, xxvi, 118, 187–88, 208–12; J. Dorsey's role in, 3, 80–83, 90, 157–58; finances of, xxvi, 5, 44, 60, 82–83, 90, 151, 157–58, 187, 208–12; B. Mandel's reaction to, 80–83, 90, 160, 212. See also Mandel, Jeanne Dorsey, affair of, with Mandel
Dorsey, Jeanne. See Mandel, Jeanne Dorsey
Dorsey, Walter, 89, 91, 93, 94

Eglin Air Force Base, Florida, federal prison at, xxvii, 12, 20, 78, 96, 122, 157, 201, 243, 244
Evidence. See Trial, hearsay evidence in; Trial, physical evidence in

Federal government, intrusion of, into state affairs, xx, 19, 26, 34–35, 37, 61–62, 102, 124, 127–28, 219; defense complaints regarding, xx, 222, 231, 245–46
Federal grand jury, 217; indictment by, xix, xxvii, 23, 47, 148
Federal jury, 175, 188, 233–34; instruction of, by Judge Taylor, xxvii, 8, 222, 223–24, 231–38, 249–51; tampering with, xx, xxvii, 8, 193, 228, 238, 239–42; verdict given by, xix, xxvii, 2, 4, 47–48, 74, 140, 151, 205, 216, 245. See also Convictions, of defendants
Federal prosecutors, 23, 26. See also U.S. attorney's office
Finney, Jervis, 155, 158, 174
First Amendment, and election financing, 41–42, 181, 246, 247

THE JOHNS HOPKINS UNIVERSITY PRESS

Thimbleriggers

*This book was set in Clearface display and Melior text type by BG
Composition, Inc., from a design by Susan P. Fillion. It was
printed on S.D. Warren's 50-lb. Sebago Eggshell paper and bound
in Holliston Roxite A by the Maple Press Company.*